Chasing the Devil at Foggy Bottom

Chasing the Devil at Foggy Bottom

The Future of Religion in American Diplomacy

Shaun A. Casey

WILLIAM B. EERDMANS PUBLISHING COMPANY

GRAND RAPIDS, MICHIGAN

Wm. B. Eerdmans Publishing Co.
4035 Park East Court SE, Grand Rapids, Michigan 49546
www.eerdmans.com

Published 2023
Printed in the United States of America

29 28 27 26 25 24 23   1 2 3 4 5 6 7

ISBN 978-0-8028-8170-0

Library of Congress Cataloging-in-Publication Data

A catalog record for this book is available from the Library of Congress.

The opinions and characterizations in this piece are those of the author and do
not necessarily represent those of the US government.

To my beloved Ann

CONTENTS

Foreword by John Kerry ix

Acknowledgments xi

1. Vote-a-Rama 1

2. The $7 Trillion Hedgehog 9

3. Male, Pale, and Not Quite Yale 31

4. Launch 67

5. The Man in the White Hat 101

6. Through the Golden Door 126

7. Conflict 153

8. Responding to the Universe 189

9. The Devil? 219

Notes 229

Index 249

FOREWORD

T HE LIST OF LIFELONG EXPERTS WHO CAN give a stirring tutorial on foreign policy is extensive. So is the universe of scholars who can cite sacred texts about religion, comparative and otherwise. But for many years, there was a sort of separation of church and state(craft)— quite literally. The worlds stayed largely separate—an irony, and a failure of imagination, in a world in which it is nigh impossible to understand either sphere sufficiently without grasping the interconnectedness of the two and the religious convictions, conflicts, and controversies at the heart of societies and peoples everywhere.

This is the difficulty that motivated Dr. Shaun Casey to lend his expertise to try to bridge these two worlds—and that is the journey Shaun retells eloquently and informatively, the work at the center of *Chasing the Devil at Foggy Bottom: The Future of Religion in American Diplomacy.*

I've known Shaun for nearly two decades, back to his time at Wesley Theological Seminary, when together we were thought partners contemplating ways to make religion a unifying tool rather than a cause of division in public dialogue. He played a similar role with me during my years as Chairman of the Senate Foreign Relations Committee, exploring new ways to engage religion as an effective tool in foreign policy. This was, of course, the path that ultimately brought Shaun into government on a formal basis, when he joined us at the State Department as the inaugural head of the Office of Religion and Global Affairs.

Shaun's academic expertise speaks for itself. But his passion for foreign policy and his willingness to wrestle with the complexity of sectarian differences to bridge gaps between the world's religions revealed a practitioner as patient as he was persistent. I was struck by Shaun's eagerness to debate and differ and push hard not to find the lowest common denominator, surface-level insights, but to really wrestle with tough issues—the history of Western involvement in the Muslim world, the Sunni-Shia split, and religious extremism—to actually find ways to advance dialogue.

These were, of course, qualities—tenacity and curiosity in particular—that prepared him well for life managing a new enterprise in the State Department, a formidable bureaucracy and an alphabet soup of acronyms and abbreviations for undersecretaries, bureaus, and special offices. It can be a lot to process for newcomers and an impossible task for many academics. To this vast enterprise, Shaun brought an often-unappreciated skill: he listened. Whether it was in the course of intransigent negotiations in Cuba, or in engagements across the Middle East and Africa, he soon became an adept thinker as well as operator. If his calling hadn't been religion, diplomacy might well have been a natural fit.

Now, in the pages of this book, we will all benefit from Shaun's expertise and perspective.

JOHN F. KERRY
68th Secretary of State

ACKNOWLEDGMENTS

I OWE MY FIRST AND DEEPEST THANKS to my family. I am grateful to my wife Ann for so much: for her love, her counsel, her wisdom, and for forty years of marriage. To my son Paul and daughter Sarah I am grateful for their manifold gifts, which continue to astound me. Paul's keen editorial advice was particularly helpful when I was stymied about how to organize the story. Sarah's unexpected and unplanned return home during the pandemic to finish her graduate work at Harvard Divinity School remotely provided me innumerable hours to pick her brain as the book progressed. And I lost my ninety-nine-year-old mother in the COVID pandemic as I was nearing completion of the manuscript. I owed so much to her and my late father.

I am thankful for the trust Secretary of State John Kerry showed to me when he hired me as special representative for religion and global affairs at the US Department of State. Without his trust this story would never have taken place. I am also deeply grateful to David Wade, Kerry's chief of staff, whose wise counsel and friendship paved our way to success on a daily basis.

I remain amazed and grateful for the extraordinary team we were able to build at the Office of Religion and Global Affairs. I owe my deepest gratitude to Liora Danan, our chief of staff, whose impact can be seen throughout the pages of this book. Others include Ira Forman, Arsalan Suleman, and Shaarik Zafar; Toiyriah Turner, Amy Lillis, Rachel Leslie, Claire Sneed, Rebecca Linder Blachly, Albar Sheikh, Rustum Nyquist, Laterica Curtis, Jennifer Wistrand, Alice Bean, Evan Berry, David Buckley, Jerome Copulsky, Priscilla Flores, Usra Ghazi, Michael Hamburger, Qamar-Ul Huda, Holly Robertson

Huffnagle, Mariam Kaldas, Helene Kessler, Alan Matney, Peter Mandaville, Julianne Paunescu, and Maryum Saifee.

The team at Eerdmans has been extraordinary. I am especially grateful to my editor Trevor Thompson, who immediately grasped the gist of this book in a manner that many of his fellow editors at several other presses were unable to do. Likewise, James Ernest, editor-in-chief, and Anita Eerdmans, president, also enthusiastically embraced the project. I want to thank my very talented and intrepid research assistants at Georgetown University: Rosalie Daniels, Julia Friedman, Madelyn Coles, and Madeline Hart.

At the end of a book project like this I am keenly aware of the multitude of people over the years who have shaped who I am and what I have been able to do. I have resisted the urge to give a lengthy recitation of their names. I am also aware of the stories I could have told but chose not to tell. Some of these omissions protect the innocent; others protect the guilty. There were so many things to tell and only so much space to do so. I will let Augustine's concluding words to *The City of God* suffice:

> And now, as I think, I have discharged my debt, with the completion, by God's help, of this huge work. It may be too much for some, too little for others. Of both these groups I ask forgiveness. But of those for whom it is enough I make this request: that they do not thank me, but join with me in rendering thanks to God. Amen. Amen.[1]

VOTE-A-RAMA

S ENATOR JOHN KERRY LOOKED OVER THE TOP of his reading glasses, trained his eyes on me as he slapped his weather-beaten diary closed, and asked, "How can I tell a story like this in public?"

He had just finished reading me a long passage from his journal, written the night he learned his friend and Yale classmate Richard Pershing had been killed in combat in Vietnam. Pershing died on February 17, 1968, during the Tet offensive, on a mission to recover the body of one of his soldiers who died in a firefight the day before. Kerry was barely twenty-four years old when he got the news of Pershing's death.

At this point in 2005 I did not know Senator Kerry well enough to know just how much spiritual and theological substance there might actually have been to the man, to say nothing of his grasp of religion around the globe. Most of what I knew about him was drawn from press descriptions of his faith during the 2004 presidential election, and those accounts were uniformly tepid, even hostile. Yet he had just given me evidence to suggest the real story was much more interesting.

The entry he read to me was a long, anguished, unvarnished lamentation addressed to God. I was astonished at the depth of his pain, grief, and confusion, and I took his question to me as a direct challenge. After his presidential election loss, I had been urging him to make his own spiritual journey public, contrary to the advice he had gotten from his brain trust during the campaign. He was wondering if such personal details and struggles could ever be revealed in the heat of an election. He wanted to talk about his faith, and he wanted to do so in a manner that was authentic and not politically exploitative. He was a Catholic raised in the pre–Vatican II era, and public personal reflection on his spiritual journey was not at the center of his Catholic experience. But it was more than that to me; this reading was a revelation of sorts. I saw that in the intervening decades since Pershing's death, Kerry had been thinking long and hard about religion, both on a personal level and on a global, political one.[1]

He had been caricatured as a fake, cafeteria Catholic during the 2004 presidential campaign, based on the attacks of Raymond Cardinal Burke, who warned Kerry publicly that he was not welcome to receive communion in Burke's diocese. Yet the truth was that Kerry had been forced to wrestle with some of the deepest spiritual questions any human being might ever face. In his case, it was confronting the violent death of a dear friend while still in his twenties. Over the years I have found myself in a handful of settings when people shared such soul-crushing stories of loss and hard times. I have learned to see these moments as sacred ground, demanding great care and caution on my part. We spent the balance of that evening alone in his hideaway office in the Senate, meandering around several subjects in between his brief forays to the well of the Senate to vote. (We were there alone for several hours as the Senate was voting on a series of budget-related bills called Vote-a-Rama that would last for several hours into the early morning.)

I learned he was a much more complicated man, especially regarding religion, than I had suspected. His personal journey, tested by the losses he saw in Vietnam and the hypocrisy of US policy there, would take him across the world, and in the intervening decades he had developed a deeper understanding of religion, had read a lot, and had met with an astonishing range of religious leaders and actors. As a senator and ultimately chair of the Senate Foreign Relations Committee, he developed a view that American diplomacy had missed many diplomatic opportunities, given its reticence regarding religion or, even worse, its willful ignorance. What emerged in his thinking was not the much-parodied "two faces of faith" stereotype in which religion is seen as either primarily good or primarily bad. Rather, he knew that religious dynamics were quite complex, and it required expertise to interpret religion in a more sophisticated manner.

I did not know where the evening's conversation would eventually lead. But I remember heading home late that night astonished at his honesty and vulnerability in sharing this deeply personal story with me. And I thought, this guy is much deeper than I had ever supposed, and it could be very interesting to work for him someday. Eight years later, when Kerry became secretary of state in 2013, he asked me to leave the comforts of academia and build an office at the State Department to institutionalize his thesis that American diplomacy could be more effective if it had a deeper capacity to interpret the diplomatic implications of religious belief and practice. *Chasing the Devil at Foggy Bottom* is the story of how I answered Kerry's call to establish the Office of Religion and Global Affairs in the US Department of State (hereafter S/RGA, the *S* signaling our location within the Secretary's Bureau). In retrospect, the primary key to our success in the office was the high degree of support and confidence Kerry invested in us. That night in 2005 was when a bond of trust was born.

In telling this story, I will answer three questions. The first question is, why is it important for American diplomacy to have a capacity to understand global religious dynamics? The second question—more interesting to me and also harder to answer—is, how does one do this sort of work? And the third question is, how do you institutionalize and expand innovation like we did in the Office of Religion and Global Affairs in one of the most sclerotic, change-resistant, and now depleted parts of the federal bureaucracy? In other words, where do you place these experts in the vast foreign-policy bureaucracy so the useful knowledge they create can get into the hands of the right senior decision makers? (This is a topic I have chased since studying with Richard Neustadt in graduate school at Harvard over thirty years ago.)

To be sure, there is deep disagreement over whether or not American diplomats should devote time and energy to understanding religion around the world. And there is not a consensus regarding how such an office should actually do such work, even if it intuitively makes sense to try. I will get at that question in due course, but for the moment I want to focus on why such a mission makes sense for US foreign policy. There are at least three reasons why the United States should care enough about religion and diplomacy to have some technical advisory capacity in the State Department to make our diplomacy smarter and better.

The first reason has to do with what makes diplomacy effective. If diplomacy is the art of leading and persuading others to pursue a more just, humane, and sustainable world, then ignoring the complex ways religion shapes the world makes no sense. American diplomacy should have a capacity to interpret religion, because religious figures and religious communities are often powerful and multivalent actors all over the globe on a wide menu of issues. And make no mistake, the US government has tried in the past constantly to grapple with religion, but almost always in an amateurish, sometimes disastrous, ad hoc manner, and it will continue to do so whether or not there is an office to assist in that task.[2] The academic study of religion has grown in recent years, yet historically, the US Department of State has tended to view religion through two relatively narrow, reductive, and insufficient windows: either through international religious freedom or as part of what has come to be known as countering violent extremism. To fully understand the political implications of religion, the US government needs, as part of routine diplomatic analysis, a deeper capacity to understand and interpret religion than what any of these paths offer. Yet, as I heard Bryan Hehir drolly observe many times, governments trying to integrate the understanding of religion into diplomacy is like performing brain surgery; it may be necessary, but it can be fatal if not done well.[3]

The second reason is ignorance of religion can be costly. For example, the willful ignorance by the US government of the power of lived religion led to unspeakable losses of thousands of American and Iraqi lives when we invaded Iraq in 2003, to say nothing of the trillions of dollars we spent and are still spending there. If US leaders had had a deeper understanding of the religious dynamics of Iraq and had understood the political and social implications of those complex dynamics, they would not have made the naïve assumptions they did about the consequences of our invasion. And they might have considered a host of options short of invasion. A similar ignorance of the religious landscape of Afghanistan led to cascading disasters there.

The third reason our diplomacy should have a deeper grasp of religion is that it is complex and controversial and should not be left solely to the untrained. While American diplomacy tends to be run by generalists, it needs expertise and training on a variety of complex subjects. For our diplomacy to be effective, it needs to understand the multiple forces that shape and underwrite the behavior of both state and nonstate actors. If the US foreign policy apparatus needs to understand the motivations of its global interlocutors, understanding how and why various religious dynamics influence action has to be a crucial part of our attempt to analyze the worldviews of friends and enemies. If, as I believe, religion is always expressed in specific contexts and embedded in history, culture, politics, and a host of other dynamics, our understanding of religion has to be nuanced and sophisticated. This is no easy task, as I soon discovered upon landing in the large and confusing structure of our foreign-policy bureaucracy. For both state and nonstate actors, the role of religion in shaping values and behavior can lead to a multitude of outcomes, ranging from war and terrorism to a remarkable set of warrants for fighting extreme poverty, promoting human rights, mitigating conflict, and a host of other issues. That is to say, religion has a multivalent impact in global politics.[4] At the outset of my diplomatic career, far too much of the analysis I saw of religion was based on the personal hunches of individual diplomats and not on solid research.

Relatedly, the unique legal and historical role of religion in the United States demands any such work be done with care. By this I mean the purpose of this analysis is not to advance a particular version of religion or to privilege certain religious communities over other forms. (There were certainly many people within the government and beyond who mistakenly assumed that I was there to promote some particular version of Christianity.) Rather, the State Department should develop a capacity to understand as many forms of religion as possible, in context, in order to discover possible avenues of diplomatic engagement. There is always the chance that a particular administration can pick favorites and also attack particular forms of religion, as the Trump administration did. But the possibility of preferential or antagonistic treatment of certain groups over others is always a danger in any administration, and internal and external critics should be on the watch for such behavior on the part of any administration.

This also means the government needs to avoid an approach to religion that simply instrumentalizes religious actors and communities. This requires the government to be transparent about the ends toward which it pursues this work and the means it intends to deploy. In other words, the US government should be able to articulate what its interests are in any interaction with religious communities. In the summer of 2013, just as I was entering the State Department, the Obama administration, through the National Security Council, issued a Strategy for Integrating Religious Leader and Religious Community Engagement into US foreign policy. While I had no hand in writing this strategy, I was a direct beneficiary, as our office did most of the engagement and analysis called for in the strategy in the Obama administration. The strategy proposed integrating religious communities and leaders into US foreign policy with special attention to building sustainable development, to promoting a diverse set of human rights, and to mitigating conflict. From the outset, we had a strategic mandate from the White House as we built our office to engage across the foreign policy apparatus of the administration as well as to engage religion around the world. And throughout our tenure we had supporters, critics, and skeptics watching us. And that was not a bad thing.

A little over seven years after my conversation with Kerry during Vote-a-Rama, in early March 2013, I got an email from David Wade, who had been Kerry's chief of staff in the Senate, asking me to come by his office at Main State, as the State Department's central building was called, for a conversation. I knew he had agreed to become Kerry's chief of staff at State, and I was excited to hear from him, to say the least. I soon found myself in his office, along with Kerry's longtime aide Heather Higginbottom, who would later become deputy secretary of state. They told me a story about one of Kerry's early briefings a few weeks before when he first landed as secretary. He was being briefed by one of the army of briefers that assaults new cabinet members, bringing them up to date on countless issues that are calling for attention and action. They told me a briefer told Kerry that, based on an executive order issued by President Obama early in 2009, he could launch a religion advisory office. Kerry interrupted the briefer, turned to Wade, and said to call me and see if he could twist my arm to join his team and launch this new office! David, Heather, and I had a forty-five-minute conversation about what I would do with such an office. By the end of the talk we had a handshake deal, and I was on my way to working at the State Department. Not much arm twisting was required.[5]

I spent the next four months completing the spring semester teaching at Wesley Theological Seminary, trying to wrap my brain around conceptualizing the office, building a staff, thinking about the issues we might work on, and waiting for my security clearance to be completed. (In this period my daughter Sarah wondered why the clearance was taking so long because I had lived the most boring life of any adult she knew.) At the time, it seemed like the days dragged, but in retrospect the time flew. While I could not have articulated it very well at the time, what I was trying to do was to theorize how our work might relate to Kerry's strategic thinking as secretary. And the best theoretical description I know of such strategic thinking today comes from the esteemed Yale historian John Lewis Gaddis, in his book *On Grand Strategy*.[6] In those early days, I was trying to do on a smaller scale what Gaddis suggests all strategic political thinkers should do.

Borrowing British philosopher Isaiah Berlin's conception of foxes and hedgehogs, Gaddis assesses a dizzying array of strategic thinkers through this construct.[7] A quick nod to Berlin's framework and Gaddis's elaboration will help illuminate how I saw our role in the office in relation to Kerry's strategic agenda as secretary. For Berlin, the ancient Greek aphorism "The fox knows many things, but the hedgehog knows only one big thing" symbolizes a promising frame for classifying great writers. Gaddis, applying the distinction to strategic political thinkers, observes that Berlin's framework in his book *The Hedgehog and the Fox*, about different types of writers, also helps to explain two different forms of strategic thinking: "Hedgehogs, Berlin explained, 'relate everything to a single central vision' through which 'all they say and do has significance.' Foxes, in contrast, 'pursue many ends, often unrelated and even contradictory, connected, if at all, only in some *de facto* way.' The distinction was simple but not frivolous: it offered 'a point of view from which to look and compare, a starting point for genuine investigation.' It might even reflect 'one of the deepest differences which divide writers and thinkers, and, it may be, human beings in general.'"[8]

Gaddis is helpful here when he argues that hedgehogs may fail to establish a proper relationship between ends and means. He notes that ends can become infinite in reality, while means are stubbornly finite. Unwavering commitment to the one big thing makes it very hard to adjust to cumulative effects.[9] Gaddis suggests that the best strategic thinkers find a way to balance the dialectic between the two different animal species. That is, in the end he argues that leaders who find a way to pursue major goals but tether their big ideas to considerations of time, space, and scale do better.[10] Let's walk through this systematically, if only briefly.

Gaddis, pointing to Abraham Lincoln's mastery of strategy in the Civil War, argues that Lincoln mastered common sense in pursuit of his success as a strategist with an uncommon mastery of scale, space, and time.[11] Scale sets the ranges within which experience accrues, according to Gaddis. Lincoln sought to be underestimated and remained resilient, accommodating unknowns more readily than someone rigidly hemmed in by history, expectations, and a desire to fulfill family history. He argues that this disposition lends itself to being more effective in responding to the unknowns of experience. Lacking such a resilience leaves little room for adapting and tends to breed entitlement and arrogance. It can lead to rigidity and a disinterest in key factors about one's alleged enemies. Space, according to Gaddis, is where expectations and circumstances intersect. In Lincoln's case, he mastered the intricacies of Northern strengths versus Southern strengths.

I'll have more to say about the relevance of the framework Gaddis commends, with respect both to President Bush's failures in Iraq and, more importantly, to the work of our office. I mention it now because from the very outset we thought very hard about the nature of our work, in order to maximize our value to the administration and to avoid simply being the smug religion experts looking down our noses at generalists in the government, to avoid being co-opted by special interests within and without the government, and to increase our chances of becoming a valued contributor to the development of better foreign policy. I can remember thinking about these issues in that time between being offered the job and formally joining the department.

If Kerry and Obama were hedgehogs, in Gaddis's terms, I wanted us to be foxes who had compasses to show senior policy makers well-informed paths. This was in contrast to much of previous US foreign policy that tended to assess religion in very reductive terms such as good/bad religion, moderate/radical religion, etc. And we needed to be tethered to the hedgehog decision makers by the quality and utility of our research and insights. I, along with my chief of staff, had to manage our team in such a way that we were providing useful information for senior leaders in a manner that did not alienate us from the broad and complex Department of State. "It's more complicated than you think" could not become our default answer to our peers and the secretary. We had to play well with others. And, to be honest, a fair number of religion scholars do not reflexively play well with nonspecialists in religion who happen to veer into "our" lane.[12]

I had studied and thought a lot about how to build a staff and how to develop a mission in the senior ranks of the State Department. Now I was being put to the test. I could make a good case for why this work was necessary to good diplomacy, and I would have to repeat those arguments on a routine basis for the next four years. But I was also in the business of actually doing our work. The two tasks remained linked. In the next chapter I will examine the question of why this work is important, but the bulk of the story will be describing how we integrated the task of interpreting religion around the globe into a more successful US foreign policy.

Chapter Two

THE $7 TRILLION HEDGEHOG

I N THIS CHAPTER I WANT TO ELABORATE the arguments laid out in the last chapter. I will take up each of the three reasons US foreign policy should be able to understand and interpret religion around the world when it is diplomatically important to do so. I believe religion is powerful and multivalent around the world; diplomatic ignorance regarding religion can be costly; and because religion is complex, expertise, not amateurism, is necessary for better outcomes.

Even casual observers cannot ignore the mounting evidence of the power of religion and religious communities in world politics since the 1980s. The list of case studies is long: the Iranian revolution; the war between the Sandinistas and Contras in Nicaragua; the role of Christian churches in the reunification of Germany; the role of the Roman Catholic Church in the ouster of Ferdinand Marcos in the Philippines; and the role of Christian churches in building, sustaining, and ultimately dismantling apartheid in South Africa, to name only a few examples. Indeed, José Casanova observed that "during the entire decade of the 1980s it was hard to find any serious political conflict anywhere in the world that did not show behind it the not-so-hidden hand of religion."[1]

By the 1990s, critical analyses of the role of religion in global affairs began to proliferate across a range of commentators, including sociologists of religion, foreign-policy practitioners, and scholars of religion. Yet interestingly, as a field, international relations remained stubbornly immune to the topic. To be sure, different sets of analysts approached the topic through particular and even peculiar vantage points. Yet religion had burst onto the public scene in new ways, and it begged for deeper understanding. As we will see later, the State Department by the late 1990s had put its toe reluctantly in this pond through the narrow frame of religious freedom, and then only under compulsion by congressional intervention.

We can learn several things by looking at this commentary from a range of viewpoints from the 1990s forward, looking at the growth of public religion in the 1980s. Perhaps the most noteworthy set of observations came from the aforementioned sociologist José Casanova in his important book, *Public Religions in the Modern World*. Casanova locates his work in the complex context of secularization theory, which in broad terms theorized that the engines of capitalism and increasing differentiation in modern societies meant religion was destined to erode and disappear in modernity. The apparent renaissance of religion globally, or at least outside of western Europe, seemed to severely undercut the saliency of prophecies about the decline or disappearance of religion. Casanova's seminal work offers a nuanced path between rejecting the secularization thesis outright and uncritically embracing the theory as still valid regarding the global fate of religion.

I cite his work here not to rehearse his interesting and compelling argument, though it is worthy of serious reflection by anyone interested in the sociology of religion; instead, what I want to show is his early recognition that religions were complex, with profound implications for understanding global politics. As he puts it: "Religion in the 1980s 'went public' in a dual sense. It entered the 'public sphere' and gained, thereby, 'publicity.' Various 'publics'—the mass media, social scientists, professional politicians, and the 'public at large'—suddenly began to pay attention to religion. The unexpected public interest derived from the fact that religion, leaving its assigned place in the private sphere, had thrust itself into the public arena of moral and political contestation."[2]

The second group of observers in the '90s who noted the public and political power of religion was an eclectic assembly of primarily American foreign-policy practitioners whose views were published in a collection of essays entitled *Religion: The Missing Dimension of Statecraft*, edited by Douglas Johnston and Cynthia Sampson in 1994.[3] While the title undoubtedly overstated the case for religion as *the* missing dimension of statecraft, the book did present a series of historical case studies, primarily focused on religion and conflict. Its broad thesis was that religion was often a driver of conflict and also a force for peace. While their primary villain was classical realism in international relations theory, which they argued had no substantive intellectual space for religion as an analytical category, ultimately the authors failed to offer much substantive advice to policy makers on just how they should proceed differently in their work even if they approved of the central thesis of the book regarding the power of religion.

They did theorize that having religious attachés at all US embassies would go a long way in making sure the US Department of State had an eye on religious dynamics. But they did not elaborate on just how these people should be trained and how to integrate such positions into the highly refined intellectual division of labor in the US Foreign Service. What kind of training would suffice? How would you overcome the latent antireligious bias in the Foreign Service? How would you convince ambassadors, to say nothing of regional assistant secretaries of state, of the added value of such a capacity? And how would you stave off the inevitable pressure to separate approved religions from nefarious ones?

The essays established that overlooking the complex role of religious dynamics and religious actors in the case studies would render an incomplete understanding of the best diplomatic avenues and options. But they did not offer a clear view of what sorts of people with what capabilities might lead to better diplomatic outcomes.

In 1996 Harvard professor Samuel Huntington wrote his controversial book *The Clash of Civilizations and the Remaking of World Order*. His book was an expansion of a 1993 article in *Foreign Policy* in which he set out a broad interpretive framework that purported to give an accurate account of the forces at work in the new post–Cold War international order. This book may have been the single most influential attempt to fill the theoretical vacuum left by the collapse of the defining metaphor of the field of international relations, the Cold War. And it was among the most wrongheaded such books in the massive literature of the day.[4]

What do I mean by wrongheaded? Simply put, Huntington's thesis reinforced stereotypes regarding "the West," Islam, and how to conceptualize religion. His framework of seven to nine civilizations proved to be a highly reductive account of the role of religion around the globe, one that proved hard to shake in the immediate aftermath of 9/11. As I traveled the world as a diplomat and met with hundreds of Muslims two decades after the book was published, it was axiomatic for many of the Muslims I met that the Huntington thesis was the dominant hermeneutical framework for American diplomatic engagement with the world. And that made my work harder. For example, when I did a remote video conference with an international relations college class in Gaza, I was asked repeatedly why the State Department's approach to diplomacy was dictated by *The Clash of Civilizations* instead of by the work of Noam Chomsky. Despite my best efforts, I could not convince them that this was not the case. I even resorted to telling them a story from my graduate-school days at Harvard Divinity School when the dean invited Huntington to a private lunch during which his ideas were serially and mercilessly attacked and mocked by the religion professors assembled there. Huntington appeared quite pleased with himself, as I recall, in upsetting the consensus of the Harvard divines.

While I cannot assess the whole meandering book, I will note the problems of its argument related to global religious dynamics with an eye to how it hampered more sophisticated views to emerge. His central thesis is that the best interpretive framework for understanding global politics is positing seven (or eight or nine, depending on where you are in the book) civilizations and charting a set of dynamics between civilizations, including the relation between power and culture, the shifting of balance of power between them, the rising cultural indigenization in non-Western societies, conflicts generated by Western universalism, Muslim militancy, expanding Chinese power, etc.[5]

More ominously, he asserts that "clashes of civilizations are the greatest threat to world peace, and an international order based on civilizations is the surest safeguard against world war."[6] These are ambitious and contradictory intellectual claims. He purports to offer the best account of the emerging world order along with the keys to manage the volatile dynamics of that order. Ironically, and perhaps unintentionally, he sets up a West-versus-the-rest map of the world that ultimately undermines his often overlooked enigmatic call in the closing pages of the work for intercivilizational dialogue as a bulwark against civilizational world war.[7] This then sets him up to miss the insight that imperialist anti-Muslim sentiment in the West might emerge as the greatest threat to world order and global stability. Those allegedly bloody Muslim borders might be there due to Western invasions or at least bad Western policies.

To see this, one has to uncover the role he assigns to religion in civilization and how his implicit definition of religion hampers his moral and political aspirations for the new world order he posits. For Huntington, civilizations represent culture writ large. And culture, he argues, is the most powerful political force shaping the globe. The clash of cultures, via civilizations, supersedes other global dynamics. "A civilization is the broadest cultural entity."[8] This paradigm, he claimed, provides not only better descriptive purchase of the global system; it also provides predictive power. When 9/11 took place, Huntington's predictive power appeared omniscient, and his at least temporary fame was secured because he allegedly predicted the coming civilizational war between the West and Islam.

What exactly is the problem with this framing? First of all, this is grand theory that flies very high over actual facts. His definitions of culture, civilization, and religion remain abstractions. He never actually offers a concise definition of civilization. Civilizations are simply the largest aggregates of ancestry, religion, language, history, values, customs, and institutions that attempt to answer basic human questions, such as, who are we? He inconsistently asserts seven, no eight, no nine recognized civilizations! In the course of two or three pages, he asserts this capacious framework essentially without argument. It is instructive that four of the nine civilizations are religion based—Islamic, Hindu, Orthodox, and Buddhist. While the West, despite his clear preference for Anglo-Catholic Christianity among the various Christian permutations in the West, is simply the West and Christendom. He is quick to assert that religion is a central defining characteristic of civilizations, citing the work of Christopher Dawson. (His debt to the Roman Catholic scholar Dawson is worth deeper exploration, but that takes me too far afield to chase here.)[9]

The upshot is that he embraces flat-footed essentialist notions of religion laced with bromides: "all major scholars recognize the existence of a distinctive Islamic civilization."[10] "Islamic culture explains in large part the failure of democracy to emerge in much of the Muslim world."[11] Likewise, the Muslim resurgence represents a repudiation of the West.[12] And, perhaps most famously, "Islam has bloody borders." While at times he notes that religions are internally plural, he ignores pluralism, because it is corrosive to his central thesis that civilizations are the largest and most important analytical units for understanding global politics. All these views share a one-dimensional understanding of Islam, a framework that sets up a West-versus-Islam global dynamic, and a capacious general theory that can absorb much contradictory data into its framework while simultaneously skating around pesky evidence that calls the ideal type into question. None of these trends augur well for a nuanced approach to interpreting religion in context. Religions are described in their alleged essences, not as complex, internally plural, historically shaped entities. And finally, he leaps over the speeding global mobility of religious adherents far beyond their purported geographical boundaries. Globalism was well under way when he was writing and has only accelerated early in the current millennium, such that religious pluralism has put the lie to any stable global framework of religious adherence by geographical location.

But the most influential publication on religion and diplomacy was former secretary of state Madeline Albright's book *The Mighty and the Almighty* in 2006. Writing five years after she completed her service as secretary of state, Albright surprised many by writing about the need for American diplomacy to build a greater capacity to interpret religion as a routine part of US foreign policy. Of all the topics a veteran American diplomat could have chosen to write about, religion was perhaps the least likely one since, as a rule, not only was religion barely on the radar screen of foreign policy practitioners but it was also virtually invisible to international relations theorists.[13]

Drawing on her experience, she noted that while religion had played important roles in varied locations, including Vietnam, the Balkans, Iran, Poland, Uganda, Lebanon, Israel and Palestine, Saudi Arabia, and Iraq, the State Department in her tenure had no experts for her to draw on with the exception of the ambassador at large for international religious freedom. And that was not enough in her view.

In contrast, she had armies of experts on economics, history, politics, military affairs, nuclear nonproliferation, and a raft of other issues to call upon when she needed advice. This, despite the obvious growing need for the State Department to be able to deal with religion. One of her fundamental arguments was that diplomacy does not move forward based on certainty, but from analysis based on good information built on good evidence. How is it possible to deal with the complexities of religion around the globe if diplomats do not have access to good information and good interpretation of religious dynamics? Rather than relying on the idiosyncratic religious personal experiences of diplomats, why not develop a professional capacity on this subject analogous to the multitude of experts the department had on other subjects?

Albright understood that various religions shaped values, policies, and methods of interpretation all around the world in very complex ways that called for more than anecdotal musings from current diplomats. Ignoring these dynamics could only lead to bad outcomes and policy disasters as well as missed opportunities to promote peace, fight extreme poverty, etc. To her credit she did not hypothesize in a grand fashion to argue, as some did, that religion was inherently bad or good as a force in international affairs. Her experience was too deep to resort to that sort of reductionism.

Another crucially important point Albright made was linking public diplomacy and good policy. That is, if a government makes colossal policy blunders, no amount of diplomacy can erase the consequences of those policy blunders. In the religion space, the terrible consequences of our disastrous Iraq policy permanently damaged US credibility in the Islamic world. No matter how many resets, or pivots, or surges were made in the decades after the 2003 invasion of Iraq, US credibility was to remain hamstrung.

For my purposes, the most important message Secretary Albright's work conveyed was the then unfulfilled mission of actually building the capacity within the State Department to engage religion as a vital and important routine function. If a former US secretary of state made a strong case for such a mission, it would be very hard to argue that the proposition was not worth considering. When the Office of Religion and Global Affairs reached full staffing in early 2015, we held a public event to celebrate the milestone, and Secretary Albright graced us with a speech noting that her call, almost a decade before, was now being heeded by Secretary Kerry with the full staffing of our office. Senior diplomatic leadership at the very height of the US government was one early key to our success.

There is a final coterie of thinkers who recognized the power of various religions in public, refusing to accept any delegation of religion to a private sphere, walled off from any public impact or consequences. These were voices from within certain specific religious traditions. For the sake of brevity, I will cite two people, one a Christian theologian and the other a scholar of Islam.

In 1991 Harvard Divinity School dean and theologian Ronald Thiemann published a collection of essays titled *Constructing a Public Theology: The Church in a Pluralistic Age.*[14] At the center of his project was a conviction that religious communities, in his case Christian communities, need not concede the relegation of their work to the private sphere by liberal democracy. Instead they could and should engage the pluralistic world in a manner that was fully, authentically anchored in Christian belief and practice, thus preserving its particularity but also contributing to public life in a manner that would support liberal democracy and see moral, political, and religious pluralism as a strength and not a weakness to be cured.

I believe he thought other religious communities beyond Christianity were also capable of similar work in the public sphere. My purpose here is not to give a comprehensive review of his argument but to note that within religious communities, thinkers, leaders, and practitioners were beginning to theorize against the widely assumed truth that religion was purely a private affair devoid of political impact or contribution to public and political life. One consequence was that Thiemann believed an American diplomatic corps that was tone-deaf regarding the public implications of lived religion was a very dangerous thing.

He argued for a form of public theology in which religious actors could move from the particularity of their religious communities into a pluralistic, liberal democratic polity in a manner that both preserved their theological particularity and worked to strengthen liberal democracy and support pluralism. In fact, he argued that particular religious communities could, more richly, make salutary political and social contributions as part of their core life and identity.[15]

One final voice to note, while not from the 1990s but important nonetheless, is the late Shahab Ahmed in his important work *What Is Islam? The Importance of Being Islamic*.[16] I cite Ahmed because he notes the multiplicity of interpretations of Islam throughout its history precisely on the relationship between Islam and modern secular/religion binaries and what he calls the legalist-supremacist paradigm. As he puts it, modern Muslims have an "altogether greater existential problem of living in terms of conceptual incoherence with their past."[17] In other words, Islamic scholars did not universally theorize a disappearance of religion or a segregation of Islam into a private sphere. It never disappeared from view in its own conceptions of politics, much to the surprise of many in the so-called West in the late twentieth century. There was no universal settlement or reconciliation within Islam to modern politics, as there seemed to be within Western Christianity, that required a privatization of Islam.

What these examples show is that in the late twentieth century the global political power of religion reemerged on the world stage in dramatic fashion and people began to pay more attention. As a corollary, the US government did not wake up to this reality in a nimble and quick fashion, to put it mildly. This leads to my second argument, that ignorance of the power of religion can be costly. We need look no further than our war in Afghanistan in 2001 and to our 2003 invasion of Iraq. Herein lies the peril part of Secretary Kerry's frequent observation that we ignore religion at our peril.

The Iraq War provides very powerful evidence that willful ignorance of religion can be costly. This became one of my stock arguments for justifying the launching of the Office of Religion and Global Affairs inside the department. I learned early in my time at State that there was near universal belief that our invasion of Iraq led to cascading disasters in terms of American lives lost, Iraqi lives lost, trillions of dollars wasted, and the irreparable damage done to America's standing in the world. The invasion ranks as one of the worst foreign policy blunders in the history of the republic, and certainly the worst such miscalculation since Vietnam. It is a cascading disaster that continues to this day. Our failure to understand religious dynamics cuts across the whole fiasco.

One need look no further than the cost of lives and dollars in our post-9/11 wars in Iraq and Afghanistan to grasp the enormity of this policy blunder. Here is a sample of what we know about the human costs, from the Watson Institute of Brown University. Seven thousand fifty-two US soldiers were killed and 8,189 contractors died. Allied troop deaths were 14,874. Opposition fighter deaths were estimated to be between 296,858 and 301,933. Civilian deaths were estimated to be between 363,939 and 387,072. Humanitarian and NGO deaths were 680. More disabilities per soldier occurred in these two wars than in the Vietnam War, the Korean War, or World War II; 670,000 were disabled.[18] Some studies estimate that 12.9 percent of Iraq veterans suffer from PTSD (posttraumatic stress disorder).[19] Three thousand four hundred eighty-one US contractors died, 12,000 national police were killed, 319 allied troops died, 36,400 opposition fighters died, and 137,000 to 165,000 civilians died, for a total of 194,000 to 222,000 deaths.[20]

As for disability claims, 895,606 veterans had been awarded them (includes all Global War on Terror veterans) by the end of 2014.[21] Estimates of the number of Iraqis who died range from 151,000 to 600,000; 307,986 Iraqis became refugees, and an estimated 3.6 million were internally displaced.[22]

The Christian population of Iraq shrank from 1,500,000 to 500,000 during the war.[23] Ironically, during my time at State, several conservative Christian religious freedom groups criticized the Obama administration for allegedly not caring about the declining Christian population in Iraq. But their memories of Iraq always seem to start on January 20, 2009, and not back in March 2003 when President Bush invaded Iraq, which was the primary force behind Christians fleeing Iraq.

The monetary costs of the war are staggering.[24] The Watson Institute at Brown University estimates the current cost of the wars in Iraq and Afghanistan, including appropriations and expenditures, future spending, and the cumulative interest through 2056 on war appropriations through fiscal year 2013, at $8 trillion![25]

But how does all of this relate to my claim that failure to grasp the complexities of religious dynamics contributed to the disaster? It is crucial for the argument of this book to see clearly that ignorance of complex religious dynamics can come with staggering price tags in terms of both lives lost and money irrationally spent. And our "forever wars" are the most palpable example of this I can point out. The politics and policies of this war failed to materialize, and willful ignorance of religious and other factors plays a huge part in the carnage. C. J. Stivers summarizes the point well:

> One of the many sorrows of the wars is that most American troops had little substantive interactions with Afghan and Iraqi civilians. Language and cultural differences, tactics, rules, security barriers, operational tempo, violence, racism, mutual suspicions, and a dearth of interpreters all combined to prevent it. The people who lived where Americans fought and patrolled, and whose protection was presented in official statements as one of the wars' organizing ideas, were often regarded by those on duty in the provinces as scenery, puzzles, problems, or worse. Citizens and occupiers had physical proximity but almost total social distance. . . . The result was that during action, and after, American combatants had little means to gain insight into the views or experience of Afghan and Iraqi civilians, as is often evident in veterans' memories and accounts of their tours.[26]

There are five points in the Iraq War where the failure to master complex dimensions of religion, among many other factors, led to disaster. If the religious dynamics had been understood properly, the invasion itself would have been questioned before it took place, and some of the horrors of the war would have been mitigated as it was prosecuted. These aspects are the following: first, President Bush's decision to invade; second, the military response to the unexpected insurgency; third, the lack of a coherent and competent governance plan for the country, including the attempt to write and force adoption of an American-style constitution on Iraq, which included inscribing American-style religious freedom language into that document; fourth, a shoddy attempt at a postconflict reconstruction; and finally, the mistaken strategic framework for the entire war. I'll take these up in order.

We really do not know how President Bush made his decision to invade Iraq. We do know that his decision was not made as the culmination of an orderly policy decision-making process curated by the National Security Council, where all the relevant policy agencies could have fully weighed in and debated the policy options.[27] The complexities of Iraq's religious dynamics between Sunni and Shia Muslims, to say nothing of the various religious minorities, never figured in his deliberations.

Instead, the three major causes were cited: to punish Hussein for his alleged weapons of mass destruction, to break the alleged Hussein–global terror axis, and to liberate oppressed people. Very quickly after the invasion, all of these justifications for the invasion were rendered false by events. These original arguments in turn fueled a narrative of preventive war that pushed aside any serious consideration of the costs of any invasion. Blind to the Sunni-Shia historical dynamics, the naïve war plan was doomed before it began, and we are still paying the price for this malfeasance. It did not have to be this way.

For my narrower concern about how a more sophisticated understanding of some of the dynamics of religion might have moved the administration to contemplate the danger of the course it set early on, it is important to see not only that the president did not consider these religious dynamics. It is even more dismaying to note that the foreign policy bureaucracy was not capable of producing a detailed assessment even if it had been consulted. There are three analytical products I know of, one from the State Department's Office of Policy and Planning and two from the National Intelligence Council analyzing the challenges posed by Iraq, and none of them convey much beyond an elementary understanding of Iraqi religious issues.[28] It isn't clear to me if the Pentagon cared a whit about religious dynamics, and if it did, it is not clear it had any influence on the war planning.

Beyond the decision to invade, the second moment when the narrow-mindedness of the administration can be seen is in the poor response to the dizzying speed of the emergence of the insurgency. There was no wisdom on how to engage the diversity of religious and political actors on the ground. A small investment before the invasion, done by the right people, could have revealed the complex role religion played in Iraqi life and politics such that any prospective invader might have rethought occupation and postconflict reconstruction as impossibly expensive projects. But invade we did, without fully grasping how a more sophisticated understanding of the religious aspects of Iraq could have prevented or mitigated some aspects of the tragedy.

By 2006 momentum was building among a cadre of younger military officers who had served in Afghanistan and in Iraq for a more robust counterinsurgency strategy designed to replace the outdated Cold War training the senior levels of the US military were implementing against insurgencies in both countries. Neither war was going well, and public opinion was turning against the Bush war efforts.[29] David Kilcullen's work chronicles the emergence of a different understanding of what was required in response to the emerging insurgencies, and to his credit, he argues that at the heart of winning hearts and minds is a commitment to local solutions based on seeking understanding of local dynamics, including religious dynamics.

But his proposals were deeply flawed both in their conception of Islam and in their confidence that military personnel could master the complex dynamics of lived religion and other cultural dynamics in environments such as Iraq and Afghanistan, where they had virtually no training in understanding Islam. The advice both from Kilcullen and in the *U.S. Army/Marine Corps Counterinsurgency Field Manual* remains highly abstract in its analysis of religion, and both sources are oddly confident that US fighting forces can acquire deep knowledge of Iraqi religious dynamics on the fly and without expert training and knowledge.[30]

While one welcomes the call to put understanding the local environments of counterinsurgency work at the center of these efforts, the naïve assumptions that untrained military personnel, or worse, military chaplains, possess the expertise to do this work is a formula for disaster. Kilcullen completely undermines a commitment to local understanding of religious dynamics in Iraq at the outset of his work when he essentializes the local phenomena he saw in Afghanistan and Iraq as local expressions of a globalized Islamist insurgency. Following his analysis, US soldiers would see any form of Muslim insurgency as part of an organized global federation. This is a presupposition that is not only wrong; it effectively undercuts his commitment at the outset of his book that local analysis is key to success.

Given the difficulty of training nineteen-year-old military personnel in a very short period of time how to fight and avoid getting killed, how does it make sense to think that in this period of time they can acquire a working knowledge of forms of a religion that is very alien to their understanding? Against that background, it is understandable why senior military leaders would turn to the notion that chaplains were a good source of engaging Muslim communities and leaders. Yet this move was not particularly wise.[31]

Most members of the various military chaplaincy corps are Christians, trained in US graduate theological seminaries. Very few have received formal academic training in interreligious peacemaking or in the study of Islam. However, on November 20, 2013, the Joint Chiefs of Staff issued Joint Publication I-05, *Religious Affairs in Joint Operations*, which added a second mission to the existing mission of the military chaplains to provide for the spiritual needs of military personnel. This second mission expanded the role of chaplains to an advisory role during military engagement at all levels of war, ranging from the Strategic National level with Joint Staff all the way down to the tactical level.

Members of the Chiefs of the Chaplains and their staff with whom I talked when I was at State expressed a high level of anxiety that the training of the Chaplaincy Corps members, both in seminary and in the military, did not equip them to properly fulfill this new role. To be sure, some chaplains had this skill set. But they were the exceptions that proved the rule that chaplains were not the right people to provide wise counsel in military theaters on understanding religious dynamics in war zones.[32]

Occupations are messy, and building bridges across deep religious, cultural, and linguistic divides rarely seems to work. We just are not any good at it, and we never will be good at it where the linguistic, cultural, and religious gaps are as wide as they were in Iraq and Afghanistan.

The next point of the Iraq debacle illustrating the impact of the lack of expertise in religious dynamics was the failure of the American effort in helping the Iraqis restore governance to the broken country, the one we broke. The literature on the war tends to focus on the decision by Paul Bremer to disband the Iraqi army and to remove the members and influence of the Ba'ath Party from public office (called de-Baathification), and rightly so. Both moves led to massive unemployment of key government experts, thus alienating a large part of the population, to say nothing of the loss of technical capacity in providing security and restoring public functions. But two other areas are more concretely related to religion: the inability of the Provisional Governing Authority to establish a working relationship with Ayatollah Sistani, and the insistence by US religious freedom advocates that the new Iraqi constitution call for a secular state and not allow an Iraqi Islamic government, in order to mimic a model of separation found in the US Constitution.

Many analysts have noted the signal failure of Paul Bremer, the Bush administration's director of the Provisional Governing Authority, to understand the importance of Ayatollah Ali Sistani's influence in Iraq. As a result, Bremer never developed an effective working relationship with the most powerful Shia leader in Iraq. The most damning testimony about Bremer's complete lack of understanding of the religious landscape in general and of the pivotal role Sistani played in Iraq's politics comes from Ravi Chandrakekaran, the bureau chief in Baghdad for the *Washington Post* from April 2003 until October 2004, who covered the Coalition Provisional Authority, which Bremer ran. On August 9, 2006, he said:

> You have to go back to June 2003. Sistani issued the fatwa saying that the constitution needs to be written by Iraqis in an elected process. . . .
>
> Bremer's plan called for an appointed group of Iraqis to write the constitution, perhaps appointed by Bremer's government folks. Well, that contradicts Sistani's fatwa. Bremer thinks that he can just get away with this.
>
> In the early months, Sistani was seen by people inside the palace as just another old man with a turban, and Bremer felt he'd be able to convince the member of the Governing Council to just disregard Sistani and push ahead with this plan. What becomes clear by the fall of 2003 is that the Governing Council does not want to cross Sistani, particularly the Shiite members. . . . It's like telling a bunch of Catholics, "Disregard the pope."

So Bremer can't get his Governing Council onboard to do his bidding. That's where it all comes crashing down. And Sistani shows himself to be far more influential and powerful than Bremer.[33]

Bremer, who had no understanding of Iraq before becoming the leader of the Provisional Governing Authority, paid a very high price for his ignorance of Sistani's influence. Ironically, Sistani was more of a democrat than Bremer or the White House, in that he believed that elected Iraqis should write the new constitution, not an ad hoc committee of Iraqis handpicked by Bremer or the White House. While Washington feared a constitution written by Iraqis for Iraqis, this ignorance-based approach eroded whatever chances there might have been for a swift transition of political power to the Iraqi people. The whole candle was lost at this juncture, and the loss was driven in no small way by Bremer's misperception of this old religious man in a turban.[34]

Irony was compounded as the United States exercised a heavy hand by insisting that the Iraqi constitution had to call for a secular, that is, a non-Islamic, government, in the name of religious freedom! This is the second area of governance in which US ignorance of Iraqi religious dynamics dominated the American approach.[35] Here again, Sistani is one of the primary characters and Bremer's ineptitude is on public display.

In short, the United States attempted to dictate a version of America's so-called separation of church and state to Iraq in its constitution. This sort of imposed constitutionalism, whose central premise was to keep Iraq from declaring itself an Islamic republic, was a naked attempt at colonial imposition, and not an act of self-determination on the part of the Iraqis.[36] Ayatollah Sistani issued a fatwa arguing that the Iraqi people should write and pass their own constitution, and not one written by America and its self-chosen dissident Iraqis. The freshly minted United States Commission of International Religious Freedom, among many others, tried to assert an American right to secure and impose an American version of religious freedom on Iraq. With no sense of irony, its conservative Christian voices argued to disempower Iraq's Muslim leaders from addressing religious tolerance on their own terms, while simultaneously arguing that back home Christian conservatives had been unfairly excluded from the public realm by raging liberals and secularists. As Anna Su brilliantly lays out, Iraq represented the latest and most sophisticated form of the United States asserting its constellation of beliefs on religious freedom by means of military and global political power. Religious freedom and tolerance was not one of a complex array of human rights we commend to the world. It was the premier human right, and one we were willing to export as part of the projection of American hard power. Religious freedom, as established by the International Religious Freedom Act, was literally weaponized as one tool in the US arsenal to export Christianity and to limit and control, in this case, Islam.

That Sistani and the Iraqi people were able ultimately to successfully subvert this conservative American religious political stratagem is a signal of many things, not the least of which is that the US international religious freedom regime is coercive and fraught with multitudinous problems and is driven more by conservative Christian ideology than by an integrated view of human rights. An approach that was more attuned to the history of Iraq on religious tolerance would have designed an Iraqi-led process for writing their own constitution while advocating for the maximal degree of religious tolerance in Iraq possible at that time. Instead, the imposed constitutional approach only delayed the production of a constitution and further eroded American credibility with the Iraqi people.

The willful blindness of US-based religious freedom advocates to what was realistically possible in Iraq simply fed the ongoing debacle that unspooled over the next decade there. Another ironic note that was missed was the fact the West took centuries across early modernity to evolve into its current highly contested conceptions of religious freedom. And yet we were arrogant enough to think we could impose a version of the current US understanding by military force and occupation, ostensibly by the barrel of gun, without any dissent from Iraqi leaders, religious or otherwise. If nothing else, this episode illustrates the coercive nature of our religious freedom rights regime and its avoidance of trying to persuade countries to embrace a modest form of religious freedom as a negative right (the right to practice one's own religion freely without coercion and restriction). This would require the United States to deploy diplomatic positive persuasion, and not threats of sanctions and other forms of punishment written into our international religious freedom structures.

The fourth area where US ignorance was made manifest was in post-conflict reconstruction efforts. Before the invasion, Army Chief of Staff General Eric Shinseki told Congress that several hundred thousand troops would be necessary in postwar Iraq for reconstruction efforts.[37] Paul Wolfowitz moved swiftly to contest Shinseki's numbers and timeline. History would prove Shinseki's case to be more accurate. A variety of actors on the ground in Iraq quickly exposed the fecklessness of the Bush "plan" to successfully rebuild Iraq. Longer-term postmortems delivered even harsher reviews. The consensus view is that the administration did not know local and national actors, including religious leaders; didn't care about their ignorance until after they got there; and then did not take adequate measures to cure their ignorance once it became apparent.[38]

The fifth and final aspect of the Bush administration's failure to understand the religious dynamics of the Iraq invasion can be seen at the strategic level. The best way I know to evaluate the Bush strategy for invading is to apply the analysis of John Lewis Gaddis's recent and rich study *On Grand Strategy*, which I mentioned earlier. Borrowing British philosopher Isaiah Berlin's conception of foxes and hedgehogs, Gaddis assesses a dizzying array of strategic thinkers through this construct.[39]

My conclusion, simply put, is that President Bush was a strategic hedgehog who thought he knew one big thing: Iraq was a rogue terrorist state in need of regime change, and the 9/11 attack presented the best opportunity for America to demonstrate, by means of regime change there, that Islamic terror could be defeated and replaced by democracy in Iraq, thus setting off a chain reaction in the Islamic world. In contrast, a strategic fox armed with what Gaddis calls "a compass" would have argued, at almost every important step in the Iraq debacle, that a detailed knowledge of the religious dynamics of the Iraq situation counseled against the ultimately disastrous decisions made by the hedgehog, Bush. Other factors, of course, would have also led to the same conclusion. By looking at several stops along the Iraq War timeline—the decision to invade, the planning for reconstruction, the writing of the Iraqi constitution, and the response to the insurgency—I showed Bush's hedgehog disposition led either to the dismissal of evidence drawn from Iraqi religious dynamics or the complete avoidance of considering such data, because it called into question the one big thing: regime change and its alleged benefits. Gaddis's two categories of strategic thinking shed light at the strategic level.

As you can see by now, I believe the Iraq War was a strategic blunder of epic proportion. At some distance from 2003, the question strikes me, why did Bush make such a strategic blunder and risk so much and create such grief and chaos? The Gaddis framework explains this and thereby highlights the significant ignorance of the religious dynamics at the center of his administration's decision to go to war.

Bush's run-up to the 2003 invasion of Iraq provides the opening scene in a drama that I see as an extreme example of hedgehog-like behavior. Throughout the period between the attack on 9/11 and the invasion of March 2003, Bush held onto a single dominant mission: to teach extremist Muslims around the world that the United States would not tolerate Saddam Hussein's alleged bad behavior such as developing weapons of mass destruction. Thus defeating Saddam Hussein and transforming Iraq into a democracy would be an object lesson that even the slowest-witted could not misinterpret. When we unpack the major elements of this vision, we see that the systematic refusal to pursue counterevidence—punishing military and diplomatic advice against the invasion—and ultimately misleading the American people combined to expose the dangers of single-minded hedgehog behavior.

Gaddis is insightful here when he argues that hedgehogs fail to establish a proper relationship between ends and means. He notes that ends can become infinite in reality, while means are stubbornly finite. Unwavering commitment to the one big thing makes it very hard to adjust to cumulative effects.[40] Bush's ends were epic, world historical in aspiration. The means he chose were shortsighted, rigid, ill-informed, unvetted, and imposed from the White House on the military, our diplomats, members of Congress, the media, and ultimately the American public. Similarly, hedgehogs tend not to tether their idea to the limits imposed by time, space, and scale.[41] What specifically do I mean?

It is well documented that President Bush decided to invade Iraq without the benefit of a thorough national security decision-making process at some point in the middle of 2002.[42] Fixated on his goal of making an example of Iraq to flout US hard power in the Middle East and to deter the acquisition of destructive weapons by Muslim terrorists or states, he had no need for extensive weighing of costs, assessing consequences, or adopting strategic goals from the vast national security apparatus of the US government.[43] In the process he overplayed poor intelligence to argue (lie?) that Iraq possessed weapons of mass destruction, which turned out in the end not to be true. Along the way he beat political opponents into submission by an effective campaign based on a Manichean framing: those who do not support us are against us. Ultimately all of this shortsightedness on means rendered the ends fruitless.

Over time he did no coordinating of his ends with the means at his disposal. Instead, aided and abetted by Vice President Cheney, he systematically silenced dissent in the Pentagon, at the State Department, in Congress, and in American society. Over the balance of his presidency, a series of military, diplomatic, and political failures in Iraq spurred a long series of unanticipated recalibrations and restarts.

Questions of means soon flooded the delusional ends of the transformation of the Middle East. Weapons of mass destruction were touted but never found. The National Security Council never conducted an organized process for the president to assess the options regarding going to war. No systematic analysis of postconflict reconstruction costs or strategy was conducted. Instead, the possible long-term outcomes were dismissed for short-term political gains. A pernicious strategic doctrine of prevention was adopted based on a policy of fear and not ethics. And at all stages, local, countrywide, and regional religious dynamics were never considered. Any concerns here were overridden by the naïve assumption that Iraqis of any and all religious communities would welcome the United States as liberators and would thank us for giving them democracy. All of this took place because the hedgehog impulse blindly pushed aside foxes who had counterevidence that might have triumphed over the delusions of the hedgehogs if given the chance.

Gaddis suggests that the best strategic thinkers find a way to balance the dialectic between the two different animal species. That is, in the end, leaders who find a way to pursue major goals but tether their big ideas to considerations of time, space, and scale do better. Bush did not tether his goal of transforming the Middle East by invasion to any of these three considerations.[44] Let's walk through this systematically.

Unlike Lincoln's mastery of scale, space, and time, I believe Bush demonstrated the opposite.[45] Scale sets the ranges within which experience accrues, according to Gaddis. Lincoln sought to be underestimated and remained resilient, accommodating unknowns more readily than someone rigidly hemmed in by history, expectations, and a desire to fulfill family history. He argues that this disposition lends itself to being more effective in responding to the unknowns of experience. Without such resilience, one has little room to adapt and tends to feel entitled and grow arrogant. Bush's sense of scale was world historic, family driven, willing to teach millions of would-be Muslim terrorists and dozens of Muslim-majority countries a lesson in imposed colonial democracy. It led to rigidity and a disinterest in key factors about one's alleged enemies.

Space, according to Gaddis, is where expectations and circumstances intersect. Lincoln mastered the intricacies of Northern strengths versus Southern strengths. Bush, by invading Iraq, opened a second war in addition to Afghanistan, and assumed a swift conquest would be followed by welcome of US troops as liberators and thus a minimal reconstruction and postwar occupation. The results of this complete failure to understand the intricacies of Iraqi "space" doomed the enterprise swiftly.

As the war effort quickly stalled and met massive resistance within Iraq, there was no nimble adaptation to these facts, much less any overt rethinking of the wisdom of the strategic framework. This strategic blunder was compounded as the administration demonstrated none of the suppleness that Gaddis commends by listening to foxes who have expertise. The Iraq War is a sobering case study on why grand strategy needs overarching visions that are tempered and modified in real time by expert judgment.

The Office of Religion and Global Affairs staff was built as an intentional den of foxes who were capable of generating deep and wise advice on how to advance American strategic diplomatic goals. An analogous source of counsel in the Bush era could have helped avoid the strategic mistakes and find better alternative strategic responses to 9/11 that would not have led to the dire consequences of the Bush travesty. Someone needs to ask the tough questions and present the good news as well as the bad news when strategy is being crafted, when strategy is not working, when strategy has utterly failed, and when strategy has worked miracles! Part of my job as director, and also the work of our chief of staff, was to try and make sure our expertise was linked to the strategic priorities of the secretary. Otherwise we were just writing memos to each other, or, as one wag put it, spending time admiring problems.

The third argument for why we should care whether or not the State Department has a capacity to interpret religion globally is related to the first argument. The point here is that interpreting the complexities of religion requires expertise and training. If diplomats are going to add interpretation of religion to their skills, it will take time and effort to understand religion and build relationships with experts and their networks.

The American diplomatic apparatus, from the staffing of our embassies and consulates to the organization of the Washington bureaucracy, is premised on understanding how and why people, states, and nonstate actors move in the world. The simple premise is that in order to be effective in diplomacy, our government needs to understand not only what people do but also how they have acted in the past, and perhaps most important, why they do what they do. The result is an impressive array of expertise in history, economics, law, science, politics, and peace across our diplomatic corps. But as Secretary of State Madeline Albright observed, she had hundreds of experts in all these subjects to turn to for advice, but when it came to religion, she had none.[46] In far too many places in America today, just about anyone can claim expertise in religion despite lack of any real study or knowledge. As one friend of mine said on 9/12/2001, there were hundreds of self-proclaimed Islamic experts born spewing hate and ignorance under the guise of expertise. As a professor of religion, I am constantly challenged by the untutored, who offer all manner of analysis of religions based primarily on drawing analogies about religions based primarily on their own religious experience. I'm sorry to say it, but the angst-ridden adolescent religious experiences of American baby boomers aren't going to generate any valid interpretations of, or fruitful analogues to, or knowledge of, contemporary religious communities around the world.

American embassies usually lack interpretive capacity on religions. The average Foreign Service officer I met in an embassy was multilingual, had lived in multiple countries, understood multiple cultures, was inquisitive, was well educated, and had completed some graduate education. But often when it came to religion, these officers were reticent, even fearful of the subject, and certainly not professionally rewarded for acquiring expert knowledge on the subject, yet frequently they admitted that knowing the subject was deeply relevant for their work, based on their professional experience. But very few would profess any deep skill in interpreting it or would say they encountered ambassadors or deputy chiefs of mission who rewarded them for developing skills in understanding the political and social implications of religion in their countries of work.

In the issues American diplomacy cares about—sustainable development, conflict mitigation, and human rights, to name only three important diplomatic topics—religious actors are forces for good, for evil, and innumerable other possible outcomes. If American diplomacy is to be effective, ignorance of these diverse influences cannot be the norm. Especially in times of crisis, embassies rarely have the time to develop new relationships. It's hard to build relationships and understanding when bullets are flying. Somehow a deeper understanding of religious communities and a set of routine relationships have to be cultivated over time between embassy staff and their host country. Likewise, the career officers in the United States need to have an analytic capacity as part of the normal business of forming and implementing foreign policy. Ignorance of religious dynamics can only lead to more mistakes and blunders.

If the case for a more sophisticated diplomatic approach to religion is compelling—that is, if you believe religion is powerful and ubiquitous, that ignorance of religious dynamics can be costly, and that religious actors and dynamics are complex and multivalent, requiring forms of expertise to decode them—the much tougher question is: How should this work be done? It is one thing to admit there is a problem; the much tougher task is to figure out what the alternative to mediocrity or neglect should be. There are many ways this work could go awry, such as promoting certain religious groups to the exclusion of others, and by promoting a particular theological position over others, as the Trump administration did with its unofficial yet official White House Evangelical Advisory Board.

Explaining how we did the work is the task of the remainder of this book. In order to tell the story of just how we did this, I need to say something about just how I became the one John Kerry picked. Doing that requires a quick account of where I came from and what some of the major forces that shaped me were. When Kerry offered me the opportunity to launch S/RGA, the twists and turns of my checkered career all began to make a lot more sense. In retrospect, I felt that much of my personal and professional meandering helped me to take on this project. In order to get to the story of how we did the complex work at the intersection of religion and US diplomacy, I need to start with my own personal journey that began in the backwaters of the Mississippi River in a strange region of the country called the Bootheel of Missouri.

Chapter Three

MALE, PALE, AND NOT QUITE YALE

I WAS FORTUNATE TO BE BORN in the small rural town of Kennett, Missouri, in the so-called Bootheel of southeast Missouri. And if I am doubly lucky, I will be buried in the Mt. Zion Missionary Baptist Church cemetery alongside four generations of Caseys, just north of Kennett, in the middle of rural Butler County. Located ninety miles north of Memphis, Kennett is, in fact, in the middle of nowhere. But I didn't escape from rural America, and I didn't bootstrap myself out of oblivion. I still have ties to that part of the world, and I am bound to the place of my birth in deep and organic ways. To tell the truth, my less than textbook pilgrimage from southeast Missouri to Foggy Bottom in Washington, DC, prepared me pretty well for my diplomatic sojourn. But make no mistake, while it was not exactly a breeding ground for future diplomats, the lessons I learned there would prove useful as a diplomat.[1]

One of the most formative teachers I had was Richard Neustadt, the beloved scholar of presidential politics and policy at Harvard. In this chapter I am attempting to do what he and his fellow professor Ernest May call "placement." The only difference is, I am placing myself, not another figure. Neustadt and May developed a technique called placing strangers, which I will follow in this chapter. I am not a stranger to myself, obviously, but I was a stranger to almost everyone I worked with at State, and I am also a stranger to most of my readers. Neustadt and May call for placing institutions in historical context in order to gain deeper insights about those institutions, but they also note the same holds true for policy makers. Even within the same institutions, different actors behave differently due to the unique contours of their personal and institutional stories. Here is how they describe the exercise:

> For effective analysis or management, the kind that is not just academically right but gets something done, it is crucial, we think, to anticipate and take into account the different ways in which different actors see the world and their roles in it—not only organizationally but also humanly as individuals. We recognize that such anticipation is mostly a matter of innately sensitive fingertips aided by experience. We recognize also that an effort to make more of it seems, at first glance, to invade the domain of psychologists and psychoanalysts, if not astrologers and shamans. We have nothing of the sort in mind. But anticipating those differences is too crucial a part of analysis and management to be sidestepped altogether, and we think that some tracking of individuals, some delineation of *their* histories—akin to time-lines for issues—if used very carefully and with awareness of limitations, can yield results useful both for making decisions and for carrying them out.[2]

Religion and politics were two constants in my childhood. And the peculiar combination of the two probably sealed my vocational fate. My father's family was Baptist; my mother's family had roots in the Churches of Christ. As was often the case in that part of the South, the mother's religion prevailed among the children. Mine was as close to an interreligious experience as people had in that part of the world in that era. And make no mistake, it was a decidedly "mixed" religious marriage. The sectarian nature of the Churches of Christ theology treated Baptists in the same way it treated hardcore atheists—they were outside the love of God and destined for eternal perdition. We were redneck, poor, white-trash Christians, and we took our religion straight, no chasers. One wag said we had three sacraments, not the usual Protestant two: baptism, communion, and arguing.[3] It wasn't exactly the textbook diplomatic training of the famous A100 introductory class for freshly recruited Foreign Service officers in the State Department. But an appreciation for the intricacies and ironies of passionately held theological worldviews would later prove to be a diplomatic advantage, even though along the line I outgrew the sectarianism of my childhood church. I don't embrace all of the quirks and cul-de-sacs of my religious upbringing, but I do have an eye for interpreting religious beliefs, practices, and idiosyncrasies that might otherwise appear opaque to others.

The hard-line biblicism of the Churches of Christ provided a moral framework of a sort. But its intricacies often proved self-defeating. One story will suffice to illustrate the point. In the late fifties, with the baby boom booming in real time, the small congregation in Kennett where my mother attended found itself bursting at the seams with kids. (I was born in 1957, the peak of the baby boom.) The church fathers decided the congregation needed to expand and build a fellowship hall adjacent to the sanctuary, or the auditorium, as it was called. "Sanctuary" sounded too Catholic and was not considered "biblical" language. As one snarky preacher put it, "If the denominations left their buildings through the door, we felt compelled to leave the building through the windows." An architect was hired, blueprints were shown, and then the hand-to-hand combat of conservative biblical interpretation lit a prairie fire. At the heart of the theological vision of the tradition was the belief that we did Bible things in Bible ways. Restoring the biblical pattern found in the New Testament was the guiding principle.

Accordingly, some hard-core folk were horrified to see a kitchen in the floor plans. They could not find a New Testament warrant for such an innovation. The "liberals" (so to speak) noted that the existing building had both a men's and a women's restroom, neither of which were explicitly warranted in the New Testament, yet no one argued against their inclusion in the church building. My mother sided with pragmatic "liberals" embracing what became known euphemistically as the "indoor plumbing" argument, which concluded in somewhat commonsense fashion that if it was all right to have a toilet in the church, it was okay to have a kitchen. Years later I would kid my mother that my theological trajectory as a digressive was sealed that day in the fifties when she fell for the liberal argument.

Church played an outsized role in my life compared to many of my childhood peers. It is hard to overstate its influence, and it is also hard to adequately describe the unique quirks of growing up in such a space. As one historian, David Edwin Harrell, writing in 1964, put it, "The twentieth century Churches of Christ are the spirited offspring of the religious rednecks of the post-bellum South." He went on to note, "Of course, the Churches of Christ have not remained an economic and cultural unit since 1906. The sociological and economic elevation of a portion of the membership of the church, especially since World War II, has motivated a large part of the church to begin the transition toward denominationalism. The result is that the movement is once again dividing along sociological lines. Conservative appeals in the movement in the 1960's have a distinctive lower class and antiaristocratic flavor, while the centers of liberalism are in the areas where the church is most numerous and sophisticated."[4]

My childhood years were lived in the no-man's-land fault line between the distinct lower class and the emerging "liberal" class in the Churches of Christ. No one should really care much about this obscure footnote on American church history in the waning days of the last millennium, but it did contribute to my peculiar upbringing and bears directly on parts of my disposition that helped position me to become a diplomat later in my adult career. My religious tribe was undergoing profound sociological and theological change precisely as I was coming of age, and my experience of that change in an odd way prepared me for a lifetime of intellectual and political exploration. If there is one dominant intellectual thread in my life, it is my utter fascination with the public and political implications of religious belief and practice. Growing up in the petri dish of this small fundamentalist sect set me up for a life of exploring the innumerable ways religious actors and their communities generate a wealth of warrants, from the benign to the malevolent, and a thousand stops in between, for all kinds of activity in political realms. If a central part of diplomacy is to understand other peoples, nations, and nonstate actors and to interpret what makes them tick, then my birth into this odd collection of pilgrims was indeed fortuitous.

One of the things I learned is that one's social location matters for how one both sees the world and is seen by the world. I have never been able to transcend completely my sense of growing up on the wrong side of the tracks. Pretty early in my life I developed a healthy sense of reveling in the fact that people would underestimate me based on stereotyping me for my low-class roots. Rightly or wrongly, I assumed I had something of an advantage if I was misjudged because of my economic origins or because I grew up a "Campbellite," a clear term of derision in the southern theological vocabulary applied to members of the Churches of Christ, for alas, Campbellites were sectarians who deluded themselves as being purer, more righteous, bearing a truer interpretation of what the Christian God demanded of his servants than other denominations.[5] I was comfortable with being underestimated. To be sure, later in adulthood, after earning three graduate degrees, from Harvard no less, I sometimes faced a different sort of reaction from people I met who assumed I came from wealth and a long line of highly educated people.

Another trait inherited from my religious upbringing had to do with a commitment to reason and argument. The historical influence of Scottish commonsense realism on American evangelical theology is well documented, and the Churches of Christ was influenced as well. Alexander Campbell, the intellectual father of the movement, was steeped in the philosophy of his day, and the earmarks of that influence were to be found in all quarters in my early church experience. Whatever the pitfalls and quirks of this philosophy, it did leave an imprint on my brain, and not all for the worse.

For example, a good sermon was constructed of dozens of proof texts strung together like so many beads. Ministers preached without notes, reciting Scriptures from memory, torn from their original contexts and stacked back to back to show that the biblical pattern of the New Testament church could be discerned and restored despite the accumulation of centuries of man-made traditions. The central task of the church was to expose these multiple errors and restore primitive Christianity, as has been the intention of the church all along. There was a certain internal coherence to the project perceivable to the initiated among the listeners, but it was an acquired skill. While scriptural warrants were deemed central to justifying the arguments, this was often matched with a heavy dose of polemics and sarcasm and just plain meanness in the pulpit.

The theology was an interesting pastiche of the Puritan impulse to purify Christianity by restoring the pattern of the New Testament combined with a large dose of Enlightenment rationality that structured one's vision of the world as composed of facts needing to be ordered by the reason of authoritative men, with a large dose of American frontier combativeness thrown in as well. My father, a Baptist by upbringing, used to tell a story of hearing a Churches of Christ preacher in the Delta of Mississippi say in the late 1940s that he would rather live with a Communist than with a Catholic. That sort of polemical homiletical bigotry drove him out of the Churches of Christ. He was not alone.

The congregation I attended in Paducah, Kentucky, where we moved when I was four, was built on the fault line Harrell mentioned above. In

1958 the church moved from downtown Paducah near the confluence of the Ohio and Tennessee Rivers to the expanding wealthy section of the west end of town, building, by local standards, a huge brick sanctuary that seated seven hundred comfortably. The cornerstone proclaimed with sectarian confidence: "Church established in Jerusalem 33 A.D. Building erected 1958." The denomination from the wrong side of the tracks suddenly had the cash, the membership, and the real estate savvy to relocate in the heart of the wealthy side of town. The congregation was populated with teachers, small business owners, and burgeoning families, and boasted a parking lot full of new cars, including more than a few Cadillacs and Buicks. Now when the congregation went looking for a minister, it sought someone with a decent theological education, not someone who had put down a plow one day and picked up a Bible the next and started preaching. And they found someone who fit the new bill, not the old brand. What I saw in my formative teen years was the deep social seismic shifts of the denomination being played out in my own congregation in the sixties.

As salaries and families grew, education levels rose. The times were pressing new questions on us, the civil rights movement was unfolding, the Vietnam War dominated the news, the sexual revolution landed in the American South, and the '50s died a very painful death. The old sectarianism of the Churches of Christ was dying, too, and as a thousand new ecclesiastical questions were unleashed, the old well-worn answers were no longer sufficient. Very few of the children born in the '50s and '60s would remain in the denomination as they entered adulthood. My conclusion, in retrospect, is that to be present during the decline of religious tradition and witness the successive waves of responses that ranged from doubling down on the old paths to complete and utter rejection of the theology of a movement, is to be educated, for better or for worse, about the subtleties of human behavior and how the power of religious communities can fragment in countless ways. Astute observers/participants can gain an education that can serve them well when they train their adult gaze on other contexts where it is important to understand the evolving political and social consequences of religious belief and practice. While I did not know it at the time, as I watched my peculiar patch of the American Christian world unspool, I was getting a pretty good tutorial in Diplomacy 101.

Several other features of the region left their imprint on my developing brain. Racial strife and tension were everywhere, even if I could only come to articulate it much later in life. Like many or, more accurately, most southern towns in that era, housing, churches, grocery stores, barbershops, parks, and schools were all segregated. While Missouri was a border state in the Civil War, the southeast corner had a somewhat unique history. Prior to the end of the nineteenth century through the first decade of the twentieth century, the Bootheel was dominated by old-growth forests, swamps, and far more mosquitoes than humans. Intense clear cutting of the old forests coupled with the beginning of a massive drainage-ditch system alongside the Mississippi River created some of the richest farmland in the world. Tenant farming came to be the dominant form of agriculture. But all of this took place well after the Civil War.

During this period of intense logging, racial tensions erupted as the population grew. The massive influx of poor white workers as well as African American workers created a new form of white supremacy. Add an interracial Pentecostal revival in this period, and the white backlash was swift and pervasive. Fledgling attempts at interracial Christian ministries were quickly quelled. In the midst of various forms of labor strife, certain strains of radical politics found at least a modest welcome. In 1912 Socialist presidential candidate Eugene Debs barnstormed across the country and gave a campaign speech in Kennett. He came in third in the 1912 presidential election in the Bootheel, trailing Democrat Woodrow Wilson and Republican Howard Taft, who were first and second, respectively, and ahead of former president Theodore Roosevelt. (I am pretty sure the current Chamber of Commerce does not promote this historical fact today.) But once upon a time there was a much more complex and interesting political landscape, and religion played a part in that.[6]

My parents styled themselves Lincoln Republicans. I grew up thinking the Republican Party stood for preserving the Union and freeing slaves. My great-grandfather, George Washington Casey, left the family farm in Wayne County and joined General Grant and General Sherman in St. Louis during the Civil War. Family lore held that George would ultimately be wounded at Vicksburg, and while being treated at a hospital, he was taught to read and write so he could tell the family back home in Missouri he was wounded but recovering.[7]

I suppose that made my family "moderates" in the region when it came to race. That moderation really amounted to occasionally noting the racial injustice all around us, without any sense that something could or should be done about it. And there was a complete blindness toward any local efforts to ameliorate white supremacy. I remember as a small child being struck by the fact of housing segregation and the ubiquity of the dirt-poor black sections of every town, to say nothing of the tar-paper shacks that lined roads everywhere.

My earliest memories are laced with scenes from small-town mid-South culture in the middle of the twentieth century: church activities, political discussions, farm-based life suffused with racial division and extended family ties. Around the time of John Kennedy's inauguration, our family moved east across the Mississippi River to Paducah, Kentucky, where I would live through graduation from high school. While Kennett had around ten thousand people, Paducah had around thirty-five thousand, and I could not escape the feeling we had left farmland and were now big-city residents.

My years growing up in western Kentucky were marked by the Vietnam War, a growing realization of America's racial injustice, a growing feeling of how powerful education was in my family's DNA, and an expanding understanding of religion, both in my personal beliefs and in understanding the wider American religious landscape. Violence, both personal and institutional, was so thoroughly woven into my lifeworld that it is only now becoming clear to me how pervasive it was in those days. All of these factors helped shape who I was to become in adulthood.

As the fourth child in a family with five kids, I got to see my eventual life unfold first in the lives of my siblings. Church activities, musical performances, lively, even heated political debates, and doing well in school were expected of all of us. I'm not a huge fan of "birth order is destiny," but by the time I reached adolescence, the bar had been set pretty high, and I didn't always match the accomplishments of my older sisters and brother. But I did find my own path.

In retrospect, I now see the centrality of public education. Both of my parents were among the first generation of their families to graduate from college, and both taught in public schools early in their careers. Eventually my mother would direct a federal educational cooperative center that delivered training to teachers and diagnostic services to disabled and underserved school children across thirty western Kentucky school districts. All four of my siblings would spend years teaching in some public educational institutions.

Educational success was encouraged, and served as the daily wallpaper of our lives. Report cards were studied by parents, and social commentary was dispensed. One quarter in grade school my teacher had the temerity to write that I had poor handwriting and that I talked too much in class. My father wrote next to his signature on my report card, "We know." Later in life my parents would complain that their children did not give them grandchildren, just more graduate degrees. They were right. The graduate degrees eventually outnumbered the grandkids ten to three. A native intellectual curiosity became an engine that propels me to this day. Learning was not an external thing to be mastered, it was an ingrained assumption as a constitutive part of a well-lived life. A deep knowledge of the biblical text, a well-digested daily newspaper, a curiosity about people and the world were similar givens.

A lower middle-class income combined with a rural heritage for my parents meant that some middle-class routines, such as hotel-based vacations, were beyond our reach. But my parents were creative, and as a result, we took innumerable camping vacations across the country. One particularly memorable trip came in the summer of 1963 when all seven of us squeezed into a Mercury Comet pulling a U-Haul trailer and headed for Washington, DC. With only slight exaggeration, we used to kid our father that he had to pull off the road to read every historical marker. All of which is to say, it was a long, slow drive. We also complained, with only slight hyperbole, that we visited every Civil War battle site east of the Mississippi.

I remember the Washington visit pretty well, as we made all the usual tourist stops: the Capitol, the Smithsonian, and the other museums. As life-long Republicans, my parents insisted that we make the obligatory semireligious stop at the Lincoln Memorial. As we neared the location, we encountered a massive logistical enterprise unfolding before us at the west end of the Mall. Something big was being prepared, as chairs and scaffolds were being set for what had to be a huge outdoor event. Only later did we realize that this was preparation for the 1963 March on Washington for Jobs and Freedom where Dr. Martin Luther King Jr. gave his famous "I Have a Dream" speech. That seemed typical for my childhood. Big events were happening around the country and the world, but usually at a distance, or at best a near miss just beyond the periphery of our awareness.

The news played an outsized role in our household. I can remember many Sunday afternoons after church and after lunch when my dad would drive the twenty-plus blocks from our house to the only bookstore in town, located near the riverfront, in order to buy a Sunday paper, usually one of the St. Louis papers, the *Globe-Democrat* or the *Post-Dispatch*, or maybe the Memphis paper, the *Commercial Appeal*. We were news junkies before that was a thing. Somewhere around the age of twelve I became a paper boy for the *Louisville Courier Journal*. In those days, the *CJ* was a grand paper, and a rare Kentucky-based window into the rest of the world. I would get up every morning at 5:00 a.m. and ride my bike twelve blocks or so to the gas station, where somebody would throw the bundles out of the delivery truck as it raced by at a pretty high speed.

I very quickly developed the habit of reading the paper before I rolled my papers and delivered them. It was a sort of unwritten rule that the *Courier Journal* should arrive by 6:00 a.m. Paducah was a long way from Louisville, so the paper was usually only read by what passed for the intelligentsia in Paducah. The local paper, the *Sun Democrat*, was an afternoon paper, so the morning news junkies of western Kentucky, such as they were, were the backbone of my customers: attorneys, teachers, stock market investors, and horse-racing fans. Since only a select few locals subscribed to the big-city paper, the routes were several miles long. My cardiovascular system was prodigious for a skinny boy of twelve. One day the district circulation manager pulled his car up to the curb of the gas station and caught me reading the sports section. "I don't pay you to read the goddamn paper, kid, I pay you to deliver it. Roll your papers and get out of here!" The pay was decent, but more than anything else, what I was learning about the wider world came via newsprint, and it made a huge impression. It was startling to visit the Newseum in Washington and scan the historical photojournalism exhibits; it was as if I were rewatching my childhood, especially when I saw the photos from the Vietnam and the civil rights era.

Vietnam was the global news background during my coming-of-age years. I am certain that any concern or interest I had in international affairs started with the realization that America was in a long war in Vietnam that was impossible to ignore. Many Memorial Days were spent driving several hours back to Missouri for Decoration Day activities at Mt. Zion Missionary Baptist Church in rural Butler County, near the farm where my dad grew up. Before a late-morning church service, families would pull weeds around family members' graves and put small American flags and handpicked wild roses on the graves of veterans. After the service, which always seemed interminable in the unair-conditioned, fully packed sanctuary, came dinner on the ground. This was a potluck feast during which one met distant cousins and old family acquaintances who were only seen at this once-a-year gathering.

To this point in my life, Vietnam was a decidedly distant affair, mediated by Walter Cronkite on television and front-page headlines describing the latest setback or victory. But in the spring of 1967 it took on a more imminent force when I happened to spy a freshly dug grave among the many headstones in the Mt. Zion Cemetery. Usually such a disruption to the well-manicured green grass in the cemetery marked the passing of a seemingly really old person. But I was struck and shocked by this headstone, with its inlaid oval photo of the face of a nineteen-year-old army private. His likeness was what sophisticates in Paducah called "a country face." It was a local boy who died in combat in Vietnam just a few weeks prior. Whatever psychological distance existed between my ten-year-old self and the war suddenly evaporated.

A few years after the Mt. Zion incident, I remember a hot summer day when the older brother of one of my best friends came home from Vietnam. Early in the war the brother volunteered for the Marines soon after high school, eventually serving as a jet mechanic at Da Nang. He gathered all the younger boys around the family front porch and told us his tale. He bought the recruitment pitch hook, line, and sinker, and told us not to fall for the propaganda. He came back embittered about the war, questioning both why we were there and how we fought it. The punchline was that if any of us ever volunteered for the war, he would personally hunt us down and, as he put it, "beat the shit out of us." This was sobering stuff, to put it mildly. He went on to say that if we got drafted, that was a different thing, and everyone had to do what he had to do under those circumstances.

I turned eighteen in January 1975, my senior year in high school. By that time the active draft had stopped and the war was winding down. Nevertheless, Mr. Ford and Mr. Kissinger were still taking names, just in case, so I had to register with the Selective Service Board of Paducah, promising to keep them apprised of my whereabouts in case the draft was restarted. I distinctly remember the lonely trek to the US Post Office in downtown Paducah, near the foot of Broadway. I had no one to talk to about this. My church was of little use, my father was a navy seaplane pilot in World War II, and I felt as lonely as I have ever felt. There was no one to turn to in order to sort out the ethical dilemmas I confronted.

Another Vietnam vignette from that era is worth telling. Apparently, the local draft board in Paducah was a "bipartisan" panel, which in that part of the South meant all Democrats with one Republican "seat." The lone Republican member died, and my father, being one of the few Republicans for miles, was asked to take the open seat. Years later my father told me the pitch was simple. As a father of three boys, one older than me and one younger, he would be guaranteed that none of us would serve in combat if drafted, in exchange for his service on the draft board. This was small-town politics at its worst, yet I suspect it was quite common across the country. My father, a patriot, veteran, and probably harboring unspoken angst about the war and the prospect of any of his three boys going into combat, recoiled in disgust. As he told me, he saw this as a deal with the devil. He would send his neighbors' sons into combat, and his payoff was to spare his own sons that risk. He was appalled.

As I think more about it, I now realize that violence was everywhere, from Vietnam all the way down to my lower middle-class neighborhood. With the stress of lower economic status came physical stress. Our neighborhood was dominated by high school males with a bent toward violence. Fistfights were common and the causes multiple: arguments over sandlot baseball games, basketball games, etc., or worse yet, just sheer malevolence aimed at the vulnerable, usually younger, weaker boys. I don't recall ever seeing physical violence against women or girls in public spaces. That doesn't mean there wasn't plenty, even a majority of the violence in that culture, against women; it was just hidden from view, as unwritten codes of southern "civility" insisted that such behavior was reserved for the privacy of one's home. But it was acceptable for older teenage boys to wreak havoc on vulnerable people.

One consequence was to develop a sixth sense while moving through the neighborhood. Many years later I learned that "situational awareness" was the equivalent term in diplomatic jargon. We biked and walked everywhere. Take this alley as a way to avoid a chance encounter with the handful of bullies who would prowl the neighborhood. A bike of one's own was the perfect platform to escape a miscreant on foot. I can only recall being in one fight, and yet I was a witness to many. My first and only fight was when I got caught napping by one of the usual bullies who just needed someone to beat up. I was a tall but skinny young kid, so to some of the bullies, that made me a legitimate target, even though I was three or four years younger than my would-be assailant. This particular guy lunged at me for no particular reason. As he sped toward me, I sidestepped him and hit him in the back as he stumbled past me and face-planted in the mud. I felt a visceral combination of nausea and pride that I was still standing, and probably too much satisfaction that I decked him, even though the credit belonged to his clumsiness and the inscrutable beauty of gravity.

The kid got up, scraped off some mud, muttered something to me, tacitly acknowledging my pugilistic luck, and wandered away. His desire for bullying was temporarily deterred. I tell this story not to promote my nonexistent fighting skills, but to say that I think my lifelong loathing of bullies may have started here. Decades later I can't say I have any real enemies, but I can now articulate, in a way I could not as a child, that bullies of any type, professorial, ecclesiastical, diplomatic or other, evoke a very primal distaste in me. The forms of power used by this current type are not physical violence in my experience, but the tools of power deployed can still be very powerful. And I didn't like it in the State Department any more than I did decades before as a kid. But I suspect some of the adult practitioners of bullying probably developed the habit early in life.

If there was an antidote to the violence of a small southern town, it was life beyond the city. My father had rabbit in his blood. Growing up on a rock farm in the Ozarks meant a childhood spent outdoors. Hunting, hiking, fishing, and camping constituted his havens, and with five kids, he was always on the lookout for companionship when he took to the woods. I logged as many hours with him on his treks and retreats as any of my siblings. It would be hard to overstate the time I spent traipsing through the woods as a kid. To this day, travel and spending time outdoors are often a cure when my soul is troubled.

My story isn't particularly unique. With parents born on farms, I paid attention to the ravages of soil erosion. Traveling in Kentucky exposed me to the devastation of strip mining of coal at an early age. Reading Rachel Carson as a teen helped transform my moral sensibilities from traditional conservationism into environmentalism. One of my earliest political acts was signing a petition opposing strip mining of coal on a stopover at Berea College on one of our family's innumerable road trips across the state. I couldn't have been older than twelve or thirteen at the time. As I grew older, I began to realize that, on many public issues, my allegedly all-encompassing faith didn't really have much to say about the threats to the natural world I saw just about every day.

There were environmental issues unique to my geography. High lead levels in the waters of the Ohio, Tennessee, Cumberland, and Mississippi Rivers were impossible to ignore. Likewise, radiation exposure to workers at the local uranium-enrichment plant became a national scandal. The most seemingly permanent "facts" of my life—the presence, beauty, and power of nature—were under direct assault. Watching the Army Corps of Engineers dam the Cumberland River to make Barkley Lake, one of the largest man-made lakes in the world, I saw the massive disruption of rural life, including the relocation of small towns and several rural churches and cemeteries, and it was like nothing I have seen since. All this led to a growing political sense of outrage that doesn't seem to have lessened much in the intervening decades. Later, of course, I would find a more robust moral language and way of life to help me engage politically on these and other issues. But this later work was anchored originally in my experience of outrage and anger regarding the environment based on my deep ties to the land.

By the time I arrived at State, climate change was front and center on Secretary Kerry's agenda, and I was eager to help in any way I could. The almost complete silence on the part of any American religious community I had contact with as a child had long since evolved into a complex landscape of religious actors, both domestic and international, for whom global climate change was a deep moral concern. These people and their institutions would play a huge role in rallying American support for the Paris Accord on Climate Change, but they would also help generate the necessary moral warrants for doing the hard work on mitigating and adapting to the effects of climate change.

Race and class were powerful drivers in just about every cultural space I inhabited. And my awareness of these complex dynamics emerged only in fits and starts. I should be quick to add that these insights still come on a regular basis as I stand on the cusp of old manhood. It never ceases to amaze me how deeply I was shaped by being white and growing up at the confluence of poor white trash and lower middle class and the separate but always nearby African American experience in the mid-South in the twentieth century. On the one hand, Jim Crow was ubiquitous. State parks and public schools were racially segregated. I didn't know of any multiracial Christian congregations. Housing was segregated, and almost all elected public officials were white. Paducah was not unique in this regard. And that is what made it so hard to see: it was so pervasive, it appeared "natural" to whites. At a much later age, I developed a deep suspicion of theological arguments based on what was "natural" that in effect baptized and sacralized institutions, social mores, sexual regulations, thus masking human social constructions as if they had fallen out of the sky from the mind of God. What seemed natural was sold as being ordained by God, thus masking baser motives of those who benefited from such arrangements. But as a child, I had some moral resources to push back on what in some quarters was known as "the southern way of life."[8]

On the other hand, desegregation of the Paducah public schools did come marginally faster to the town than to some cities in Kentucky, but I am not sure this is really noteworthy. In the 1967–1968 school year, the dual "separate but equal school" system desegregated, apparently under the leadership of a moderate school superintendent, Newman Walker. As I mentioned earlier, my parents were racial moderates, which in this case meant they supported the desegregation but were not actively pursuing this end in local politics. We watched and read about the freedom movement as interested parties, quietly and hopefully following the larger cultural tectonic shifts. But I do not recall any energy being spent on helping the cause.[9]

As I prepared for my fourth-grade year to start, I began to notice an uptick in explicit racial epithets on the tongues of the kids in my all-white neighborhood in anticipation of desegregation. I was stunned. We were not allowed to use racist language in our family, so it was a shock to hear friends routinely using this prohibited vocabulary. It was quite the surprise when I arrived at George Rogers Clark Elementary School that fall to discover my science teacher was a young African American teacher, Mrs. Rice. Looking back, I cannot imagine the pressure she must have been under as one of a very few young African American women public school teachers in our town. I also developed a schoolboy crush on her, which, needless to say, I told no one about.

But even this form of racial progress imposed costs. Many of the administrators in the separate black school system were stripped of their administrative posts in the new desegregated system and moved back into the classroom. I don't think any white school administrators underwent this fate. In my elementary school, which encompassed the wealthy white neighborhoods and a couple of lower middle-class neighborhoods like mine on the west side of town, we were buffered by geography from having many African American students from the rest of the city. In other words, the cartographers of the school boundaries could still protect the richer, whiter elementary school by drawing school boundaries to exclude many blacks. My elementary school of almost five hundred students had, at best, only a handful of black students after "integration." With two junior high schools and one senior high school in Paducah, it was increasingly harder to avoid making the schools much more representative of the racial makeup of the city.

Against the backdrop of what was happening across the country in the civil rights movement, in some ways my experience seems sedate. But I also know that it could not have been easy for my African American classmates. Perhaps my town muddled through in a better way than some towns in the South. My own social location in a lower-middle-class family no doubt blinded me to the depths of our racism. At the same time, I felt a good bit of distance from the lives of many of my best friends, who grew up surrounded by incredible wealth. The income inequality that we currently take for granted in America was manifested in its own way in Paducah.

I remember coming to school the day after President Johnson announced he would not run for a second term as president in 1968. One of my fifth-grade classmates casually announced to us that his dad was borrowing $100,000 from the bank to purchase Bell Telephone stock, to take advantage of the inevitable stock-market slide at the opening bell that day. This had the casual tone my parents might have used to tell us they were heading to the grocery to buy more milk. I had only the foggiest notion of what the stock market was. I did not know a single adult who played the market, much less anyone who could walk into a bank and get a $100,000 loan on the spot. I asked my classmate why his dad would do that. The answer was, telephone company stock would go down along with the general market, driven by fear of who might succeed Johnson, but as a blue-chip stock, Bell Telephone would inevitably soon rise back to its normal higher price before long. His dad would buy low and sell high and make a killing. This was the equivalent of discussing quantum mechanics in my house. We discussed many current issues at the Casey dinner table, but stock speculation was not one of them.

The gulf between my rich classmates and my own family's poor and lower middle-class roots was always apparent. Many of my friends' families vacationed around the country, had large houses even by today's standards, and paid hefty country club dues to play on Robert Trent Jones–designed golf courses. All that is to say I straddled some divides in my childhood, and saw the ones I didn't straddle at pretty close range. All in all, I had a sense of distance, never fully belonging in the culture, but never fully alien to it either.

After I graduated from high school, I spent four years in West Texas trying to get an education at Abilene Christian University (ACU), a college affiliated with the Churches of Christ. Several important things transpired there for me. First, I discovered a version of the classic Christian vocation of faith seeking understanding. In an interesting irony, the Churches of Christ valued education, and in my congregation were many teachers, administrators, and school board members. The number of my church peers who pursued graduate education was well above the average for a town that size in the mid-South. At ACU I found a subset of faculty for whom learning from the best was seen as an asset and not a threat. Learning for the sake of learning was promoted, and I was fortunate to find myself drawn to an amazing set of professors who had found their way to West Texas.

The second thing that happened was meeting Ann, my future wife. Our getting to know each other was a harbinger of many good things to follow. Ann was at Tufts University in Boston, and while her friends were taking their junior year abroad in places like Paris and Vienna, she chose to do so in Abilene. We were in the same section of a large church history two-semester survey class, in the second semester. Our professor, LeMoine Lewis, was a Harvard Divinity School–trained church historian who in many ways was very old school. When he distributed the graded midterm exams to the class, he would, with great ceremony, hand out the highest-scoring exam first and recognize that student by name. In the fall semester, I had earned the highest grade on the midterm, so I was already prepping for my five seconds of fame when the second-semester midterms would be returned. Much to my chagrin, Prof. Lewis announced the highest score went to Ann Wallace. As the paper passed my desk on its way to the back of the room, I followed its path back to her and resolved I had to get to know this beautiful woman as soon as possible!

The third main thing that transpired was my discovery that one could study religion at the graduate level at places like Harvard and Yale and Chicago. Of course, I knew people who had gone to these schools to study a multitude of subjects, but I was fortunate to meet three professors at Abilene who had trained at Harvard Divinity School (HDS). It didn't take long before I found myself trying to imagine what this path might look like for me.

While ACU might strike most people as an unlikely training ground for such a pilgrimage to Cambridge, Massachusetts, the truth was that path was well trod by the time I arrived in the late '70s. Lewis graduated from Abilene Christian in the mid-'30s, and, after a couple of years of preaching in Texas, he enrolled at HDS. He told me that when he presented his Harvard dream to his Abilene professors, they told him that if he preached for two years, they would write letters of recommendation for him. They undoubtedly thought this strategy would deter him from his Harvard dreams. But he was not deterred.[10]

At that point the academic reputation of Abilene Christian would not impress the powers that ran Harvard Divinity School. But Dean Willard Sperry was impressed with his transcript, especially his credentials in biblical languages, which exceeded those of the more typical HDS students. Sperry took a risk and offered Lewis provisional admission. If he succeeded in his first year, he would be allowed to stay. Not only did Lewis succeed but, upon finishing at Harvard, he returned to teach at Abilene and sent dozens of students to HDS over the next three decades. I was the last of his students to attend Harvard.

One of the other Harvard-educated professors at Abilene Christian, Thomas Olbricht, had an equally profound impact on me. I took every undergraduate course he taught. Olbricht read voraciously and taught an astonishing range of subjects in theology, biblical studies, and philosophy. He modeled a form of scholarly engagement with the current state of affairs in the academic study of religion that was confident, not fear based, and displayed an intellectual integrity and vocational joy in teaching that remain a model to me to this day. Several of Lewis's and Olbricht's faculty peers did not share their support for my pilgrimage to Harvard, and said so to me or indirectly through others, but I was overjoyed when I was admitted. And the prospect of reuniting with Ann in Boston was also part of my joy!

The weekend of my graduation in May 1979 marked a deep personal loss and a disruption of a magnitude I still cannot fully describe, because my oldest sister, Karen, committed suicide. For my purposes here, the details don't really matter as much as what I learned at the young age of twenty-two. Forty years later I am struck by the wisdom of Wendell Berry's observation that we live the life given, not the life planned. At twenty-two, there was a sweet rationality about the universe and my role in it. Karen's death created a large hole in that worldview, but it took quite some time to be able to articulate that change. Certainly, losing a sibling at that young age was never something I could have imagined. Finitude is something many baby boomers came to know over time, but it came early in my adulthood.

I have found myself drawn to people over the years who know something about suffering early in life. They often seem to have a capacity for empathy and compassion that sometimes is lacking in people for whom suffering is a theoretical concept. Likewise, I have tried to look a little deeper when I encounter people driven by anger or a will to dominate, or those who see others as means to ends and not as ends in themselves. Bullying played a role in Karen's suicide, and that hasn't helped my childhood-shaped dislike of bullies. I know I should look into why adults rely on bullying tactics as a staple of their professional identity, but I struggle with that. All of these dynamics are important, especially when you must interview lots of people in a start-up situation like I had at State. When you wade through dozens if not hundreds of applicants for a handful of slots, the ability to perform at a high level personally and as part of a team is a huge asset. One inadequate personality can sink an entire office.

At a minimum, I had to learn to develop a capacity to embrace indeterminacy, mystery, and some degree of peace with not being able to resolve or completely understand every event or adventure. I think I have learned to try to be clearer to people, especially those I love and care for, about my feelings and thoughts. I certainly have not been perfect in that enterprise, but I remain deeply committed to the ideal.

Cambridge, Massachusetts, proved to be the tonic my soul needed, given how my Texas sojourn ended. My father and I drove from Kentucky to Massachusetts with all my possessions in a trunk. One link to my past my father gave me was an arts and craft rocking chair that was part of the Casey household when he was born in the Ozarks in 1919. I would spend more hours in that chair in my monastery-size room in Rockefeller Hall at Harvard Divinity School in the next three years reading than any other human activity. My dad never fully understood my attraction to the study of religion. As the youngest child in a large extended Baptist family, he had given up somewhere along the way trying to live the peculiar strictures of rural Baptist life. As he once told me, he just knew he couldn't live up to those standards. But he was proud of his kids and their graduate degrees, even if he didn't fully comprehend why some of us might choose religion as the subject matter.

In 1979 Harvard Divinity School was an institution in transition. I was in no position to understand this nor did I care. I was too young to know what I didn't know, and I wandered through the curriculum, torn between vague thoughts of becoming a professor and even vaguer thoughts of trying to help my peculiar subtribe in American Christianity become more open and progressive. There were old lions on the faculty such as Krister Stendahl, Wilfred Cantwell Smith, C. Conrad Wright; ghosts such as Amos Wilder and James Luther Adams; scholars entering their peak years such as Harvey Cox, Helmut Koester, Gordon Kaufman, Preston Williams; and young, rising stars like Margaret Miles, George Rupp, and Peter Gomes.

Somewhere along the line I read the journalist Theodore White's line about being a Jewish kid from Dorchester who got admitted to Harvard College in the thirties and how he approached the endeavor with the mind of an intellectual thief: he was going to take every idea he could from the place. As a Church of Christ kid from the cow college in West Texas, I completely understood what White was getting at. LeMoine Lewis gave me his valedictory lecture in his office in Abilene, and I recall a couple of pieces of advice. First, success at Harvard was 90 percent perspiration and 10 percent genius. He told me to outwork my peers. Second, he told me to spend my summers in manual labor in order to sweat any acquired arrogance out of my body, if not my soul. I'm pretty sure I didn't perfectly absorb either of those lessons, but they did make an impression.

Some of the major lessons I learned in this my first round at Harvard Divinity that have served me well were, first, no one is the smartest person in every room all the time. Those who thought they were were shot down in flames pretty fast. Corollaries to this were, you might be the smartest person in the room for the next ninety seconds, so use them wisely, but smarter still was knowing when to shut up and learn from the people who were smarter than you until your number came back up. In other words, in a roomful of very smart people, chase the knowledge and don't worry about the source. Even though in divinity school we were measured by our own individual work product, the real education resided in learning from the teacher and one's student peers.

Closely related was the discovery that the best professors found ways to convey their knowledge and wisdom, but they also found ways to elicit more knowledge from the students than we knew we had. And they were not afraid to affirm the smart insights that came from their students. I once heard a friend describe Harvard of that era as "a praise-free zone." In my view, that is a horrible indictment, if true. But I don't think it was completely accurate. It would be many years before I began to seriously think about pedagogy in an intentional way. I was shocked to discover how obediential and hierarchical the State Department was. I initially found midcareer Foreign Service officers reticent to add their voices to discussions in our office. When I queried some them about this privately, they replied that in many of their international postings it was made explicitly clear that they had not attained sufficient seniority to speak up unless directly addressed by a superior. This struck me as incredibly stupid. I was in search of the best answers and analysis, even if it came from the summer intern who was a rising junior. It would prove to be a hard point to convey in Foggy Bottom at times, but eventually it began to kick in. My best teachers at Harvard were interested in good arguments, and they maintained a rough form of democracy, particularly in seminars, where the quality of the ideas carried more weight than did the relative status of the source. They weren't saints, but they weren't all devils either.

Another lesson Harvard drilled into my head was the classic Enlightenment insight to return to the sources. Too often in my undergraduate years we read about historical figures; at Harvard we read what the historical sources said. Immersion in primary sources was the bread and butter of my early graduate studies. This is one of many reasons I believe that our diplomatic corps will always be best served with officers who have a liberal arts education and see lifelong learning as a fundamental aspect of the job.

I remember vividly my second conversation with Ambassador Martin Indyk. He was telling me a story from an encounter he had in his earlier diplomatic days, and as he neared the conclusion of the tale, I had a smirk on my face. He interrupted himself in midsentence and said, "You know how this story ends! You've read my damn book?!" I had only met him the week before, but in the time between the two conversations I learned of his latest book, *Innocent Abroad*, and I had ordered it and read it. I replied to him, "Of course, I've read your damn book! That's what professors do." Now, it is true that most State Department professionals read mounds of internally produced products, memorandums, cables, intelligence assessments, etc. But my view is that one has to fight hard to create the space to keep learning and discussing with a broad range of people to stay sharp and informed.[11]

The last lesson that I picked up during my time at Harvard is to choose your partners well, which I did in marrying Ann as I was finishing up my degree! Shortly after we married, we headed to Mississippi, where I became the minister of a small, allegedly progressive congregation of the Churches of Christ in suburban Jackson. We now refer to this period, somewhat tongue in cheek, as our period of foreign missionary work. The cultural leap from Cambridge to Jackson in 1983 is hard to exaggerate. I thought I was a southerner based on my Kentucky childhood, but I very quickly learned I was wrong. I radically misjudged where my denomination was going as well as just how long my ministerial talents would hold up. After two years, we beat a hasty retreat back to Boston in search of more graduate work for both of us. But it was hardly a waste of time. While it was a time of racial retrenchment, to put it mildly, in the Deep South, there were heroes all around, and we met a few of them along the way.

When Ronald Reagan began his 1980 campaign for the presidency with a speech at the Neshoba County Fair, near Philadelphia, Mississippi, just a stone's throw from where the civil rights martyrs James Cheney, Michael Schwerner, and Andrew Goodman were buried in an earthen dam in 1964, it was impossible to miss the symbolism. Reagan's speech was not a racist dog whistle; it was a racist declaration written in letters ten feet high. The Republican Party was doubling down on making Richard Nixon's earlier southern strategy a pillar of the party, and white conservative Christians were on their way to political power. That strategy had its apotheosis in Donald Trump. But we did not know that until much later.

Our small congregation, located on the shores of the Ross Barnett Reservoir (!), owed its existence to a lurch rightward in the large, close to downtown Church of Christ congregation in Jackson proper. It is not worth rehearsing the idiotic theological quarrels that led to the exodus. But I found myself ministering to a small congregation of young professionals united at least in their common belief that they were no longer the narrow sectarians they had left behind. But knowing what you are against does not tell you what you are for. Almost without exception, every adult in my congregation had grown up in abject poverty in southern Mississippi, and as adults, they were making more money than their wildest childhood dreams would have allowed.

I was making $18,000 a year and could not believe my good fortune. But we were out of our element. At one small dinner party with church members, a good-natured but serious argument broke out over whether the London cast of *Cats* was better than the New York cast of *Cats*. This was not an abstract debate, as every couple there, save the Caseys, had seen both versions of the play in the last twelve months. While the Churches of Christ in some quarters had clearly crossed the symbolic railroad tracks from my childhood, its theology had been completely co-opted by the nascent Republican Party's handmaiden, the Religious Right. Voting a straight Republican Party ticket fulfilled the Christian's duty in public life. There was no theology of public life. Within the property lines of the congregation there was incredible charity. Outside the property lines, many of us were indistinguishable from the rest of Mississippi society. And our traditional theological teachings, such as they were, were no match for the conservative political winds. Race, poverty, and nuclear weapons buildups were not fit topics for church folk.

By some miracle I fell into a ragtag group of young clergy from a broad range of Christian denominations who were feeling varying degrees of discomfort in our respective traditions and in the Mississippi political environment. Not unlike my congregation, we were united by what we did not like, but we were scrambling to make sense of what was going on around us. We met regularly in the Office of Evangelization of the Natchez-Jackson Diocese of the Roman Catholic Church. We decided to read one of the draft versions of *The Challenge of Peace*, the pastoral letter written by the US Conference of Catholic Bishops in response to the radical nuclear policies of the Reagan administration. Father Bryan Hehir, a diocesan priest of the Archdiocese of Boston, was the principal author of the letter. Little did I know that a decade later I would be studying under him back at Harvard. For that short time in Mississippi, it was intellectual manna from heaven, consumed by this marginal Harvard-educated pastor adrift in the Deep South. Exile never feels very good at the time. But in retrospect, seeing the world from the margins of one's vocation, far away from true community, and wondering if one's career was over before it started, can be a useful exercise. Ultimately I had no answers about what I was supposed to be doing with my life. My tradition was bankrupt and unable to fund a vision of how to navigate the exodus from sectarian Protestant theology with some semblance of plausibility and fidelity. The reigning option of joining the GOP revolution was intolerable. Before we knew it, we were speeding back to Boston.

Once back in Boston, my dismay over any effective current Christian political engagement deepened. This eventually led me to head to the Kennedy School at Harvard to pursue another master's degree, this time in foreign policy. The most noteworthy lesson I learned while there came at the hands of the legendary Harvard professorial figure Richard Neustadt. Late in the summer when we received our letters naming our academic advisers, I felt I won the Massachusetts Lottery when I read that I had been assigned Neustadt.

Neustadt's major work, *Presidential Power and the Modern Presidents: The Politics of Leadership from Roosevelt to Lincoln*, was a classic, and he was celebrating the success of a more recent book he wrote with fellow Harvard professor Ernest May, *Thinking in Time: The Uses of History for Decision Makers*. Here was a stereotypical Harvard professor: a top theorist in his field, adviser to presidents, down-to-earth and unpretentious (okay, not so typical for a Harvard prof), and a truly generous and great teacher. If there was one lesson I took away from his courses, it was that the way decision-making structures of government are designed and function can be crucial for the success or failure of policy. Being smart, being feared, and being loved are in no way guarantors of policy success. How you structure the information flow in a bureaucracy is crucial to making better policy decisions. His courses were case studies examining multiple failures in US policy caused by the right information failing to reach the relevant principals who were making the policy decisions. When I arrived at State, I was deeply aware of the bureaucratic challenges attached to a new office with no history of operation either within the State Department's deliberations or in the even more vexed interagency process run by the White House. While we did well in the internal State deliberations, I found cracking the White House code to be much more difficult.[12]

I also took away a very nice personal affirmation. As a divinity school graduate lurking the halls of the Kennedy School, I felt out of place on multiple occasions and wondered if I really belonged in the very different ethos at the southern end of Harvard's Cambridge campus. I will never forget near the end of that year when Neustadt told me I had the chops to play in the policy and political worlds. That single affirmation went a very long way in quelling whatever anxiety I might have had about whether or not I belonged there. I ended my time there with a strong grounding in US foreign policy and in the nuts and bolts of how policy was made. It also marked the end of the Cold War, and the defining metaphor for the field of inquiry of international relations died with its passing. So much of the content of what I learned was seemingly obsolete on graduation day.

At the end of that academic year, I took a year off to be a full-time stay-at-home dad with our newborn son, Paul. In 1988–1989 one did not see a lot of men pushing baby carriages around Harvard Square full time. A few years later I had the opportunity to do the same with our daughter Sarah. I am not nominating myself for sainthood, and I would not trade the time with my kids that most men of that era never got. At a minimum, it made me less of a jackass. Or so I am told.

On something of a lark during my final semester at the Kennedy School, I skimmed the divinity school catalogue and I noticed that the new dean, Ronald Thiemann, was teaching a course on religion and public life. I decided to venture back to my old haunts at the northern end of the campus, intrigued that someone there was mucking about at the intersection of religion and American public life, the very issue set that drove me north away from Mississippi.[13] It would prove to be a momentous decision.

It was a new era at the divinity school compared to my first sojourn there. Under Thiemann's leadership, a new generation of more publicly engaged scholars came. People like Bryan Hehir, Cornel West, Evelyn Higginbotham, and Francis and Elisabeth Schüssler Fiorenza represented a much-needed cadre of scholars who were not just interested in a provincial approach to the study of religion. In very different ways, they were exploring the public implications of religious belief and practice at the very time I was searching for better answers to those questions myself. I entered the doctoral program in Religion and Society and could not have been happier. It is pretty hard to reduce eight years of your life into a few hundred words, so I'm not going to try. But there were several things that sped me on my way far better equipped to make a go of things in Washington.

First among these was meeting and studying under Bryan Hehir. Hehir is a diocesan priest who happens to be one of the foremost scholars in ethics and international affairs. In his illustrious career, he worked for the US Conference of Catholic Bishops as director of their Office of Peace and International Justice; was the principal author of their pastoral letter, *The Challenge of Peace*; won a MacArthur Genius Award; was president of Catholic Charities, USA; was dean of Harvard Divinity School; and recently retired from teaching at the Harvard Kennedy School and serves as secretary of Health and Social Services for the Archdiocese of Boston. It's impossible for me to overstate his influence on my life and career. He chaired my thesis and prepared me for a successful academic career launch.

The rest of my eclectic thesis committee was comprised of Harvey Cox, the late Ronald Thiemann, and Francis Schüssler Fiorenza. I wrote a thesis on preventing the proliferation of nuclear weapons, a policy nexus firmly nested in the purview of the State Department. I got exactly what I sought from Harvard between the Kennedy School and the Divinity School. And that was a deeper understanding of how particular religious communities can and should move into a wider, pluralistic, and secular public policy realm in a manner that was authentic to the particular theological tenets of a Christian tradition, but that also respected the pluralistic nature of American public life. To be sure, there were, and still are, vociferous critics of any such movement. But I came away convinced that such engagement and excursions beyond the boundaries of Christian communities were actually at the heart of what Christianity was supposed to be about. Loving one's neighbor meant, in part, promoting justice, loving those at the margins of society, and doing so in a manner that did not replicate so much of the hegemonic pathology of so many contemporary Christian "leaders."[14]

When I started, I was convinced my old tradition, the Churches of Christ, had very few resources to do this sort of work. By the time I left, I was more confident there were ample warrants for doing precisely this sort of work from an eclectic roster of theological sources across contemporary theology. I remember vividly, after passing my oral defense of my thesis, visiting Bryan in his office to discuss the latest job openings in my field. Wesley Theological Seminary in Washington, DC, was looking for a theological ethicist with a specialty in theology and public policy. Part of the duties included running a long-standing, semester-long program, the National Capital Semester for Seminarians, open to any divinity school or seminary student to come to Washington and learn about the intersection of theology and public policy. When Bryan read the ad, he put down the paper and said, "Shaun, this is you! They don't know it yet, but this is you!" I remember hoping that his prophetic powers were on par with his intellectual powers. In time, he was proven right!

I could prattle on at great length about my thirteen years teaching at Wesley, but instead I will focus on the items that helped me on my eventual path to State and the relevant lessons I learned along the way. We arrived in the Washington area in the summer of 2000, in the waning days of the Clinton administration. I was able to attend a small gathering at Howard University on December 1, 2000, World AIDS Day, where President Clinton gave remarks and the air was heavy with nostalgia and fear about the apparent Bush election victory. (*Bush v. Gore* was issued less than two weeks later.) It was an odd and surreal time in Washington, a harbinger for what would transpire over the next twenty years.

Many things shaped my future in Washington during my Wesley days, but a few stand out. The first was a clear signal from Wesley's president, David McAllister Wilson, and Dean Bruce Birch that any work I did in Washington public life—lectures, media, think-tank work, consulting—would count as service to the institution for any tenure and promotion consideration. As David said, "As long as they spell Wesley correctly, I'm happy for any public work you do." It is impossible to overstate how liberating this was in my academic career. I had seen at Harvard how professional jealousy easily sprang up against scholars whose work violated the provincial boundaries of centuries of dusty publications that were read by only a handful of like-minded scholars. Being a public intellectual was not frowned upon at Wesley. To this day many, perhaps most, religion scholars labor in academic environments where public scholarship can be used against one in the sketchy ethical world of tenure and promotion, especially in the study of religion. But I had a license to print money. As I often said, teaching ethics, theology, and public policy in Washington means never running out of material to work on. From my days of doubt in Mississippi about the ability of theology to contribute to public life, through my years of doctoral education, now I had landed in a place where I could teach exactly what I was trained to do. It was a very good feeling, in that two decades of preparation had paid off in the form of a job located at the intersection of religion and global politics.

My first real shot at engaging the Washington chattering classes came with the run-up to the Iraq War. As the last chapter should make clear, I opposed the war on moral and policy grounds. By late 2002, it was clear to me that the Bush administration was laying the public groundwork for invading Iraq. From where I sat, the moral debate had been deftly derailed by Bush's "those who are not with us are against us" rhetoric. Democrats were cowed into supporting the war out of fear that opposition to it could be used against them in later years. I set out to see what an unknown professor might be able to do as a complete naif and outsider in Washington. To make a long story short, I hit the airwaves and spoke at innumerable churches. I also debated a who's who of neoconservative fire-breathers who were drafted by the White House to stamp out any moral resistance to the invasion. That crew included George Weigel, Jean Bethke Elshtain, Michael Cromartie, and Richard Land. As Iraq rapidly spiraled into horror, these and their like retreated into a sort of moral witness-protection program, but some of them would reemerge later in the Trump era, giving new meaning to resurrection. I like to think I more than held my own. I also managed to get a sense of how the conservative foreign policy machinery worked, and that would serve me well later on while at State. Their cynicism appalled me, and the willingness to manufacture and tailor "moral" arguments to blindly support such a blatantly unjust war was a good lesson for me to take to heart for the Obama era and the Trump dumpster fire, where conservative Christian leaders mutated into willing intellectual shepherds to herd their masses into mewling compliance with Republican national leaders.

At Wesley I ran a unique program in American graduate theological education called the National Capital Semester for Seminarians, where any seminary or divinity school student in the country could come and study the intersection of theology and public policy with me in the spring semester. In addition to a traditional graduate seminar, the program included an afternoon of site visits each week, which would introduce students to the jungle of nonprofits, service providers, politicians, think-tank analysts, professors, journalists, rock throwers, and peacemakers who constituted the insane cacophony of Washington voices at the intersection of religion and public policy. It was a town armed with thousands of unguided missile launchers, and I loved just about every minute of it. And perhaps most endearing of all, twenty years ago when I landed in Washington, if you called up just about any of this cast and told them you had twenty graduate students in tow who wanted to learn what this or that particular organization was doing in public life, from the right or the left, they would try to work with you to meet your students.

The major benefit for me was an ever-growing network of contacts on the left and the right. I was one or two phone calls or emails away from a lot of people. Washington has always been a very tribal town in the worst sense of that term. But I found a niche when I arrived that gave me access to some very peculiar bedfellows. As the political sectarian divide, which accelerated in the Gingrich era, began to hit light speed, many of my ties to the right began to strain.

Two relationships that began in my early years in Washington have continued to help me to this day. I met Mike McCurry early in the twenty-first century when he became a member of the Wesley Theological Seminary's board of governors. McCurry had served as President Clinton's spokesman in the White House, and he also happened to be a pretty serious Methodist, hence his willingness to join Wesley's board. I remember meeting him for the first time at one of those endless ceremonial dinners that seminaries and divinity schools put on that board members are obliged to attend. I have no recollection of what the dinner was about. But I do remember telling myself how lucky I was to be seated across from him at the dinner, where I got a master class in DC politics. It would be the first of countless conversations over the next fifteen years.

I could tell many stories about McCurry and extol his many virtues, but from the time I met him I was impressed not just with his network—he seems to know everyone on both sides of the aisle—but with his willingness to connect people to each other. While the District of Columbia is very tribal and networking is a primary vehicle for success here, it contains two major types of people: those who hoard their connections and those who share their connections. McCurry is the pinnacle of the latter class. And I was, and am, a major beneficiary of his largesse here. He was, after all, the one who connected me to John Kerry.

The second important person I met was just starting out in Washington and not a grizzled veteran. And our meeting is another classic tale of Washington connectivity. Wesley's president, David McAllister Wilson, is no slouch himself when it comes to networking chops. He got to know John Hamre, president of the Center for Strategic and International Studies (CSIS) in Washington who had served earlier as deputy secretary of defense in the Clinton administration. Hamre had studied a year at Harvard Divinity School back in the '60s on a Rockefeller Brothers Foundation grant, making him a very rare bird in Washington as a senior international security official with some real training in religion. CSIS had just won a sizable grant from the Henry R. Luce Foundation to produce a study of how the Bush administration approached religion in its foreign policy. David recommended me as someone who could provide some guidance to the CSIS project, and Dr. Hamre reached out to me and asked me to meet with his Post-Conflict Reconstruction team that was running the grant project.

The CSIS project would produce a pathbreaking report, *Mixed Blessings: U.S. Government Engagement with Religion in Conflict-Prone Settings*. My contributions were marginal at best, but the most important aspect of that enterprise was meeting Liora Danan, the lead author of the report. Liora was a couple of years out of Rice University and managed this large grant with a major report due on essentially an unparalleled topic, how the Bush administration and the US foreign policy bureaucracy engaged with religion. It was not a mission for the fainthearted. I remember being impressed—after all, my career was spent working with twentysomethings—with her drive and organizational and writing skills, to say nothing of turning the word salads an army of security and professorial types were throwing at her into an elegantly conceived and written report. I told myself, I thought she would go far and that CSIS was lucky to have someone so preternaturally talented. The project ended, and I had no further contact with her until I arrived at State a few years later.

During the middle of the decade 2000–2009, I was rummaging through dozens of archives researching a book on the role of religion in the 1960 election, when John Kennedy narrowly defeated Richard Nixon. Kennedy's Catholicism made him politically vulnerable, while Nixon waged a secret war to gin up Protestant anti-Catholicism in order to win. Kennedy realized Nixon was weaponizing religion in a new way, so he dedicated significant campaign resources to counteract Nixon's deviousness and won the race as a result. Inevitably I started to share lessons I had learned from the Kennedy story around Washington, and I found a small coterie of interested conversation partners in the press and in Democratic circles. I turned in my manuscript for *The Making of a Catholic President: Kennedy vs. Nixon 1960* the week before I headed to Chicago for my reeducation training at Obama '08 headquarters in the summer of 2008, when I joined the campaign.

When Obama, Hillary Clinton, and John Edwards were ramping up their campaigns, I became friends with Joshua Dubois, Obama's religion staffer, and I knew Burns Strider, Hillary's religion person, from previous work together. My theory was that the more Democratic campaigns got smarter on religion, the better for the eventual nominee, who would have to face the phalanx of Christian fundamentalists the Republican nominee would have, no matter how implausible or inauthentic that candidate's personal life might look through the evangelical lens. I constantly sent Joshua and Burns, on the same email, articles and suggestions. I wasn't sure how long I could keep that up without choosing between their bosses, but if they didn't like that they never told me. Eventually the Obama team asked me to do press for them on religion, and I faced a tough choice. My heart was with Obama for many reasons, not the least of which was his opposition to the Iraq War, but Hillary was killing him in the polls. I conferred with veteran Democratic friends, most of whom said, without missing a beat, that I should join Team Obama. Hillaryland was overflowing, and there would be no room for a neophyte, they argued. Instead, I might be able to make a difference with the Obama team.

My value got tested early. In March 2008, I was out to dinner with my family when Joshua Dubois called to tell me ABC News was going to run a story on Obama and Rev. Jeremiah Wright, the soon-to-retire pastor of Trinity United Church of Christ, where Obama became a Christian and was a longtime member. ABC was offering the campaign a chance to respond to the story live, and Joshua said the campaign wanted me to appear with Chris Cuomo, host of *Good Morning America*, after they ran the story early the next morning. My first reaction wasn't no, it was "hell, no." I told Joshua I was honored, but there had to be dozens of better choices than me. I told him to call me back in thirty minutes if they didn't have anyone else. In the meantime, we finished our meal and headed home.

Joshua called back and said they still wanted me. The implication was clear: they needed an older-looking white guy, academically sound, who could remain cool in the face of some heavily slanted reporting, to say nothing of the likely visuals. Later that night I had a long phone call with David Axelrod and Bill Burton from the press team. I felt well prepared, and overnight I read a ton of press material sent to me by the campaign. I had my talking points. I didn't get much sleep that night, and the car to drive me to ABC's *Nightline* studio in Washington came very early in the morning. On the ride in I began to have severe doubts about my sufficiency for the task ahead. By this time, I had done a fair amount of media in Washington. And I liked live television the least. Radio was fine, but newspaper reporters were the best because one could toggle between off the record and on. But television tended to be unforgiving, and quickness usually counted more than depth. Most professors can't clear their throats in thirty minutes, much less say anything coherent in thirty seconds. And there was my made-for-radio face. But I had volunteered, so I headed to what I began to feel were the gallows without much semblance of dignity in my head. I felt my political career might be ending just as it started.

When I was dropped off at ABC's *Nightline* studio in DuPont Circle, I followed a handler into a very tiny studio room, crowded with a large camera, a cameraman, my handler, and one other person. By then it was about 5:15 a.m., and *Good Morning America* would start live at 6:00 a.m. I was to see the taped story by Brian Ross, and then Chris Cuomo would interview me for about ten minutes. My segment would be edited down to a few minutes and dropped in after Ross's report, making my remarks appear to be live. It dawned on me then that whatever I said could be edited to Cuomo's advantage. I felt even worse at this point.

When I saw Ross's taped story, I felt both better and worse. Better because I had seen this movie before. Ross had done no original reporting. Instead he had obtained DVD discs of Wright's sermons that the congregation itself sold. There was no interview of Rev. Wright, just excerpts taken out of context from multiple sermons, all designed to make Wright look craven. Interspersed between quotes were scenes of African American women dancing in traditional African garb, all designed to reinforce stereotypes of African Americans seemingly "out of control." I felt worse because I had naïvely assumed an updated version of *The Birth of a Nation* would no longer be a template for mainstream news.

When our interview started, it was clear to me that the Ross-Cuomo team thought this was the beginning of the end of the Obama candidacy. All they needed was for me to say the wrong things. I was asked how could a man who preached the need for unity and reconciliation endorse such inflammatory remarks and sit under the tutelage of such hate for so many years? I calmly said that Senator Obama did not endorse any of the political views expressed by Wright, and if ABC had any evidence that Obama did support such views, why didn't they show the clips in the story? Cuomo was not amused. He asked the question a second time, and I stuck to my line: there was no evidence Obama shared Wright's views on racial injustice in America. I kept calm and pitched the question back to him. The third time he asked the same question, his voice was rising and his frustration was mounting. That time I countered by trying to draw an analogy between his father, Governor Mario Cuomo, and Cardinal O'Connor, the archbishop of New York, when his dad refused to be linked to some of the cardinal's views. Before I could get a full sentence out, Cuomo began shouting that this story had nothing to do with his father's ambivalent relationship with the Catholic Church back in his day. I was stunned. I couldn't believe he had lost his cool, but I didn't interrupt him when he began to fall into an angry spiral.

Apparently, someone spoke to Cuomo through his earpiece, and the next thing I know, Cuomo is thanking me between gritted teeth and telling me we were out of time. In the immediate aftermath, I felt I had blown my assignment because I triggered Cuomo's temper even though he didn't trigger mine. In the small room as the lights came up and the feed to New York was cut, all three staffers were laughing and telling me they had never seen anyone get under Cuomo's skin like that and cause him to lose his cool. That was cold comfort to me, because the interview had devolved into a one-man shouting match. As it turns out, ABC edited out the third question, sparing Cuomo the embarrassment of losing his cool after I punched major holes in the story they thought was going to shoot down the Obama campaign. The short of it was, the campaign senior leadership was very happy with my performance, and I was the opening act of a longer strategy to counter the guilt-by-association campaign trying to kill Obama by linking him to Wright. I have no illusions that my performance ended the controversy. That happened days later when Obama made his famous speech on race in Philadelphia. But I may have won my eventual invitation to join the religious-outreach staff for the general election campaign that day.

There isn't much to tell about the general election campaign. There wasn't an owner's manual for Democratic presidential campaigns on how to do outreach to religious communities. We were a bit of a novelty act, and the team never developed a strategy, so we became a confederation of free agents left to our own devices. As the only one they could find dumb enough to take the job as national evangelical coordinator, I had to make bricks without straw. I worked my reporter network, spent a lot of time on evangelical college campuses, and helped prevent some political mistakes that otherwise would have cost the campaign among progressive and centrist evangelicals. Many people see presidential campaigns as romantic, idealistic causes, fueled by idealism and hope. There is a certain element of that. But, in reality, at the working level the work is tedious, hard, and often feels like a slow-motion train wreck, until Election Day. Along the way I never won the confidence of the boss, Joshua Dubois, and as a team we never won the confidence of either the senior leadership or the various regional field directors. Friends later told me Joshua "banned" me from any position in the White House. At the time, that didn't really phase me, as I had always planned to go back to Wesley full time. The Wright debacle taught the brain trust the painful but incorrect lesson that religion was a political third rail, to be avoided at all costs. Sadly, this viewpoint carried over long into the administration.

As one friend of mine put it, over the course of the campaign and into the early White House era, Barack Obama was transformed from an adult convert to Christianity who suggested religion need not be a force solely for dividing the country into a "none," that is, an unchurched person for whom religion was not meaningful. That is an overstatement, to be sure, but a central feature of Obama's life and public narrative certainly was curtailed by the campaign apparatchiks because of the Wright episode. I would give the religious outreach team a C plus for our work on the campaign. He won, and that is what mattered most.

What did I learn from this campaign that helped me five years later when I found myself at Foggy Bottom? First, the Republican Party really, really works hard to maintain its self-perceived exclusive right to dictate just what religion means, who counts and doesn't count as true experts on religion, and they will fight to the death to maintain control over these narratives. They hated the fact that Obama demonstrated some credibility and authenticity as a person of faith. From the birther lies to the Jeremiah Wright attacks, one cannot help but see a form of white Christian supremacy at work on the part of the GOP.

The press is all over the map in terms of competency in covering religion and politics, to say nothing of religion and international affairs. Far too often when religion stories deserve political attention, editors would pass the story from seasoned religion reporters to national political reporters. I recall one bizarre conversation with a nationally known political reporter who revealed she did not know that all evangelicals were not Pentecostals. The sophistication of most national political reporters on religion remains rudimentary at best. The care and feeding of the press is hard work, and many people inside the government have given up trying, especially regarding religion.

I also learned that high-functioning teams are crucial to success, and that they are very hard to build and even harder to maintain. Campaigns are temporary bodies, but bureaucracies live longer, are burdened with more inertia and groupthink, and can melt into dysfunction rapidly. One inadequate personality can poison an entire office. It takes a clear vision, vigilant leadership, and a willingness to speak clearly and quickly to aberrant behavior, all while moving a hundred miles an hour while staying focused on the strategy and goals of the organization. High-performing teams rarely appear spontaneously, and they die without care, energy, and leadership.

Finally, I learned the need to speak up. Professors are trained to react over time. We are not rewarded for constructive, nimble leadership. Learning how to balance speaking up in real time with not being a carping, critical voice is a very delicate dialectic to master. And learning how to raise one's voice is also dependent on the ability of peers and superiors to hear one's words and act on them. I found that drawing on history often worked. I think this is due, in part, to many leaders in government having some sense of participating in a historical drama of sorts, and they want to do well under such conditions.

In the four months between Kerry's invitation to me to join the State Department and the day I was sworn in, many of the twists and turns in my pilgrimage from the Bootheel of Missouri to Foggy Bottom made a lot more sense in hindsight. The old aphorism of the State Department being the haven of "male, pale, and Yale" staff did not fully capture who I was. And I saw my somewhat unusual path to be something of an advantage.

Chapter Four

LAUNCH

MY FIRST DAY AS A POLITICAL APPOINTEE on the senior staff of the US secretary of state was beyond surreal. First thing in the morning I was processed, which meant signing innumerable forms; getting my badge, which I had to display around my neck when present in the building; swearing a brief oath with just the oath giver present; and then riding an express elevator to the seventh floor for the secretary's Monday morning senior leadership meeting. This meeting was to become an important weekly ritual, but the first time I walked through those doors it was more than a little intimidating. I was about thirty seconds late, and Kerry had already started. All seats were taken, so I stood just inside the entrance where the fifty or so people present were staring at me, wondering who this new guy was.

When Kerry introduced me, I perceived a range of reactions in the room, from bemusement (we need a religion guy?) to curiosity (I've never heard of this person!). Here were the various undersecretaries; the more numerous assistant secretaries, or their acting placeholders; and representatives from most of the offices and bureaus in the sprawling State Department apparatus. What I realize now, which I didn't at the time, was that the people in the room were still taking their measure of Kerry himself. He had been secretary for all of five or six months, and for many of the people in the room, these Monday meetings would be their major interaction with the secretary. As it turned out, I was one of the first wave of his political appointees to be onboarded. Since I did not require Senate confirmation, I arrived at the tail end of his first wave of personnel picks. While I suspect my deer-in-the-headlights appearance was obvious to all, in short order the strangeness a newcomer inevitably feels began to wear off. In time these meetings proved to be incredibly helpful, as they were not only an opportunity to hear Kerry's commentary on what was going on around the world but also a chance to hear from the senior department leadership about the major issues occupying their attention. The next few months were a whirlwind.

The single most pivotal moment in those early days was a serendipitous encounter. I was entering one of the outlying State Department buildings just north of Main State, heading to one of the dozens of introductory meetings I embarked on at the outset. I passed by someone on my way who looked familiar, but since this was all alien territory, I knew it couldn't be anyone I actually knew. I have been told that I suffer from a sort of absent-minded professor stupor when I walk around; I prefer to call it deep thought, but the part of my brain processing real-time information is sometimes on tape delay, since the internal conversation is often what dominates my brain. I remember saying to myself, a few steps after seeing and passing this person, "That woman is a dead ringer for Liora Danan." A few steps later I realized, "You moron, that probably was her!" I pivoted around, as she had, and we stopped and had a brief conversation. She had joined the State Department in December 2012 and was working at the Bureau of Conflict Stabilization and Operations. We set a time to grab coffee and catch up. It would prove to be a fortuitous conversation.

The upshot from that and subsequent conversations was that Liora agreed to be detailed to my office, for a temporary period. In short order, it became apparent to me that she had all the skills necessary to be my chief of staff and then some. Landing her allowed me to check the first and major hiring task off of my list: finding the right chief of staff. I had been torn between someone with vast experience in the department and someone who had a deeper commitment to innovation and team building and who possessed deep subject matter knowledge on religion and policy. I opted for the latter in Liora; as a result, I had the partner I needed to navigate the launch of our office in a very complex political and policy environment. I interviewed multiple candidates for the job, and it became apparent quickly that she had the right set of gifts for what was needed.

In retrospect, I am amazed at how lucky I was so early in my tenure. If I had gotten this hire wrong, we never would have soared. I have told my students over the last two decades that Washington is a very tribal and politically sectarian city, and that networking is a precious commodity. And my story at State proved this to be true. Even though Liora and I had not stayed in touch in the years between my consulting gig at CSIS, when she paid my salary, and my joining the State Department, I knew when I saw her at State that I had to reconnect, pick her brain, and see how she might help my new adventure. In my notes before our coffee meeting, among the questions I wrote was, "What are you good at?" Her answers convinced me. One of the crucial items I was looking for in a chief of staff was the ability to disagree with me. I told her I would always support her in public and reserve any questions or disagreements we might have for one-on-one conversations. I tried to empower her to establish her own authority and independence in the office and beyond. I would estimate, over time, that we agreed about 85 percent of the time. And I quickly learned that I needed to listen to her very carefully, especially when we disagreed. That ratio kept things interesting. There were several crucial tasks that descended on us quickly. I can say with complete honesty that it was the best hire I made at State.

One of the first things I learned is that real estate matters at State. This is ironic on so many levels. At Wesley Theological Seminary, my office was in the subbasement of an ancient dormitory that was slowly turning to dust. Students used to come to my office, or more accurately, my monastic cell, and they would wonder out loud, "Professor Casey, who did you piss off to get exiled down here?" My faculty sisters and brothers and I, encamped in the basement of Straughn Hall, reveled in our outcast geographical status. But State was different, and this time I hit the lottery. I was given an office on the seventh floor, which is where the secretary's suite is located, thus putting me in the best neighborhood. This was no accident, and it sent a strong signal from the top that Kerry wanted me to succeed. In addition, we were on the third corridor, between the historic Office of Policy Planning and what eventually became the Office of the Special Presidential Envoy for the Global Coalition to Defeat ISIS, occupied by General John Allen. We had windows facing west with spectacular views of Arlington Cemetery. This was historic territory, and the career folk knew how to read these sorts of signs. I felt grateful but also a bit wary. Most offices of the so-called Specials often had a principal, a staff assistant, a secretary, and a location that was hard to find. I embraced the territorial status, but I kept a wary eye out for any jealousy it might provoke.

The late great Texas governor Ann Richards once chided President George W. Bush for being born on third base but growing up thinking he had hit a triple. I had no such illusions. I knew I landed where I did because of Kerry, not because I had slowly climbed the ranks of American diplomacy. My office was a spacious, beautiful, dark-paneled room that had served as the office of the assistant secretary for legislative affairs. Outside the door was a wall full of the portraits of the previous occupants, people like Dean Acheson, Thruston Morton, Douglas MacArthur II, Brooks Hays, and Wendy Sherman. The whole place was dripping with history. And, fairly or not, lots of people in the building noticed us for our location, if not our mission.

Codifying our mission, recruiting staff, meeting with interested external parties, and learning the complex structure of the department dominated the early days. We quickly developed a threefold mission statement that actually held up very well over the course of the next three and a half years. Our first mission was to advise the secretary when religion cut across his portfolio. If we were going to maintain the proper fox/hedgehog relationship, we had to connect our work to Kerry's. And that task fell to me and Liora. If you have even a nodding acquaintance with John Kerry's work during his stint as secretary, you know that religion cut across his priorities on a regular basis. Our job was to provide him with the best analysis we could muster, or to convene the best interpreters of religion we could find in order to provide him with good answers. We also built a very strong set of relationships with our next-door neighbors in the Office of Policy Planning.

David McKean, Kerry's Senate chief of staff and also chief of staff of the Senate Foreign Relations Committee, was an old friend and great partner. David had Kerry's trust, a deep intellect, and a keen sense of history. In the four weeks between my first day and the public rollout event for my office, I mentioned to him that George Kennan, the founder of the Office of Policy Planning, and perhaps the most well-known American diplomat in the twentieth century, once hired theologian Reinhold Niebuhr as a consultant. Without missing a beat, David proposed a deal. If I never compared him to Kennan, he would never compare me to Niebuhr! I assured him we had a deal. Relationships and collaboration would prove to be the key to success in the State Department, and our work with Policy Planning over the next three and a half years exemplified that activity. The speechwriters in Policy Planning became our good friends, and we constantly worked with them to highlight for Kerry where engaging religious actors could advance our diplomatic goals. Lauren Baer, who managed an array of issues in that office, proved to be an invaluable source of wise counsel as we grew rapidly in the early days. She had done a lot of the preparation work inside the State Department for the creation and launch of S/RGA.

Our second mission was to increase the capacity of our embassies and posts to engage with religious actors and to assess religious dynamics more effectively. My theory was that our office was there to put itself out of business. In other words, we tried to model a more sophisticated approach to religion in order to address Kerry's intuition that US foreign policy could do better at interpreting religion, and in modeling a higher standard of analysis, we would also train career diplomats to do better. If we were successful in teaching an innovative set of approaches, there would come a time when a shiny office in the Secretary's Bureau to promote the issue was no longer needed. We got about a quarter of the way to this goal by the end of the Obama administration.

An academic friend visited me pretty early in our run, and she told me there were two major critiques of my office in the professorial religion guild. My first thought was "huh, only two?" but I kept my mouth shut. She said the first complaint was that Kerry should have hired one of them instead of me. I didn't really have a response to that one! Obviously, I thought Kerry made a pretty good choice. The other was that I wouldn't have enough staff to make a difference. I told my friend to tell her complainants they should be patient and just watch and see how many people I get. Some in that guild thought I would only hire cheerleaders bent on puffing Christianity at the expense of allegedly disfavored religions, none of whom actually had any sophisticated training in religious studies. By the end of our run, we had over thirty staffers who had earned over twenty graduate degrees in religion or a cognate field. We could have run a leading liberal arts religion department with our talent. Between my personal history with Kerry going back several years and the very smart people I found who could fill in my knowledge gaps both on the department and on the contours of global religion, I was pretty confident we were going to be fine.

Our third mission was to be the portal for any external group, individual, or government that wanted to explore possible collaborations, clarifications of policy, or connections to the wider department on issues of mutual concern. The opening tsunami of visitors surprised me. I knew there was pent-up interest, for an array of reasons, from wanting grant dollars, to self-promotion, to just plain curiosity, to say nothing of a desire to help the US government improve its mixed record on global religion. But when hundreds of people showed up in the opening months, I was caught off guard. But I swore we would not fail because we mismanaged the high level of interest from around the world. I learned a lesson from the travails of the White House Office of Faith-Based and Neighborhood Partnerships back in early 2009. I started getting a steady flow of emails and phone calls in late spring from several important national religious leaders I had met during the campaign. The message was always the same: the White House Faith-Based Office was not returning calls or emails, and people were wondering why had they fallen out of favor. My response was simple: they were understaffed and overwhelmed by the volume of interest. I took every meeting request I got in those first four months, and it was exhausting, but it was important to do so.

One example is typical. I got an email from Jay Kansara, head of government relations with the Hindu America Foundation. Jay came by to introduce himself and asked for some help. Over many decades tens of thousands of Bhutanese refugees had been resettled all across the United States, and there was anecdotal evidence to suggest that many of them were being targeted for proselytization by various Christian organizations. Jay asked me if the State Department knew where these refugees were currently living. If his organization knew that, they could offer programming and support, particularly to the Hindus among the Bhutanese refugees. I gave what became a constant refrain for an answer, and that was, I don't know, but I will find out and get back to you.

I asked Anne Richard, assistant secretary for Population, Refugees, and Migration, for an answer to Jay's question. She introduced me to her staffer, Barbara Day, who ran the refugee-resettlement section. Barbara said the US government did not keep records of where refugees currently resided, but they could document where refugees spent their first ninety days in the country. She said research showed that refugees do move around in the country, but a healthy percentage of them stay in the places where they spend those first ninety days. I put Jay in touch with Barbara so she could share with him the data they had on where Bhutanese refugees first lived in the United States, and the Hindu America Foundation was able to program accordingly.

I also made a promise that our office would meet with anyone willing to come see us. Some critics suggested we were really in the business of establishing approved groups and not-approved groups. This was false. We met with everyone who wanted to meet with us, with one exception, which I will describe in a moment. We didn't ask who people voted for, nor which political party they were affiliated with. We worked for the American people, not on behalf of any religious community or organization or political group. We met with people who wouldn't have been caught dead in the same room with one another. We had to be radically inclusive, and that made things interesting.

At some point my executive assistant, Toiyriah Johnson, got a call from someone representing Doug Coe, founder and director of the shadowy conservative Christian group known as the Fellowship or the Family, which, among other things, runs the National Prayer Breakfast. Coe wanted to meet and summoned me to the group's northern Virginia compound, known as the Cedars, for an all-day conversation. I told Toiyriah to offer Mr. Coe an hourlong appointment in my office, which was my standard reply to these sorts of requests. It was unfair and unrealistic to spend a whole day off-site with him. A few days later I got a call from the director of one of the Obama administration's faith-based offices, who asked me if I knew who Doug Coe was. I said I did, and the director said I couldn't talk to him the way I had in my reply! I was nonplussed, to put it mildly. I told my administration colleague my reply had been entirely professional and reasonable. A fellow administration member was telling me I had to answer Coe's summons, and to do anything less was being disrespectful! I demurred but was more than a little stunned that the Fellowship had the sort of power to try and coerce me into meeting with them by enlisting the aid of an administration member. After time, Coe's intermediary reached out again and proposed we meet in a coffee shop instead of Main State. Again, I offered to meet him in my office, and he declined.[1]

In February 2014 I did accompany Kerry to the National Prayer Breakfast, and it was interesting, to say the least. I was walking behind Kerry as we were led to our tables near the front of the very crowded ballroom, and I noticed a bit of a kerfuffle in the direction we were heading. I couldn't make out exactly what was going on, but it looked like a gentleman was being strong-armed out of his chair and taken away. I made a mental note to ask a friend of mine who was big in the Fellowship and an usher at the breakfast just what took place.

According to my friend, a scuffle broke out when one of the ushers realized the person slated to sit next to Kerry was a Russian mobster! Needless to say, they moved the guy back to the cheap seats. I have to say I have heard more stories since that day from State Department colleagues that international mobsters routinely apply for tourist visas to the United States ostensibly to attend the event, and use the balance of their time doing business in the country. It was also shocking to me to see how many low- to mid-level US government employees volunteer to usher at the breakfast. In my view, the shadowy, right-wing, dark-money international apparatchiks who attend the breakfast are not the types US presidents should be speaking to every year about "the teachings of Jesus."

As part of my landing I tried to make a series of Hill visits, and in the process a very depressing trend emerged. Democrats were happy to meet and interested in our mission. Republicans beat me like a rented mule. One notable reaction was with three of Senator Marco Rubio's staff. Two of the staffers were cordial and seemed mildly interested. The third staffer snarled that they all knew why Kerry had hired me. That struck me as odd, but I couldn't resist asking him just what he meant by that. He insisted that Kerry's plan was to generate publicity for my new office and, while no one was looking, to shut down the Office of International Religious Freedom. That struck me as outlandish, but it would not be the last time I heard this theory. It became clear that the inside-the-Beltway International Religious Freedom crowd did not like any challenges to their hegemony and sole ownership of religion and diplomacy. Any different forms of engaging religion in US diplomacy were seen as an existential threat to Republican dominance of religion. I told the staffer that was a novel idea, but it was wrong. The International Religious Freedom Office was a congressionally mandated office, and to shut it down or reduce its budget or head count would take an act of Congress. Neither the secretary nor the president could kill or curtail the office by fiat. I then needled him a bit, probably unwisely, that the Republicans would never let that happen. I assured him the administration had no such plan. He was not placated and raised the issue two more times in the hourlong meeting, ultimately embarrassing his two colleagues. It would not be the last time Rubio's staff tried to make my life miserable. But it symbolized the rank partisanship Republicans flashed regarding religion and diplomacy in my presence.

What few Republican offices that would meet with me tended to be cold but not as rude. I saw that State had very weak connectivity to Congress in general, but relationships with Republican members were scandalously bad. John Kerry's relationships, built over his decades in the Senate, were exponentially stronger than the rest of State's juice with Congress combined. State will never regain its stature on Capitol Hill without a major expansion of its working-level communication with members and staffers. The Pentagon, in contrast, has a vast apparatus on the Hill, and at the end of the day it shows. Senators and representatives can make political hay at State's expense back home with impunity, while very few dare to criticize the Pentagon among their voters for fear of political backlash. That political calculus needs to change.

Our third mission was also crucial because of some internal preparatory work done under Secretary Clinton. Early in her term, Secretary Clinton had established the Strategic Dialogue with Civil Society and hired Tomicah Tillemann to run these dialogues as senior adviser for civil society and emerging democracies. A working group on religion and foreign policy was established along with several other dialogue groups. It was cochaired by Chris Seiple of the Institute for Global Engagement, an evangelical Christian organization established by his father, Robert Seiple, and William Vendley, secretary-general of Religions for Peace, all representing civil society. Representing the US Government were Undersecretary for Civilian Security, Democracy, and Human Rights Maria Otero; ambassador at large for international religious freedom, Susan Johnson Cook; along with Joshua Dubois and Mara Vanderslice from the White House Office of Faith-Based and Neighborhood Partnerships from the administration. Over the course of 2012, this entity would make a series of recommendations to Secretary Clinton regarding what to do in the religion and foreign policy space. These sorts of dialogues make a lot of sense, as they increase the communication between the department and important stakeholders, providing in some cases knowledge the department might otherwise not hear, serving as something of an early-warning system if issues begin to coalesce on a subject, and serving as a conduit for disseminating policy information to civil-society actors. But this sort of partnership works best when there is a formal designated entity in the department that manages the relationships. This was, of course, missing in the State Department regarding religion.

The hundred or so members of the dialogue on religion and foreign policy had more than a few self-promoting types who saw themselves as the perfect candidate to land the job leading any office that might emerge as the locus of a new mission or office of religion and foreign policy. As is often the case in these sorts of task forces, Washington-based people can show up and dominate the proceedings in such a way that work products tend to favor those who show up and produce the paper, and not the out-of-towners.

Many of the original A-list academics who were recruited to join the religion and foreign policy working group saw this dynamic and voted with their feet and stayed home. To further complicate matters, some on the government side also saw any potential office emerging from the dialogue as a prime perch to which they might be able to get a friend or themselves appointed. In late 2012 the working group on religion and foreign policy recommended to Clinton that she establish an Office of Religious Engagement and also make their advisory group permanent. To compound the intrigue further, when Kerry first learned from his initial staff briefing that he had legal authority to launch an advisory office on religion, he knew nothing of the work of the civil society dialogue group working on these issues. Yet many of the members of that group told me later that they assumed Kerry saw the wisdom of their recommendations, and that was what drove his decision to hire me.[2]

What did this mean for me? At a political level it meant that I had a hundred or so "parents" who thought I owed my job to their brilliant work with Secretary Clinton! It also meant some people in the working group and a handful in the State Department also thought they were perfect candidates for the job I got. And they all assumed it was their work, not Kerry's own insight, that accounted for the existence of my office. All of this unspooled to me over the course of the first six months of my tenure. Needless to say, there were lots of people with mixed motives coming to see me in the early days to take my measure. And as I inherited the maintenance of the ongoing work of the religion and foreign policy working group, I had to tread very carefully, as some of them were less interested in helping me with policy development and more interested in their own organizations' ongoing interests on a host of fronts, especially receiving government funding. I would eventually be able to bend these groups to my needs, but it came at some cost, as I will discuss later. Not only did I have to meet with hundreds of people in those early days who were seeking new relationships with the department, I also had to manage this existing cohort of insiders who thought they were special while I knew their narratives of how I got to State were mistaken. We could not afford to mismanage either cohort if we were going to fulfill this third mission of being the walk-up window for those interested in learning more about what State did at the intersection of religion and diplomacy.

In addition to drafting a concise mission for the office, Liora and I spent a lot of time planning how to organize the office, making an effective case for the number of staff we needed to do the mission and then recruiting the best talent we could find. Here Lauren Baer on the Policy and Planning Staff proved to be a crucial ally. She has been at the center of Secretary Clinton's attempts to launch a version of our office, and she knew the politics and organization of the building with a depth I would never be able to muster in the early days. She observed that the key to our success in socializing our mission in the building was connection to the six regional bureaus. They were, in a sense, the marines of US diplomacy in that they were our ongoing presence at the country level around the world. If we could convince them that S/RGA could help them be more successful in their regional strategic goals, that would go a long way in making engaging religious actors and assessing religious dynamics a normal part of our diplomacy. Lauren recommended hiring six regional advisers, and I quickly saw the wisdom of this.

When we started recruiting for these slots, ideal candidates would have studied religion in their region, preferably at the graduate level; lived or traveled extensively in the region; and had a firm grasp on US foreign policy in the region either by virtue of government experience or by study. In addition, they should have an active security clearance! Very few people had the full set of qualifications. But we built a remarkable staff. One of our central teams was our set of six regional advisers. We found a spectacular team lead in Amy Lillis, a career Foreign Service officer with extensive experience around the globe, possessor of a formidable linguistic talent, holder of a graduate degree in conflict analysis and resolution, and boasting an impressive set of contacts both in the department and around the world. She would time and time again provide priceless leadership and mentoring to our regional advisers and make me much smarter than I would have been otherwise. She was one degree of separation from just about every post. In many ways, this group was our heart and soul, since our relationship to the regional bureaus connected to all the US embassies and consulates around the world. If we were going to prove our worth to the rank and file of the State Department, it would depend on the work of this group.

We also established a functional team to liaise with the multitude of crosscutting functional issue offices and bureaus led by Claire Sneed from the Bureau of Conflict Stabilization Operations. Claire brought to her position connections with a global network of peacemaking groups, a background in training expertise, and deep knowledge of the Bureau of Conflict Stabilization Operations, where we had many allies. Once we were up and running, we built a public diplomacy (PD) team to run our communication programming, connect us to the department-level public diplomacy and public affairs apparatus, manage the relationship database we were building, and run dozens of external meetings across an impressive range of policy issues. The PD team, under the estimable Rachel Leslie, another career Foreign Service officer, helped put us on the public map and magnified the State Department's messaging around the globe.

I met Rachel on my first trip to Israel, where she was my control officer. Every time a Washington-based "principal" travels to a country, the embassy or consulate appoints a control officer, who manages the principal's schedule, transportation, lodging, etc. I quickly saw that these liaisons have a very tough job, particularly if a principal were a prima donna, as more than a few senior leaders at State were rumored to be. I sought to convey to those Foreign Service officers who served as my control officers that I was low maintenance. I usually did that by asking them questions about where they were from, what postings they had had in their careers. On the drive from Ben Gurion Airport to our hotel in Jerusalem, I peppered Rachel with my usual questions. Her answers set her apart from most of her peers!

I learned that she had taken a year off recently and earned a master's degree from the University of Chicago Divinity School, writing a thesis on what the State Department should do to develop a better approach to religion, if they were ever smart enough to try! I insisted that she send me a copy of the thesis, which I devoured when I got back Stateside. I had found a kindred spirit who, while on the public diplomacy team at the US consulate in Jerusalem, had built a deep portfolio of the dizzying array of religious communities and actors in Palestine. At the end of our visit, I told her if she ever needed a Washington-based rotation, to let me know. She soon needed such a post, and we recruited her. Like Amy Lillis, not only did she launch and manage one of our core teams, but she was also great at interpreting department culture for us, making our work more effective internally as well as externally.

The final piece of the design of our work was the integration of three previously existing offices into S/RGA: the Special Representative to Muslim Communities, the Special Envoy to Monitor and Combat Anti-Semitism, and the Special Envoy to the Organization of Islamic Cooperation. All three of these offices were nested in disparate corners of the department with minimal staffs and even less technical capacity to accomplish their diplomatic objectives. The proliferation of "Specials," that is, small offices with concentrated missions that often did not fit in the larger bureaucracy, was a fairly recent development. Usually the history of such offices could be traced to one of several sources: congressional energy and funding, a recalcitrant department that did not want to innovate and had trouble adjusting to emerging global issues through either a regional bureau or a functional bureau, or a flagship issue for a new secretary. Bringing these three into Religion and Global Affairs allowed them to multiply their impact through the synergy of sharing a much larger research and analytical capacity, and they were all now located in the Secretary's Bureau, where they would have more visibility and resources. In each case, the bureaucracy reacted differently. For us, it meant that our internal political map became much more complicated. But it also meant we had more opportunity to add staff, and it mitigated the rather lame charge that we were somehow a pro-Christian enterprise. I'll have more to say about the work of these offices in a later chapter.

Liora and I made two agreements with each other in the early days. First, we wanted to be intentional about office culture, and second, we had to agree on all hires, in part, because of the intricacies of office culture and also because we each brought a different set of skills and experiences to recruiting. As a graduate-school professor, I had never organized anything larger than a graduate seminar of fifteen people, and those disbanded after fourteen weeks. But throughout my life I had seen many institutions thrive and many fail because of inattention to organizational culture. I knew that good working environments sometimes happened by accident, but I couldn't afford to take a chance on that. Liora felt similarly, and luckily for me, she had more experience in policy-driven work spaces on these themes. She ended up being much more of the driver, curator, and leader on this. I think it made a huge difference in our recruiting and in the culture that emerged.

We developed a short list of office values and used them both in our recruiting discussions and in creating something of a culture of accountability where I, or anyone else, could be queried about behavior that did not comport with our expressed values. What we came up with was pretty simple and straightforward, but also somewhat countercultural at State. In many respects, the details were less important than creating an ethos where these issues could be discussed and legitimated as being at the heart of our enterprise. We might ultimately fail to implement our threefold mission, but it would not be because we didn't care about the strength of our work culture. Here is our list, with commentary.

Find joy in your work. Determine what brings you joy and how to engage in roles that do so. State was typically not a warm and fuzzy place to work, or so I was told over and over again. Yet State was rated in annual surveys as one of the best places to work in the federal government! I saw the full range of human emotion on display across the sprawl of the department. Joy is an elusive and all-too-rare quality. I am convinced that naming it as a pursuit can aid in its acquisition. We had been given a rare gift, and that was the chance to shape the manner in which the US government approaches religion in its diplomacy. As part of my pursuit of joy, I wanted an office of people who could find ways to see the possibilities in that mission and help others find joy and purpose in their work.

Treat others with dignity. Keep an open door and never be dismissive. Pitch in when needed and manage your own ego. We hired a lot of ambitious, successful, highly motivated employees. I had enough experience to know that treating people around you well isn't always part of the default package with type A personalities and, dare I say it, among academics. We had to signal respect externally as diplomats. I felt diplomacy began at home. At its height, our suite was crowded with staffers engaging people from all over the building and ushering hundreds of visitors, interlocutors, critics, and international diplomats into our space. As a part of the Secretary's Bureau, we had to meet a very high bar of professionalism and hospitality. And we had to comport ourselves in the same manner as we met with thousands of conversation partners around the globe.

Continue learning. Share articles, organize brown-bag lunches, and talk to colleagues. Define and pursue your professional goals. We had so many people who had deep expertise in religion and diplomacy, yet our diversity created so many moments when we all needed deeper learning to manage the complexity of the issues we worked on. It wasn't always easy. But we consumed a very high volume of information and communication on a daily basis, and some very interesting relationships and discussions emerged along the way, especially with scholars beyond our staff. In my case, I spent far more time knocking around in the Orthodox Christian world than I would have ever imagined before I joined the State Department. I am embarrassed to say that in all my years of graduate study in religion, outside of the first three or four centuries of Christian history, I had read very little Orthodox thought. I turned to the Center for Theological Inquiry (CTI) in Princeton, New Jersey, where my good friends Robin Lovin and Will Storrar were working on a project to rethink international religious freedom. CTI had a unique capacity to bring together an impressive array of American religion professors in short order, to make a dent in my ignorance of the Orthodox world. These very smart people remained a valuable resource for me far beyond their original crash course.[3]

Support a flexible workplace. Be accommodating when others have personal issues. Prioritize your own family and relationship obligations. Over the course of almost four years, with over forty different people working at various times across that period, life happened. Serious relationships began, others ended. Children were born, parents died, siblings got sick, children graduated, children got married. My mother had just turned ninety-two when I started. I knew the phone could ring at any time requiring me to drop everything and go. We had to have our backs covered. When major crises hit, I told people to go and tend to their needs and we would cover for them. And from time to time when these things took place, I was confident we were able to liberate people to leave and not to have to worry about their work at the office.

Do collaborative, creative work. Share ownership and prioritize partnerships. Aim for work that fills a gap and has impact. We faced an endless set of potential collaborations across the department and around the world.

I believed if we had clarity of mission, we would be able to say yes to the right things and avoid less meaningful work. In short order we found ourselves as an attractive destination for many other offices who sought out our analysis and collaboration.

Drive out fear. Share your ideas and voice your concerns freely. Create a safe space for colleagues at all levels to speak. This might have been the most important single part of the platform. I have worked in fear-drenched work-places, and I know all too well what that is like. It would have been very easy to slip into this mode, and there were shops at State that prided themselves in destroying any pretense of work/life balance. I once served on a short-lived innovation team populated by senior State Department leaders, and at our first meeting a woman assistant secretary pronounced words to the effect of, "Let there be no talk of a work/family balance in this meeting. Everyone know the Bureau I lead is where that stuff goes to die." No one challenged her pronouncement. I was determined to set a different standard.

Secretary Kerry spoke at a public rollout event for the office in August 2013. The event was held in the Benjamin Franklin Room on the seventh floor. The press was there, as were family, dignitaries, and lots of interested parties. My friend Melissa Rogers, who was the director of the White House Office of Faith-Based and Neighborhood Partners the year before, also spoke. It was a great day for me. I had had a brief tenure of four weeks between my official start and the official launch of the office. The tsunami was about to start, and I was prepared. In my remarks I thanked Kerry for his trust and his vision that the State Department could develop a more sophisticated approach to religion. It was time to test his thesis, and he gave me wide latitude to develop a plan and the resources to enact it. I also cited Reinhold Niebuhr, who in an earlier era of great turmoil in the international political system warned against two American temptations: hubris and isolation. Two of my religion professor friends in the audience that day, Michael Kessler and Jerome Copulsky, got the reference. Writing at the end of World War II and on the cusp of the Cold War in his book *The Irony of American History*, Niebuhr counseled avoiding hubris that somehow America had all the answers or the luxury of assuming that America no longer had a role to play in the international system.[4] When it came to religion, there were people in Washington who believed the former option was still the best one. Only in 2013 that meant exporting conservative Christianity to save the world. Some people mistakenly thought that might be my mission. Others thought America should stay away as far as possible from any attempt to get a more sophisticated grasp of how global religion shaped diplomacy. I signaled to those who had ears to hear that neither of these paths struck me as the right way to go.[5]

Once we were up and running, I quickly ran headlong into two camps within the department where religion was a primary locus of interest and action. The first camp was International Religious Freedom, which had been around for fifteen years after Congress enacted the International Religious Freedom Act (IRFA). The second camp was countering violent extremism, or CVE, in what was then current policy jargon. CVE was a new framing of, or better yet, a vestigial restating of, the Bush administration's global war on terror.

When ISIS invaded northern Iraq in June 2014, suddenly all of Washington was awash in CVE talk. The simplistic theory was that ISIS was all about religion, and now that CVE policy jumped the tracks into a global policy issue, naturally people in the State Department had all kinds of ideas for how the Office of Religion and Global Affairs should play a role. And not all of those ideas were compatible with what I wanted to do. A confluence of bad ideas, not particularly well-informed senior department leaders, and the usual push to "do something quick" in the face of the terrible atrocities ISIS committed created a bit of a maelstrom for us that required some delicate internal diplomatic efforts. The lack of a consensus regarding the wisdom and efficacy of CVE "doctrine" created just enough space for us to navigate a path forward without being co-opted by much of the theoretical nonsense that passed for orthodoxy in parts of the CVE ecosystem.

The place to begin is to chart the evolution of CVE as a policy trope throughout the Obama administration. Originally CVE was conceived as a set of policy initiatives designed to prevent radicalization of domestic actors. The English translation was that the Obama administration needed a better strategic approach to engaging American Muslim communities than the Bush umbrella of the Global War on Terror. In August 2011 the Obama administration issued a strategy paper entitled "Empowering Local Partners to Prevent Violent Extremism in the United States."[6] On the one hand, the strategy moved away from any vocabulary related to the rhetoric of the Global War on Terror, while on the other hand, it proposed to partner with local government and various civil society groups to prevent radicalization.

But the strategy could not avoid leaving the distinct impression that the administration felt American Muslims were at significant risk for being recruited by foreign Muslim terrorist groups.

Despite the fact that this strategy marked a huge improvement over Bush administration policies on potential domestic terrorism, critics abounded. A representative critique was authored by Will McCants and Clinton Watts from the Institute for Public Research at CNA in 2012.[7] They complained that there was no clear definition of CVE, that the strategy was based on flawed theories about what actually works, and that its proponents had yet to question whether CVE is worth doing at all. These same critiques would come to plague the US CVE efforts abroad. Once ISIS exploded on the international stage in June 2014, it was perhaps inevitable that someone would suggest that the domestic CVE strategy be globalized. Sarah Sewall was confirmed on February 11, 2014, as undersecretary of Civilian Security, Democracy, and Human Rights at State. She would become one of the, if not the premier, drivers of a new global CVE policy.

In many ways the approach to religion that was woven into the CVE strategy represented a 180-degree turn from our approach to religion and diplomacy. Despite Sewall's appointment, multiple other centers of power in the State Department were claiming some equities in the CVE space, and Sewall's inability to corral all those interests set off an internal competition that ultimately undercut any policy process coordination.[8]

There were several elements to the emerging strategy. First, the strategy was based on an outdated and discredited theory of human behavior. In multiple speeches throughout 2015 and 2016, Sewall invoked psychologist Abraham Maslow's hierarchy of needs and pyramid of self-actualization as the theoretical lens through which to understand why people were vulnerable to recruitment by violent extremist groups. While Sewall was always careful not to directly stereotype Muslims as being especially vulnerable to radicalization, it was nevertheless clear that ISIS and its potential appeal to Muslims around the world was the main problem driving the CVE initiative. She also was vigilant to say we don't fully know why people become radicals, yet she consistently stuck to invoking Maslow's analysis.

In her telling, Maslow posited a hierarchy of human needs ranging from critical needs such as food, shelter, and safety at the bottom of his "pyramid" to needs at the top of the pyramid, like finding love and belonging, self-esteem, and purpose. Not fulfilling the bottom-rung needs can create "push factors" that make people vulnerable to extremist recruitment. Likewise, unmet needs at the top of the hierarchy can allow religion to create a "pull factor" that might also entice people to join extremist groups. Let me just say that this theoretical approach to religion and CVE is not evidence based. Ironically, Maslow's famous 1943 work was based on his assessment of eighteen Western, primarily white male subjects he believed had achieved self-actualization. This is hardly a sufficient sample from which to draw broad conclusions about human happiness and motivation, to say nothing of explaining why some people are more vulnerable than others to joining violent extremist groups. But it makes an easy framework to explain an otherwise complex nexus of issues. It is not based on any local research into how the fraction of a fraction of a fraction of Muslims around the world ended up being recruited by the likes of ISIS. But Maslow helps Americans knit a theory that underwrote the securitization of much of American diplomacy in the face of an allegedly existential threat from Muslims.

While simultaneously extolling the need for more research into regional differences regarding violent extremism, Sewall helped construct a global coalition of over one hundred countries who purported to buy into her universal explanation of the push/pull factors that explained radicalization. The call for more research rang hollow. What were needed were "deliverables," in policy speak, and she wasn't particularly interested in getting advice from actual experts on Islam. She was interested, however, in drafting "talent" into the CVE mission, and that is where things began to get dicey for me.

Sewall was commissioned to design and run the White House CVE Summit in February 2015. In the lead-up to that show, she invited me to come by to talk about what our mission was in S/RGA, as a courtesy, but she had an agenda that went beyond the meet-and-greet. She proposed that S/RGA take up one of the lines of effort coming out of the CVE conference, and that was producing deliverables in the form of an imam-training curriculum that Muslim majority countries, primarily in the Gulf, could implement. Seven or so months later, President Obama could then announce our success in producing a stream of moderate imams at the opening week of the United Nations General Assembly in New York. My head almost exploded at the many problems I saw in that proposal. I demurred and said there were multiple problems with that idea, and I promised her I would take it to my staff and we would get back to her with our analysis.

After I described our mission, she said very matter-of-factly that she wanted me to detail one of my senior advisers, Peter Mandaville, to her front office. Peter, a professor of Islamic studies at George Mason, who had done a turn in the Office of Policy Planning under Secretary Clinton, had agreed to join my staff but had not begun his tenure yet. Knowing that Peter did not share Sewall's CVE views, and believing that I deserved a shot at being fully staffed before I let other offices poach my staff before they got to be my staff, I said no. This did not go down well. As she applied the pressure, I simply replied that I worked for the secretary, not for her, and if she had a problem with that she needed to take it up with him. I told her I was on the cusp of having as much analytical power in understanding Islam in the world as any office outside the intelligence community, and thus I would be happy to advise her on her CVE policy. But we were not going to be writing an imam-training curriculum.

I did run her proposal through my staff's brains, and they universally objected. The consensus was that the US government had no business nor competency writing such a curriculum, to say nothing about the possible receptivity in the targeted countries. In fact, in many of those countries, it was precisely in the ministries that regulated imams that much mischief was nurtured and funded. The sight of the State Department writing a curriculum in this manner would have made us look like imbeciles. The capper was that the belief that a reform curriculum drafted by us could produce "moderate," retrained clergy in a few months was not credible. We made our case to one of her senior aides, and his negative reaction demonstrated that the goal was delivering action, not necessarily doing something smart.

To get a grasp on just how farcical this idea was, imagine this scene for a moment. The president and chief imam of Al-Azar University, the oldest Muslim university in the world, come to the United States to meet with the chairman of the Joint Chiefs. Once they are seated in his office, they announce they have come to America to help us counter our violent extremism problem in the US fighting force. They have read the accounts of thousands of reported sexual assaults within our military. And they also note with extra consternation that a significant percentage of these acts pertain to male-on-male violence, which is clearly prohibited by our Jewish and Christian Scripture.

They go on to say they believe the problem lies with clergy in the US military chaplaincy corps who are teaching a violent perversion of true Christianity. Their solution is to engage their school's theological faculty, who are trained in the appropriate ancient biblical languages, to write and then teach a reformed clergy curriculum to our chaplains, which embodies true, nonviolent Christianity and not the current, apostate, violent type. They are confident that their better curriculum could reverse the errors of the chaplains' current training and in short order counter the current violent extremism problem in the US military.

Why couldn't we see the preposterous nature of our CVE work?

In a nutshell, here is what was wrong with the international CVE strategy of the Obama administration. Perhaps its largest defect was, despite occasional denials from the CVE mandarins, that its overwhelming focus was Islam, and everyone knew this. Even though countering violent extremism was a vast improvement over the Global War on Terror rhetorically, the focus remained similar. It just had a kinder, gentler framing. It still had the effect of essentializing Islam as inherently suspect when it came to violent tendencies. Bad religion, as in bad Muslims, was a bedrock assumption, and this only compounded problems because it nicely reinforced the West-versus-Islam narrative being peddled by some terrorist groups.

Further compounding the problem, CVE was a top-down enterprise, despite all the rhetoric about empowering local communities to counter violent extremism. Hundreds of millions of dollars went to summits and to the Department of Defense, and precious little went to expand embassies' capacity to understand the religious landscapes in their countries and to build robust relationships with different religious communities as a result. As one of my staff put it, "CVE is a theory-rich, evidence-poor enterprise." Becoming smarter on the contextual local dimensions of conflict, and whatever role religion might have played in any conflict, just wasn't as sexy as White House and UN summits, where theories and untested analogies could grow like weeds.

In my travels, I discovered the single greatest complaint by Muslim leaders was, in fact, bad US foreign policy. And by that they meant two things: the Iraq invasion and the ongoing US support for the occupation of Palestine by Israel. I did not attempt to justify the Iraq invasion, much to their surprise, and often to the surprise of my embassy-based control officers! In fact, my first real foray into Washington politics was leading a coalition of ethicists in publicly opposing the invasion. On the Israel-Palestine front, I was able to demur that I was involved in the current ongoing efforts to broker peace between Israel and Palestine. Needless to say, the CVE policy made no mention of the folly of our invasion of Iraq, thus ignoring the elephant in diplomatic conversations all over the planet.

I am aware of no evidence that any of the hundreds of millions of US tax dollars spent in the name of CVE prevented any violent extremism anywhere. The global top-down approach that ironically claimed to want to empower local communities and fund evidence-based programming never reaped results. Other people began to notice the policy impacts. On July 20, 2015, in the middle of the ramp-up of the new CVE policy, a coalition of forty international development agencies, many of whom received US foreign development funding, wrote a stark letter to the administration expressing their alarm about the emerging CVE policy and gathered a lot of global attention with their complaints.[9]

They noted that the CVE strategy risked repeating the same mistakes as other post-9/11 stabilization initiatives: prioritizing securitized responses over investments to address the structural causes of instability, and coupling the two lines of effort, creating confusion and working at cross-purposes. More specifically, they cited these concerns: that civilian-led development, prevention, and peace building that support locally led solutions to the root causes of insecurity are chronically underfunded, especially in relation to military efforts; and that subordinating development assistance under a CVE approach risks undermining US foreign assistance. They saw too much linkage already between development and security operations, which damaged the trust of local stakeholders. Clear boundaries between development assistance and security are better; CVE efforts to reduce extremism with communities are not being accompanied by governance reforms, social inclusion, and accountability by governments and institutions; and the over-reliance on military or aggressive security responses to threats when social and political solutions are needed can fuel grievances, encourage violence, and undermine CVE objectives.

So, how did our countervailing ideas play? (From time to time we jokingly referred to our work as CCVE, as in countering countering violent extremism.) We knew our small office was in a precarious position. On the one hand, we did have a great depth of understanding of the vast contours of global Islam and its complexities, and a wealth of relationships with academic experts on the subject, which meant people came to us for advice and answers. On the other hand, we were a very small unit up against the vast number of offices that claimed ownership of CVE at State and elsewhere in the administration. We tried to find a prudent path and choose our battles wisely. This produced a series of tactical moves consisting of pushing back on the really bad ideas like writing an imam-training curriculum and officially partnering with problematic global religious entities and networks that some in the department thought were sterling partners on CVE. We also cultivated allies within the department and also in the intelligence community, who shared our misgivings about CVE and possessed a much deeper knowledge of religion in local and regional contexts. We also tried to push back tactically when ideas gained traction, like the notion that we needed to develop a counternarrative on social media to refute the ISIS message that the United States was waging a war on Islam. The State Department could never effectively engage in a tweet-for-tweet war for hearts and minds against ISIS. The very idea that the US government would ever have the credibility to write a counternarrative with even marginal plausibility was beyond belief.

Our aspiration was that each US embassy and post would have a curated landscape of lived religion that allowed them to develop a deep knowledge of the religious communities and actors in their host country and to build a working relationship with as many of them as possible. The typical post knows all the political actors and parties in a country and routinely stays in communication with them. It constantly engages all manner of civil society groups in order to understand the politics and social dynamics of a country. Staff are well trained in the country's history and that of the region. Religion should be no different. I was prone to saying that when bullets start flying, it is too late to establish lines of communication that might help mitigate a crisis or catastrophe. When it came to conflict and overt violence, it was impossible to "manage" a crisis from half a world away in Washington. If our posts had a deep knowledge and an array of deep relationships with religious groups, this would go much further in mitigating conflict than any US government–led or UN-led summit in the States. The fact that most of our posts lacked this capacity was what underlay much of the aspirational language of the Washington-based CVE mandarins. Knowing we lacked an on-the-ground capacity to interpret the drivers of violence when ISIS erupted, they had to resort to a top-down Washington-centered approach. This was never going to position the United States to actually move events anywhere in the world without local capacity to understand facts on the ground. But even if they had wanted to develop a sophisticated understanding of local dynamics, these mandarins did not have the slightest idea how to do that.

Over the course of time from June 2014 until the end of the second Obama term, CVE lost steam and standing across the administration. I think there was general fatigue with the public relations hoopla that never actually delivered on its own hype. There was also a fair amount of infighting across the competing circles of power, each of which had its own mandates on countering ISIS and most of whom chafed at the attempts by Sewall to dominate the whole space. No single person or office was in charge, and despite Sewall's public profile on CVE, there was not a unified department behind her, and that, in no small way, was her fault, given her "my way or the highway" approach.

Religion in the abstract is easy to hypothesize and market. Religion embedded in national, local, or regional contexts is diabolically hard to understand. It takes patience, humility, deep study, and collaborative interrogation to begin to find understanding. Under the pressure of an alleged global crisis, this sort of work dies a swift death, in my experience. The analytical reservoirs in the US government on religion, such as they are, get kicked to the curb pretty fast because they don't generate lists of talking points for senior policy leaders who do not want to hear, "I'm sorry, Madame Secretary, it is more complicated than that." The result is millions of wasted dollars and, sadly, in some cases, lost lives.

What is my counsel on the future of CVE policy, especially with respect to religion? I agree with most of the analysis offered by Peter Mandaville and Melissa Nozell in a recent paper, "Engaging Religion and Religious Actors in Countering Violent Extremism," although I would go further in my conclusions than they do in that I believe it is time to bury CVE as an analytical and policy approach. (Since this is a publication from the US Institute of Peace, a US government agency and recipient of CVE funding, I suspect it simply isn't politically expedient for them to conclude that CVE is no longer an appropriate approach to religion and conflict.) Nevertheless, let me summarize their major observations about the role of religion in CVE.[10]

They argue that there is not a single root cause of violent extremism. Yet, most people working in CVE operate with the assumption that religion is part of the story, even if they cannot fully explain what that part is. To me, this is the fundamental flaw I saw in the State Department's approach. So many lines of action flowed from this fundamentally flawed assumption. A more sophisticated approach would be to abandon the great hope of CVE that elevates and separates religion as the major approach to mitigating conflict globally. The department has deep resources all across its complex organizational chart to parse and analyze the complexities of conflict. The varied and complex role of religion should not be exclusively pumped at the expense of all the other factors that create and sustain conflict. Blow up CVE and put religion and conflict back in a less prominent fashion into the existing bureaucratic DNA in places like the Bureau of Conflict Stabilization Operations and in the regional bureaus.

Mandaville and Nozell further state that while the CVE orthodoxy calls for engaging religious actors and communities, there is no consensus on just what this means pragmatically for policy. Instrumentalizing religion for national political ends is morally fraught and shortsighted. They cite three dangers here. The search for "moderate" voices is more complicated than a short glance would suggest. I would argue that the US government has no competency to offer a theological judgment that the term "moderate" suggests. Looking for "credible" religious voices as partners in CVE likewise presents dangers. At its worst, such a label can actually pose an existential threat to anyone so labeled in their own political context. And governments adapting religious language in their messaging strategies are also dangerous and can be counterproductive in that they can enforce the idea that indeed the US is trying to control, co-opt, or ultimately destroy certain aspects of Islam.

Mandaville and Nozell present a number of smart recommendations, but as I noted above, they do not come to the logical conclusion their arguments point to, and that is, if we want to "rightsize" the role of religion in countering violent extremism, we need to abandon the CVE frame altogether and relocate religion in a broader diplomatic framework of mitigating conflict. This would eliminate the overt anti-Islam bias that is inherent in the CVE approach. It would also prevent traditional diplomatic subjects such as good governance, fair elections, humanitarian aid and development, anticorruption programs, country-to-country citizen engagement, cultural exchanges, and a host of other historic forms of diplomacy from being assimilated into the intellectually bankrupt Borg-like CVE entity. It would also redirect hundreds of millions of dollars back into traditional diplomacy that actually makes a difference in preventing and mitigating conflict around the world.

Despite these two deeply flawed approaches to religion and diplomacy I encountered when I first arrived at State, there was one small but interesting contrast, and that was the approach I found in the Bureau of Conflict and Stabilization Operations (CSO), under the leadership of Assistant Secretary Rick Barton, whom I first met at CSIS. Just about the entire CSIS professional staff in the Post-Conflict Reconstruction project ended up in the State Department in the Obama years. CSO was a Secretary Clinton initiative designed, in part, to have a force of diplomats ready to move into postconflict arenas as soon as security would permit. Their mission would be to deploy the necessary resources to jump-start a vast array of reconstruction efforts to speed up postwar efforts to move to stability. Engaging with religious dynamics would be a part of the CSO toolkit in this work. Neither traditional religious freedom nor CVE efforts were at the heart of their methodology. I met a receptive crew there, including Rick, his deputy assistant secretaries Pat Haslach, Karin von Hippel, and Jerry White, and, of course, Liora Danan and Claire Sneed. Their mission was severely undermined when Undersecretary Sewall dismissed Barton early in her tenure. CSO never fully recovered a coherent mission, and a major source of research and innovation eroded in the interregnum between assistant secretaries after Barton's unfortunate departure.[11]

The balance of my first six months flew by quickly, but four memories stand out and are worth mentioning. The first thing Chief of Staff David Wade asked me to do was to join an ongoing discussion about the fate of the UN Convention on the Rights of Persons with Disabilities, or the Disabilities Treaty, its shorthand title. The last piece of legislation Kerry had worked on in the Senate as chairman of the Senate Foreign Relations Committee came to the floor for a vote in December 2012. Senate Majority Leader Harry Reid brought the treaty to the full Senate, having every reason to believe this treaty, negotiated in the George Bush era, would easily reach the needed two-thirds vote of the Senate. But things went horribly awry at the last minute when a significant number of Republican senators walked away from their commitments to vote for the treaty and voted no, despite the heroic efforts of former senator Robert Dole, who was present on the floor of the Senate when the rebuke took place. The Senate voted 61–31 in favor of the treaty, but it failed to reach the sixty-seven-vote threshold required for passage of a treaty.

Why did the vote fail? The short answer is that a national association of homeschoolers, the Home School Legal Defense Association, carefully crafted a public relations blitz among a few thousand conservative Christian homeschooling families to swamp Senate offices with calls to urge voting against the treaty. Enough Republican senators were intimidated and changed their votes to defeat treaty. This right-wing group, led by Mike Farris, founder and president of Patrick Henry College, sagely launched the attack and carried it out by mobilizing tens of thousands of evangelical homeschoolers to directly lobby senators. The Democrats were caught off guard; they ignored the campaign, never taking the threat seriously. Neither Kerry nor Reid was happy with the outcome. Because conservative evangelicals were at the heart of the defeat, Wade asked me to join the discussions to see if engaging a broader range of religious communities in an education campaign might prove beneficial.

The arguments launched by these fundamentalist Christians were drawn from very old far-right tropes that have been used against the United Nations from its inception. The structure of the argument is simple: the United Nations is the first step toward world government, which by definition means a surrender of US sovereignty, with international law superseding American law. While the treaty embodied the standards of the Americans with Disabilities Act and did not require any change in US law, the clinching argument of the Farris crowd was that the UN would have the legal right to dictate homeschooling practices for families with disabled children. This lie proved to be powerful enough to intimidate enough Republican senators to vote against the treaty, thus assuring its demise. Republican fear of losing conservative evangelical political support is as close to political kryptonite as exists in American politics today.

The State Department had a small task force working on raising awareness of the Disabilities Treaty, led by the department's special adviser on disability rights, Judy Heumann. Judy is a legend in the human rights world, given her pioneering work over a long career fighting for disability rights. She also happens to be a great person, a brilliant strategist, and a relentless advocate. She welcomed me into the task force, and I quickly became a fan.

I assessed the possibility of raising awareness about the treaty among American religious groups and concluded that the only way to change the dynamics was to inform Catholic, Mormon, and evangelical leaders and communities about what had transpired and to educate them on what the treaty was about. The short version of the story is that I spent a lot of time and energy but ran into a very powerful wall of fear in all three constituencies. And the fear was a combination of not wanting to cross the Republican Party leadership and not wanting to risk alienating a powerful, if obscure, substrata of the evangelical underworld; and also, frankly, a sense that there wouldn't be any fatal political consequences from disabilities groups for remaining on the sidelines.

We raised the treaty with the Vatican. My research indicated that in 2009, when the treaty was promulgated, the Vatican did not endorse or oppose it but expressed some anxiety that it could be read to support abortion rights. They never warmed to the idea of supporting the treaty. I met with several nationally known evangelicals. Russell Moore of the Southern Baptist Ethics and Religious Liberty Commission told me that if a white Republican president walked this treaty to the Senate floor, it would pass 98–0! Despite his candor, he said that neither he nor his organization could support the treaty, well, you know, for political reasons. Meaning they did not want to be seen as attacking homeschoolers, even though he acknowledged the treaty would transform the lives of countless disabled children and adults worldwide. So much for moral absolutes. Knowing what we know now about the internal corruption of the Southern Baptist denomination, it was not going to happen. To their credit, the National Association of Evangelicals did endorse the treaty. Since they are a membership organization of many denominations and move by consensus on policy issues, it took them a year to reach that decision. By that time the prospects for another Senate vote had disappeared. But I was pleased with their moral courage and due diligence in sorting out the issue. I flew to Southern California to talk with the famous Rick Warren, the senior pastor of Saddleback Church. We had a good discussion. As was often the case, I tried to establish some sort of connection with the person across the table from me. It turns out that he attended Hardin Simmons College in Abilene, Texas. He was surprised to find a member of John Kerry's staff who graduated from Abilene Christian! But he was cagey. While he told me he would discuss his views with various senators personally on an upcoming trip to Washington, he didn't really tell me where he stood on the treaty. And he did not agree to raise awareness of the treaty in his vast global network of stakeholders. Once again I got the feeling he did not want to cross conservative Christian homeschoolers who might be able to undermine his brand.

I also made a multiday pilgrimage to Salt Lake City, Utah, to engage senior Latter-day Saints leaders. I wasn't able to convince senior leadership of the Mormon church to take a stand on the treaty, even though they distribute tens of thousands of wheelchairs to children around the world each year. They were sympathetic to my case that the treaty would create a greater demand for their services. I don't think they were able to get over their traditional reticence about taking policy stands in public, given the strong negative backlash they received from their opposition to gay marriage. Likewise, while they took some very strong progressive stands on immigration issues, I think they found dealing with public policy issues to be exhausting and fraught with difficulty. While I had lengthy conversations with some leaders, I was never granted access to Dieter Uchtdorf, a member of the First Presidency. He was in a position to make a difference.

I got a hearing in all three communities; I just wish I had been more successful. The Disabilities Treaty should have united a broad range of US religious communities. But it was not to be. Partisanship was poisoning our foreign policy, and religion was a driver of some of that partisanship.

The second episode I remember vividly from the first six months was an invitation to travel to Vienna for a global conference on interfaith dialogue convened by the King Abdullah International Center for Interreligious and Intercultural Dialogue, or KAICIID, as it was known. The center had been established by the Saudis the year before and was headquartered in Vienna. Another global interreligious entity, Religions for Peace, also held its international gathering immediately after KAICIID's event, in the same hotel in Vienna. It was my introduction to interfaith dialogue as theater. It turns out I could have been in a great global city just about every month of my entire State Department tenure, attending these sorts of expensive extravaganzas; staying in the same five-star hotels; signing the same utopian, highly eloquent statements on the need to stop violence in the name of religion; and helping to advance the not-so-opaque political aspirations of the various nations, individuals, and NGOs (nongovernmental organizations). The pursuit of cash was at the heart of much of this vast global interfaith network. This ecosystem has only exploded since my first trip in late 2013. Too much of the broad field of religion and international affairs is orchestrated by wealthy elites who have leveraged their prominence into a state of permanent globetrotting to very expensive convenings. I decided early on that this was not what S/RGA was going to concentrate on. I did attend a handful of these gatherings. But it was almost always a means to meet with important people under the cover of a large gathering to try and advance specific policy initiatives. KAICIID, in those days at least, was the glitziest and best funded. That ecosystem has only grown, but the fiscal resources are beginning to dry up now, primarily because there are too many networks seeking money and the actual delivery of change on the ground seems small. In the absence of any significant impact on the ground, the future of this sort of approach is bound to recede.

But there I was in Vienna, with lots of people who were curious about the new American guy. And I have to confess, a lot of that interest seemed to be tied to whether or not the Office of Religion and Global Affairs would have millions of dollars of grant money to distribute around the globe. And that was precisely why I never wanted such funding. Whatever the problems were at the intersection of religion and US diplomacy, they were not going to be solved by dispersing large funds of money. Nevertheless, I didn't have much downtime in Vienna.

The meeting was surreal. A made-for-television stage, complete with a smooth-talking host who dominated the sessions, made the whole aura hard to believe. I do not recall a single woman or a Jew on the main stage during the conference. It was choreographed, but one could not miss the main deliverable, which was a message that the Saudis were among the good guys on religion, no matter their reputation or the message about religion they were exporting to vast regions of the world.

The most interesting moment for me came at the very end of the conference when I was asked to make a short set of remarks on the concluding panel. It was a bit of a high-wire act in that the invitation to speak came after the conference started and I did not have time to get my remarks "cleared" by the dozens of offices and bureaus back home who would have taken a keen interest in me not causing an international incident on my first international trip. My remarks were, intentionally, unremarkable. I cited a couple of things President Obama had said in his 2009 Cairo speech, thinking that I could not cause too much of a stir back home by hewing to Obama's lines. But the last speaker on my panel, on the whole conference, was the secretary-general of the Organization of Islamic Cooperation, Iyad bin Amin Madani. Madani had studied in the United States and cut a striking figure. His remarks consisted of an analysis of John Ford's classic film from the fifties on American racism, *The Searchers*. It was a brilliant exposition, and he was updating Ford's narrative that tried to condemn the American racism of the 1950s by shining a light on an earlier era of white American racism against Native Americans. It was hard to miss his swipe at American attitudes toward Muslims. I'm not sure how many in the international audience knew either Ford or his movie, but I was impressed. When the panel was over and the conference concluded, I stood up to shake Madani's hand and speak to him. Instead of shaking my hand, he pivoted around me, just out of my hand's reach. As he moved by me he said, "Do you speak to your president?" Before I could sputter an answer, he continued around me and said, "If you do see him, tell him we need action. We don't need more pretty speeches!" I was caught off guard by his response, but I had to give him credit for his style. He made his point in dramatic fashion, and there wouldn't be any cheesy diplomatic handshake photos of our meeting. Mentally I gave myself a C minus for the trip. I hadn't made a fool of myself with any public gaffes, but I could hardly claim I made a connection with Madani. Luckily, I would have the opportunity to try and rectify that later.

The third episode from the early days was in January 2014, when I took my first trip with Kerry. This marked the end of the first phase of the office's development and the beginning of S/RGA attaining a degree of impact in a growing number of issues with a larger and increasingly talented staff. Kerry was on the road, flying to various meetings in Europe, with a final stop in the Middle East. Unexpectedly, one of his European meetings was dropped, and he had an extra day in Europe before heading to the Middle East. Pope Francis had just been named pope a few months before, and Kerry wanted to call on his counterpart in the Vatican, the newly appointed secretary of state,

Archbishop Pietro Parolin. David Wade told me Kerry wanted to use the extra day to go to Rome. Our ambassador to the Holy See, Ken Hackett, sprang into action and set up the spur-of-the-moment meeting between the two.

Wade had me draft a memorandum for Kerry outlining the issues Kerry should advance as well as the issues the Vatican was likely to raise. This was the first memorandum I had to write for the secretary, and I had literally no time to shop the paper or have it vetted through the cumbersome formal vetting system called "the Line." This had to be a fast product for what would become one of Kerry's most enduring diplomatic relationships, with Parolin. I needed to get this one right, and I felt like I didn't have much of a safety net.

Fortunately for me, Pope Francis made his first annual address to the Vatican diplomatic corps just before Kerry's scheduled meeting; in it he outlined a number of his diplomatic priorities. I quickly surveyed a number of people in my networks about what Kerry should say to Parolin. I ended up counseling Kerry to start the meeting congratulating Parolin on his appointment and on his impending elevation to cardinal. In terms of substance, I suggested beginning with the state of the negotiations on Middle East peace, discussing global climate change, and raising the Disabilities Treaty with his counterpart, along with a few more issues. I briefed Kerry in his compartment on his plane, and we walked systematically through the memo. He liked my framing and peppered me with questions. At the time, I reflected on the irony of a low-church Protestant guy, raised in an obscure, rabidly anti-Catholic corner of America, advising the Catholic secretary of state on what to say in his first meeting with the Vatican.

Once we arrived at the Vatican, we were escorted into a room, where Parolin welcomed Kerry and our delegation warmly. It was fascinating watching these veterans of global diplomacy and international politics engage swiftly, intelligently, and productively. When Parolin quickly realized that Kerry was sharing details of where the Israeli and Palestinian process was, he knew this was going to be more than a meet-and-greet session. Pope Francis was scheduled to travel to Jerusalem later in the spring to meet with his dear friend, His All Holiness, Bartholomew, the patriarch of Constantinople, and the global leader of the Orthodox Church, to mark the sixtieth anniversary of Pope John VI's historic meeting with his Orthodox counterpart, Patriarch Athenagoras, in Jerusalem. But Pope Francis also wanted to aid the current Middle East peace process. The Vatican had heard from Israeli prime minister Benjamin Netanyahu as well as from Palestinian leader Mahmood Abbas. Parolin quickly saw that Kerry wanted Pope Francis to know the American view of the state of affairs. It was the beginning of a very fruitful relationship between Kerry and Parolin.

I was impressed with how Kerry had digested my memo and, without notes, walked systematically and impressively through the menu of policy issues I had outlined. He had Parolin's rapt attention, and it was captivating to see these two policy veterans communicate and build what would become a deep friendship. It was a command performance on Kerry's part that built a strong foundation that would serve them both well in coming days on many issues. I heaved a deep sigh of relief when the meeting concluded.

The final important milestone in the early days was the beginning of our work with the Office of the Special Envoy for Israeli Palestinian Negotiations. Ambassador Martin Indyk, the special envoy, had assembled his team to revive the negotiations, and at his suggestion, David Wade convened a group of us to think about how we might build support from all sides, in the geographical space of Israel and Palestine as well as with their supporters in the States. Indyk thought the United States had not done as much as it might have, among the three religions, Judaism, Islam, and Christianity, to rally public support for the two negotiating parties as they did the hard work of closing the negotiating gaps. As we were committed to aligning our work with Kerry's to the greatest extent possible, this was a golden opportunity for us to come alongside the negotiating team and play an ancillary but potentially important role in the process.

I knew enough about the history of these peace negotiations to know that I was in no way an expert in this realm; I had a steep learning curve. And it was helpful to work alongside Liora, who had more background on the issue set. Over the course of the next several months, we would invest a lot of time engaging religious actors both in the United States and in Israel and Palestine. I'll have a more detailed account of this work later. But it was a sign of how important the department saw our work that Kerry would suggest to Indyk that we could be useful on this, one of Kerry's priority issues. And it is a credit to Indyk that he saw a role for us to play. No one could say we were just window dressing.

As the onboarding of staff picked up pace, and as more and more substantive work came to us, by mid-2014 we were up and running and building an expanding work portfolio. We were successfully launched, and, as is usually the case in foreign policy, unanticipated real-world events began to overtake the plans and issues the administration had designated as priorities. One of those issues the universe tossed our way was the hemorrhaging global refugee crisis that caught the world's attention with the rise and rapid territorial expansion of ISIS in the second half of 2014. Given the role religion played all across the global refugee crisis, it was inevitable that we would have a role to play.

Chapter Five

THE MAN IN THE WHITE HAT

THIS CHAPTER WILL TELL THE STORY of how we contributed to the Obama administration's efforts to fight global climate change. Religion was not the main story in that policy effort, but it was a significant factor. This is an example of what we came to call informally in the office "rightsizing religion." We weren't roaming the halls of the State Department claiming to see a religious angle in every policy discussion in order to create work for ourselves or to exaggerate the prominence of religion everywhere. Climate change cut across two of our missions, to advise the secretary when religion cut across his portfolio and also to seek to engage actors outside the department who wanted to work on issues of mutual interest. Religious leaders, formal religious institutions, religion scholars, and religious activists all across the planet were weighing in on climate change.

Our job was to see where and how understanding the presence of religious dimensions in a policy arena might lead to greater diplomatic success. In terms of the environment, religion played a modest but noteworthy part in the effort of the administration to win significant public support for the Paris Climate Accord and its implementation. After the success in Paris, we began to turn our attention beyond advocacy to see how religious actors might participate in the climate-change adaptation and mitigation efforts to be funded by the Green Climate Fund. The success of Paris was one of the signal accomplishments of the Obama presidency. Trump quickly withdrew the United States from the Paris Agreement, and now President Biden has rejoined the Paris Accord. I see the work that Kerry did in negotiating the agreement as even more historic now. Over the course of this chapter, I will

show how we approached a policy priority, did our research and reconnais-
sance, developed a plan of action, and executed that plan while leveraging
partners within and beyond the State Department, all in the name of advancing a strategic diplomatic initiative.

My last class at Wesley Theological Seminary before joining the State
Department in July 2013 was a two-week intercultural immersion trip to the
Greater Yellowstone Ecosystem. One of the unique features of Wesley's curriculum was to require all master of divinity students to take an intercultural
immersion class. I watched with no small amount of envy over the years as
my faculty colleagues trekked the world introducing their students to various exotic places and teaching cultural and religious literacy. By the end of
most spring semesters, I was wrapping up my National Capitol Semester for
Seminarians program, which required me to schlep a semester-long seminar
of students all over Washington, DC, to dozens of sites, and I was usually exhausted. The prospect of leading a group of graduate students halfway across
the planet did not have a lot of appeal on the heels of such a semester. My
stack of summer reading and my writing commitments added a guilt factor,
sealing my fate not to travel and teach over the summer break.

In the summer of 2009, I was hiking in Yellowstone with my family, and
it struck me as we were walking one of my favorite patches of earth that we
were as far away from Washington culture as we could imagine. The next
thought was what a moron I had been not to see earlier that the Greater
Yellowstone Ecosystem was in fact a distinct culture, and I could bring a
cohort of students here to probe the scientific, moral, policy, and theological
aspects of global climate change. I had a surprisingly easy time persuading
the curriculum committee that this would make a legitimate contribution to
the curriculum. It took several years of planning to build a great pedagogical
platform, but by May 2013, I was bound for Montana with a class in tow!

For several years I had been ignoring a voice in my head that had only
been getting louder. That voice produced a steady commentary that global
climate change might represent the largest global moral issue of our day. As I
continued to find a multitude of reasons to silence that whisper now grown
to a full hundred-decibel scream, I came to realize my hesitance was due to
the complexity of the issue and especially the political complexity of addressing it successfully. So many forces were arrayed against any solutions. It was
a complex collision of academic topics that easily allowed paralysis and for-

bade easy solutions. It was, as one scientist called it, "a diabolical problem."[1] But I eventually realized I could no longer avert my eyes or stop my ears.

As a teacher of ethics, I came to see that there were moral, theological, policy, and scientific aspects of the problem, and very few people had the tools or energy to see all these dimensions at once. The cultural and political climate generated responses ranging from anger and rage, to willful ignorance, to cynical, well-funded right-wing efforts to deny that climate change was induced by human behavior. This combination did not yield an adequate set of local, regional, or global solutions. It was completely understandable why so many of us labored to ignore the issue. To this day I fear we may have waited too long to rectify the catastrophic damage to our planet. And higher education, with its hyperspecialization and territorial intellectual silos, was increasingly ill equipped to teach all the dimensions of the problem and its possible solutions. But I went to Montana to try my best.

As it turned out, Yellowstone is the perfect place to address the policy, the science, the ethics, and the theological dimensions of the problem.[2] Proximity to the tangible effects of global climate change is a powerful and necessary impetus for addressing the problem. And that requires leaving the classroom and immersing students in the outdoors. Or better yet, it requires moving the classroom outside traditional indoor classrooms. Students can master some of the science; they can tour the halls of Congress and master the policy details; they can read and study the moral and theological aspects of the problem in a traditional seminar format, but without seeing the devastation of climate change in different natural environments, they are unlikely to ignite the moral passion necessary to address the problem.

When I arrived at State, I knew from my first meeting with Kerry many years before in 2005 that climate change was one of his deepest policy commitments. I met Mike McCurry back in the early part of the twenty-first century when he became a member of the board of governors of Wesley Theological Seminary. Kerry recruited McCurry to join his presidential campaign in the waning weeks of the 2004 campaign, and of course, Kerry lost the election to George W. Bush and, in the process, came under attack from a small set of Catholic bishops over his stand on abortion. The campaign ultimately chose not to directly respond to the charges against Kerry that he was not a true Catholic. In the days immediately after the election, Kerry called McCurry as he was sifting the campaign and the topic of religion came up in

the conversation. Kerry asked McCurry how he might have responded differently. McCurry demurred and told Kerry he needed to meet an assistant
professor, Shaun Casey, at Wesley Theological Seminary who was writing a
book on the 1960 presidential election between John Kennedy and Richard
Nixon. A few days later I got a call from one of Kerry's Senate staffers invit-
ing me to meet with several staffers in Kerry's office. After a meeting with
advisers like David McKean and David Wade, I was asked to pull together
a list of religion scholars and practitioners to meet with Senator and Mrs.
Kerry for dinner and conversation about religion and American politics.

As I walked into the living room of the Kerry home, I saw Kerry surrounded by some of the early-arriving guests, listening to Kerry excitedly
describe a meeting he had had that day with a group of scientists who were
sounding the global alarm about the threat of climate change. I saw his passion in action on climate change before I had a chance to shake his hand for
the first time.

I was determined to see how S/RGA might align with this Kerry priority from the outset. But I have to confess, it wasn't at all clear how I was
going to do that. Here is what I knew when I arrived. Based on my decade
and a half in Washington, I knew there were three relevant sets of actors in
the space at the intersection of religion and climate change. The first set of
actors were the religiously affiliated or adjacent organizations. Some represented specific religious communities such as the US Conference of Catholic
Bishops. Some represented wider traditions such as the Evangelical Environmental Network. This landscape was complex, and the size of these organizations ranged from the mom-and-pop variety to the large and well run.
The policy sophistication of these groups also ran the gamut from virtually
none to highly skilled. They were united by their passion and something
of a chip on their shoulder because the other two parties, the mammoth
secular environmental groups and the Obama climate policy offices, tended
to ignore them.

These secular environmental groups, the second set of actors, included
the likes of the Sierra Club, the Nature Conservancy, and the Natural Resources Defense Council. These were large, well-funded, politically savvy
Washington players. They tended to see the religious groups primarily as
lightweights, politically naïve but useful from time to time for their grassroots advocacy utility. In Washington parlance, they were "Collars for Cam-

eras," that is, clerics in their religious garb, useful at public events. But by and large, they didn't spend much effort consulting with the religious crowd.

The third set of actors were the climate policy shops dispersed across the executive branch of government. They respected the secular behemoths, and their feelings for the religious groups ranged from fear, based on the common perplexity faith-based advocates often evoke in Washington, to respect for the passion and knowledge the faith-based groups had earned over the years. Among the latter was Todd Stern, the special envoy for climate change, who was the chief US negotiator for the 2015 Paris Climate Agreement. Stern once told me that the key to a successful agreement was securing the support of three American constituencies: the business community, the international security sector, and the American religious communities.[3] Stern had hired Karen Florini as his deputy special envoy for climate change; she, among other things, headed their civil-society engagement efforts. With Karen as our partner, and with Stern's explicit approval, we built and implemented a strategy of bringing together all three groups to work together to secure as much support as possible for the strongest possible agreement in Paris.

In the first meeting we called in May 2015, I attempted to craft and test a narrative of the state of uneasy relationships among the three parties, and, if they agreed with my assessment, to sketch a way forward for the next few months leading up to the global meeting in Paris to complete the global agreement. In our office, I termed this the "Can this marriage be saved initiative." I saw our role as mediating the tensions, whether large or small, and bringing these three partners together to transcend whatever friction had emerged among them over past years and unite them around building stronger lines of communication so they could combine assets to increase the chances of a successful outcome at Paris.

It's always interesting to see how people enter a large conference room and choose their seats. We had too many people crammed into this room, and it wasn't possible to do the normal State Department protocol of setting up name placards and arranging the seating before the meeting. As I recall, my spot was reserved at the head of a long conference table, and everyone else chose their own seats. The administration policy folk stood against the wall behind me, the mammoth environmental groups took one side of the table, the religion folks took the other, and my staff were backbenchers taking the seats against the other walls. I got right to the point. I laid out my thesis that everyone in the room wanted the most aggressive agreement possible, and yet there was a level of mistrust among the parties that might interfere with achieving that goal. The religious folks felt looked-down-upon by the behemoths, and the big guys saw the religious folks as amateurs. But both groups feared that the policy teams wanted or needed an agreement so badly they would settle for a weak treaty, and the policy people seemed pretty uncomfortable listening to both sets of advocates take shots at them. After setting this out, I then said, as diplomatically as possible, "prove me wrong." For a few seconds, there was silence, which I took to mean I had struck a nerve.

Over the years in classroom settings when dramatic silence emerges, I reflexively became uncomfortable. Somewhere along the line I realized that such silences often portended significant breakthroughs or spiraling chaos. Now I am no longer afraid of them because of the transformational opportunities that sometimes emerge. This particular moment was exactly what I was hoping for. I was not disappointed. Silence represents opportunity.

Steve Colecchi, from the US Conference of Catholic Bishops, broke the awkward silence and quickly agreed with my thesis. He also, in his powerful, kind way, challenged the big environmental group directly. He told them that the pope was about to release his encyclical on the environment, *Laudato Si*, and they should not attempt to co-opt the pope's message. He anticipated that the pope's message would get hijacked, and in the process, he would be reduced to just another secular figure in the coming political battle between the administration and the Republican-controlled Congress. He asked the secular groups not to jump on the public bandwagon and enlist Pope Francis as just another political endorser of a strong Paris Agreement. The US Catholic Church had a communication plan for the rollout of the pope's encyclical, and they wanted to magnify his message without getting stomped on by secular environmentalist appropriation. He asked for a few weeks before the big guys launched their own campaigns based on the new encyclical. That lit a fire in the room, and a truly wild conversation erupted. By the time it was over, we had a new set of relationships and the outlines of a plan going forward.

The rest of the room promised to try not to hijack Pope Francis and his message for their own publicity purposes, acknowledging their gratitude to the Catholic Church for the huge contribution the pope was about to make with the release of his encyclical. The Obama policy shops promised to welcome the queries and aid the advocacy groups. All the advocacy groups, secular and religious, were happy to hear this. I was especially happy that we were the ones to properly assess the tensions among these vital stakeholders and that we were on our way to building a communication strategy to aid in the pursuit of a strong agreement, which was precisely what everyone in the room was seeking. We ran an ongoing series of briefings with a wide range of Obama policy officials for an expansive group of religious actors, where a give-and-take dialogue took place.

The next hard step was to assemble a team out of thin air that could organize the issue set for us across all three broad sectors: religious groups interested in environmental policies, the secular environmental giants, and the diverse policy shops. Diagnosing a problem was one thing. Staffing an initiative and implementing a strategy was quite another. As usual, Liora, our chief of staff, was way ahead of the curve. Many months earlier she had noticed a broadcast email sent to every State Department employee announcing the Jefferson Science Fellowship (JSF) program. This program was a decade old and was administered by the National Academies of Sciences, Engineering, and Medicine and was designed to allow senior scientists to help formulate and implement US government policy by working for a year as a Jefferson Science Fellow. A dozen or so scientists were picked every year, and once picked, they interviewed with dozens of State Department offices to find a place that matched their interests.

The department offices were required to write position descriptions for the fellows, so they could indicate which specific offices they wanted to be interviewed by during interview week. Liora noted that we might be able to snag someone with an interest in climate-change policy to work with us in the lead-up to the December 2015 Paris climate talks. We wrote up the position description, and I promptly forgot about it. I remember telling her, no scientist is going to want to work for the Office of Religion and Global Affairs, given the amazing array of science-related policy issues and offices in the State Department. A few months later, interview week arrived, and almost all the scientists signed up to interview with us. I was stunned. Of course, what I learned, and should have known, is that almost all the fellows spent the week interviewing with almost every office that had posted a position! After all, they were all collectors of data, and we were something of a unicorn among the other offices, so they all wanted to get a glimpse of the outlier.

When the dust cleared from the selection process, Professor Alice Bean, an experimental particle physicist from the University of Kansas and member of the Compact Muon Solenoid (CMS) Collaboration at the large Hadron Collider, agreed to be the Jefferson Science Fellow for the Office of Religion and Global Affairs, with a position description calling for her to lead our efforts to support the Paris Climate Accord.[4] In our first conversation, I asked Alice to do three tasks, thinking these would keep her busy for several weeks: map the domestic terrain for the major religious groups working at the intersection of religion, the environment, and public policy; outline the major secular environmental groups working in public policy; and map all the offices in the executive branch of the US government working on environmental policy. Since these were the three groups found in my original hypothesis, I needed Alice to draw us a map of who populated these three groups and then to build relationships with them. It took Alice only days to track down all these different players instead of the months I thought it would take her.

Alice's research empowered us to start contacting all three constituencies and building relationships in order to convene the first of what proved to be many different gatherings in many different formats over the next year and a half. Without this foundation, we would have floundered and had no real impact in addressing the problems between and within the groups.

This line of our work culminated in a symposium we cosponsored with the Berkley Center for Religion, Peace, and World Affairs on November 9, 2015, a few weeks before the final negotiating session in Paris. Over the course of two days we had panels that reflected the intersection of science, religion, and environmental public policy. The two days had something of a celebratory feel, as everyone believed the outcome in Paris was going to be good. I was especially happy because we had taken up Todd Stern's challenge to engage religious communities to enlist their feedback and gain their support. We assembled a talented team and engaged a wide array of American religious communities, who in turn challenged the administration not to settle for a weak agreement just to be able to say they got an agreement.[5]

It's worth recounting why Pope Francis was the man everyone was talking about at our original meeting in early May 2015. Certainly, he was the most important religious actor in the lead-up to the Paris Agreement. The release of his first papal encyclical, *Laudato Si*, in May 2015 and his visit to the United States in September 2015 dramatically shaped the environmental-policy discussions in America. Why did his encyclical and his subsequent visit make such a difference? The simple answer is that *Laudato Si* was his first encyclical, published barely two years after Francis was elected pope, when he was riding a wave of unprecedented global popularity. He was a global rock star, and, given the lengthy list of global social issues to choose from, he chose to write about climate change. In addition, the world was coming together in Paris seven months after the debut of the encyclical to try and craft a global environmental agreement. The moral stars were aligned in a very rare constellation. The encyclical did not underperform.

As a scholar immersed in Catholic social teaching for almost forty years, I have to remind myself that the genre of this type of literature is not familiar to most Americans, even to most Catholics. Forty-five-thousand-word theological tracts are alien to most Americans. But this one was stirring a fuss in the halls of Congress and in the office of the State Department, and even the mainstream media was anticipating the release of this new pope's first encyclical. I think it is important to assess the content in order to better understand what all the interest was about. When it came out, I sent a copy to Secretary Kerry, along with a memo of analysis. A year and a half later, in December 2016, when I accompanied Kerry to his private meeting with the pope at the Vatican, the pope gave Kerry a bound copy of the encyclical.

In many ways *Laudato Si* looked a lot like a typical papal encyclical. It was addressed to the whole world, not just Roman Catholics. It invoked past popes and councils. It resembled the famous encyclical of Pope John XXIII, *Pacem in Terris*, in that it concentrated on the whole planet and it shaped a US president, in that case John Kennedy. Even its paragraphs were numbered in the traditional manner, which gave it a certain gravitas not common in the digital age. At the same time, it was quite different. It was the first encyclical of a new and charismatic pope, Francis. It was promoted by a vastly more sophisticated communication strategy and team than other popes had employed. It was published barely six months before the final negotiation session of a UN climate-change policy process. And the pope himself was coming to the United States to address a joint session of Congress, in addition to participating in a number of other events in the United States, in September 2015, between the release of the encyclical and the UN climate negotiations in December. It's hard to understate the novelty and brilliance of those months between the release of the encyclical and the culmination of the Paris Accord negotiations.

It's worth taking some time to describe and assess the document itself. The pope begins by quoting a canticle of his namesake, Saint Francis of Assisi: "Praise be to you, my Lord, through our Sister, Mother Earth, who sustains and governs us, and who produces fruit with colored flowers and herbs." He immediately adds: "This sister now cries out to us because of the harm we have inflicted on her by our irresponsible use and abuse of the goods with which God had endowed her. We have come to see ourselves as her lords and masters, entitled to plunder her at will. The violence present in our hearts, wounded by sin, is also reflected in the symptoms in the sickness evident in the soil, in the water, in the air and in all forms of life."[6]

This is no benign call for a general survey of the debate on whether or not climate change is man-made. It is a call for the world to come together seeking authentic social and moral progress in the face of a global threat to the planet. One that we made ourselves. The dire nature of the threat to our common home means that nothing in this world is indifferent to us. He makes a case for the universal solidarity of humanity in light of the dangers we have created that threaten human existence. Here he is echoing the words of the final document of the Second Vatican Council, issued in December 1965, *Gaudium et Spes*, which states, "The joys and the hopes, the griefs and the anxieties of the men of this age, especially those who are poor or in any way afflicted, these too are the joys and hopes, the griefs and the anxieties of the followers of Christ."[7]

Francis is grounding his plea to the world to respond to the threat of climate change in the theological framework of his tradition, even though that tradition has only devoted notional energy and thought to the environment as a topic of moral concern. He is continuing more recent Catholic efforts to address all people of good will in a dialogue to make moral progress and not to rely on a solely technocratic scientific approach to climate change. Unlike many conservative Christian voices in the West, he does not disparage science, as he has graduate-level scientific education himself. He notes further that his concern overlaps the concerns of many other theological voices, including his friend Ecumenical Patriarch Bartholomew, also known as the Green Patriarch, as well as numerous others who have enriched the church's thinking on the environment. He closes the introductory section

with an appeal for the world to come together to seek a sustainable and integral development to protect our common home. He expresses a particular
appreciation "to those who tirelessly seek to resolve the tragic effects of
environmental degradation on the lives of the world's poorest."[8]

He calls for a new dialogue to combat indifference, obstructionist attitudes, resignation, or blind confidence in technical solutions. "We need a
new and universal solidarity." He closes with a quick list of the themes he
will elaborate: the intimate relationship between the poor and the fragility
of the planet, the conviction that everything in the world is connected, the
critique of new paradigms and forms of power derived from technology,
the call to seek other ways of understanding the economy and progress, the
value proper to each creature, the human meaning of ecology, the need for
forthright and honest debate, the serious responsibility of international and
local policy, the throwaway culture, and the proposal of a new lifestyle.[9]

Space doesn't allow me to analyze the whole document, but what you
see in the early pages is enough to begin to show why the work had such an
immediate impact. The most popular religious figure on the planet issues
his first encyclical to address the hottest current global political topic in the
midst of a global political process that will culminate in a global agreement
in a matter of months after the publication of the letter. He has waded into
a hornet's nest of policy, moral, and economic arguments and fights with
boldness and verve. The timing could not have been better for those in the
global diplomatic arena.

When Speaker of the House of Representatives John Boehner invited
Pope Francis to address a joint session of Congress in March 2014, he had no
way of knowing the speech would come four months after the release of *Laudato Si* and three months before the meeting in Paris of the parties finishing
the global climate accord. Francis was coming to the United States to attend
a meeting on the family in Philadelphia, but he came to Washington, too,
and made a total of seventeen separate sets of remarks while in the United
States. If the visit had many purposes, the pope's stay in Washington made
at least one political difference: it made it very difficult for Republicans to
attack the Obama administration's aspiration for the strong results in Paris
at the end of the year.

In June of 2015, Senator Ed Markey had invited me to the Hill to talk
to the Senate Climate Caucus about the pope's upcoming visit. In addition

to Senator Markey, I recall Senator Al Franken and Senator Chris Murphy were there. After I made a quick set of initial remarks, the senators peppered me with questions, most of which signaled some political anxiety that the pope would be attacked by climate-change deniers on the Republican side of the aisle. I remember Franken in particular being animated over how the Democrats could support the pope in the face of the anticipated reaction on the right. I asked him how many followers he had on Twitter. As I recall, the number was in the range of five figures. I noted that Francis had millions of followers at that point. I then said I thought the pope could hold his own in the court of American public opinion, and any Republican who attacked Francis during his visit was probably not doing the climate-change denial cause any favors. Franken said he took my point.

The day of the pope's speech, I got a ticket from the White House to sit outside the Capitol on the west side with a large crowd of dignitaries from a wide swath of Washington public life. I was happy to find myself seated next to James Zogby, founder and president of the Arab American Institute, and his wonderful wife, Eileen. We were able to catch up while soaking up the very unusual sight of Washington Republicans and Democrats sitting together, listening to the pope address the joint session of Congress, and then witnessing the pope and leading congressional figures from both parties standing on a balcony above us and waving to the crowd. I had never seen such a sight in my twenty years in Washington. And there was no hint of criticism of the pope to be heard.

His speech was daring and bold. In fact, both his address to Congress and his remarks earlier at the White House were compelling. The congressional address was a call to Congress to do its job! And the heart of the speech concentrated on four Americans, Abraham Lincoln, Martin Luther King Jr., Dorothy Day, and Thomas Merton, and their specific contributions to American moral and political life. It was a deft and eloquent speech that drew on the words and deeds of this American quartet to urge Congress to fulfill its mission to address and heal the divisions of the country. I do not know who drafted this speech, but it was compelling, and, if nothing else, it muted, if only for a while, the right-wing Republican noise-machine criticism of the march toward Paris in less than three months. Two passages near the end of the speech are worth quoting:

From this perspective of dialogue, I would like to recognize the efforts made in recent months to help overcome historic differences linked to painful episodes of the past. It is my duty to build bridges and to help all men and women, in any way possible, to do the same. When countries which have been at odds resume the path of dialogue—a dialogue which may have been interrupted for the most legitimate of reasons—new opportunities open up for all. This has required, and requires, courage and daring, which is not the same as irresponsibility. A good political leader is one who, with the interests of all in mind, seizes the moment in a spirit of openness and pragmatism. A good political leader always opts to initiate processes rather than possessing spaces (cf. *Evangelii Gaudium*, 222–223).

Being at the service of dialogue and peace also means being truly determined to minimize and, in the long term, to end the many armed conflicts throughout our world. Here we have to ask ourselves: Why are deadly weapons being sold to those who plan to inflict untold suffering on individuals and society? Sadly, the answer, as we all know, is simply for money: money that is drenched in blood, often innocent blood. In the face of this shameful and culpable silence, it is our duty to confront the problem and to stop the arms trade.

Three sons and a daughter of this land, four individuals and four dreams: Lincoln, liberty; Martin Luther King, liberty in plurality and non-exclusion; Dorothy Day, social justice and the rights of persons; and Thomas Merton, the capacity for dialogue and openness to God.

Four representatives of the American people.

Moments later, as he concluded, he said:

A nation can be considered great when it defends liberty as Lincoln did, when it fosters a culture which enables people to "dream" of full rights for all their brothers and sisters, as Martin Luther King sought to do; when it strives for justice and the cause of the oppressed, as Dorothy Day did by her tireless work, the fruit of a faith which becomes dialogue and sows peace in the contemplative style of Thomas Merton.

In these remarks I have sought to present some of the richness of your cultural heritage, of the spirit of the American people. It is my desire that this spirit continue to develop and grow, so that as many young people as possible can inherit and dwell in a land which has inspired so many people to dream. God bless America!

The day before the speech to Congress, during his joint remarks with President Obama on the South Lawn of the White House, he signaled to the world in the first of seventeen sets of remarks he would make while in the United States, that climate change was on his mind.

Mr. President, I find it encouraging that you are proposing an initiative for reducing air pollution. (Applause.) Accepting the urgency, it seems clear to me also that climate change is a problem which can no longer be left to our future generation. (Applause.) When it comes to the care of our common home, we are living at a critical moment of history. We still have time to make the change needed to bring about a sustainable and integral development, for we know that things can change.

Such change demands on our part a serious and responsible recognition not only of the kind of world we may be leaving to our children, but also to the millions of people living under a system which has overlooked them. Our common home has been part of this group of the excluded, which cries out to heaven and which today powerfully strikes our homes, our cities, our societies. To use a telling phrase of the Reverend Martin Luther King, we can say that we have defaulted on a promissory note, and now is the time to honor it. (Applause.)

We know by faith that the Creator does not abandon us; He never forsakes his loving plan or repents of having created us. Humanity has the ability to work together in building our common home. As Christians inspired by this certainty, we wish to commit ourselves to the conscious and responsible care of our common home.[10]

The overall visit accomplished at least four things in a very fraught political moment leading up to Paris. First, these speeches demonstrated the overlap between Catholic social teaching and the American tradition of liberal democracy. Second, the pope argued that through dialogue problems could and should be addressed, and he made that case in front of the least deliberative body of 535 Americans, the US Congress. Third, he tried to point them to action and solutions to some of the most intractable issues of the day by drawing on a diverse set of four exemplars. It was as if he was saying Congress needed to rise to the heights of its better angels. And finally, whether by design or by accident, his presence and eloquence blocked the worst tactics of the Republican climate deniers and created a wider political space for the Obama administration to finish the job of the Paris Agreement. Todd Stern's vision of persuading America's religious communities to support the Paris process and results was secure by the end of Pope Francis's fall visit.

As the fall continued, I drew a lot of satisfaction that the administration's efforts were coming to a climax in Paris. Our outreach to religious communities grew as we convened numerous calls and face-to-face meetings between administration policy makers and interested religious communities. We had successfully built a platform for dissenting groups to meet with policy shops and give their feedback and express their hopes of a tough accord. The Georgetown meeting was the closest thing I saw to a celebration of a long and successful policy effort. I was particularly proud of how we had found a way to make a modest contribution to one of the signal policy achievements of the Kerry State Department. With virtually no new internal funding, we found a way to access new resources through the Jefferson Science Fellowship and funding from the Luce Foundation in partnership with the American Academy of Religion to hire expertise at the intersection of climate change and religious scholarship.

Once the ink was dry on the Paris Agreement, we pivoted to a strategy of education and implementation, and not simply advocacy. But before describing the pivot, we should examine the Paris Agreement itself. Despite the political maelstrom about the Paris Agreement in American political discourse, very few people have actually read the text. In fact, very few people have ever read any sort of United Nations convention, much less an agreement that takes place in the context of a UN convention framework, as the Paris Agreement does. This makes propaganda easier, since habitual critics of anything related to the United Nations are seldom actually held accountable for their lies, as I learned in my work on educating religious communities regarding the UN Convention on Persons with Disabilities.

Perhaps the most important aspect of the Paris Agreement is the set of preliminary remarks before the twenty-nine articles of the agreement. Here, as in many UN documents, a set of moral and political principles are set out, describing the underlying commitments on climate change. Many of these principles are drawn from the 1992 United Nations Framework Convention on Climate Change. It is important to see that the Paris Agreement is the latest iteration in a process that is over two decades old. The most noteworthy of these multiple principles are the principles of equity and common but differentiated responsibilities and respective capabilities.[11] The commitment to common but differentiated responsibilities signals that all nations are responsible for combating climate change, while acknowledging that not all countries bear the same moral and political duties. This is a significant moral and political claim.

Paying attention to how this plays out over time in the implementation of the agreement is huge. Countries vary in their carbon emissions. Countries vary in their ability to make fiscal contributions. Some countries suffer more than others in the face of climate change. Taking full account of these considerations has to be at the heart of the work of the parties to the agreement. Likewise, the agreement is further nested in recognition that countries must respond in the context of sustainable development and the eradication of poverty. This section culminates, "Acknowledging that climate change is a common concern of humankind, Parties should, when taking action to address climate change, respect, promote and consider their respective obligations on human rights, the right to health, the rights of indigenous peoples, local communities, migrants, children, persons with disabilities and people in vulnerable situations and the right to development, as well as gender equality, empowerment of women, and intergenerational equity."[12]

These are the sorts of moral statements that drive antiliberals and right-wing populists nuts, because the moral principles represent an overlapping consensus that does not give priority to any single moral tradition as supreme. But the parties drafting the Paris Agreement can be forgiven for not writing a thousand-page preamble that privileges only Christianity, or any other single moral or religious tradition. Before the current rise in white Christian nationalism, the United Nations enjoyed strong support from many American religious communities, but that is less true today. But a moral framework is explicit in the UN environmental proceedings.

Article 2 of the agreement sets out the concrete policy goals.

1.   Holding the increase in the global average temperature to well below
     2 degrees C above pre-industrial levels and pursuing efforts to limit
     the temperature increase to 1.5 degrees C above pre-industrial levels,
     recognizing that this would significantly reduce the risks and impact of
     climate change;
2.   Increasing the ability to adapt to the adverse impacts of climate change
     and foster climate resilience and low greenhouse gas emissions develop-
     ment, in a manner that does not threaten food production; and
3.   Making finance flows consistent with a pathway towards low greenhouse
     gas emissions and climate-resilient development.

Article 2 concludes by saying the agreement will be implemented to reflect
equity and the principle of common but differentiated responsibilities and
respective capabilities, in light of different national circumstances.[13]

Each party is to announce its targets for reducing greenhouse gas emissions reflecting its highest ambitions in order to achieve the global goals
listed in article 2. Rich countries will assume a greater burden, and mechanisms will be established to finance the mitigation and adaptation efforts of
developing countries to reflect the commitment to common but differentiated responsibilities.

Several things are worth noting. First, the system is completely voluntary
and lacks any global enforcement apparatus to monitor and force compliance.
Likewise, the financial mechanisms are voluntary. And it is far from clear
that our current anarchic nation-state system is capable of sufficient action
within this voluntary framework to meet the temperature goals envisioned
by the agreement. In my view, the key will be whether or not the financial
resources necessary to fund adequate adaptation and mitigation efforts will
be sufficient. Or, put another way, the massive costs attached to this global
plan are not specified well, and the sources of this unspecified amount are
not laid out with any specificity. I think a logical, responsible, and necessary
next step is to answer the fiscal questions, if the agreement has a chance of
achieving its high aspirations. There is an emerging climate-change financing
system that bears scrutiny, as does the role of religious communities in that
system. Far too often religious communities believe their role is simply to

advocate for political action without including themselves in the politics and financing of the political remedies.[14] In the long run, the size and effectiveness of the financing of mitigation and adaptation efforts will be the key to saving the planet from the most catastrophic consequences of climate change. The combination of public and private financing will determine our fate.

The state of that emerging financial system is mixed at best. The UN environmental program estimates that developing countries will need $300 billion a year by 2030 to deal with climate change.[15] The early years of such funding are falling short of that goal. In 2009 wealthy countries pledged that, by 2020, they would contribute $100 billion per year in financing through multiple sources including government, multilateral institutions, and private sources to assist poorer countries in mitigating the consequences of climate change. Estimates by the Organization of Economic Cooperation and Development show that financing was still short by $20 billion in 2018.[16] To add further alarm, most of that funding has come in the form of loans rather than grants. Alice Hill and Madeline Babin note that in 2018 loans constituted nearly three-quarters of the $78.9 billion of overall climate funding developed countries pledged in 2009. To make matters worse, in 2018, more than sixty countries could access loan capital only at interest rates higher than 18 percent for projects longer than two years. This is clearly not a path to successful climate-change mitigation and adaptation.

They go on to note that between 2010 and 2015, the United States mobilized $15.6 billion in climate finance. President Obama pledged $3 billion to the UN Green Climate Fund (GCF). Due to President Trump's removal of the United States from the Paris Agreement, the United States has paid only $1 billion to the GCF. President Biden has announced that the United States is rejoining the Paris Agreement; he also announced the allocation of $1.2 billion for the GCF in fiscal year 2022 and pledged to raise its overall financing of development banks to $5.7 billion annually by 2024. This figure was widely criticized for being too low.[17]

Media accounts of the effectiveness of the GCF in the early years are also not encouraging. After a very slow start in receiving funding of early country pledges and a very slow dispersal rate of those funds, the GCF seems to be reforming. In 2019 the GCF improved its leadership staffing and replenished its funding, thanks in no small part to countries such as Germany and Norway, and a little later the United Kingdom, France, and Canada. In mid-2022, the GCF will start its next replenishment process, and its future viability will be questioned.[18]

After the successful negotiation concluded on the Paris Agreement, S/RGA continued its engagement with religious communities, particularly on the topic of climate-change finance. Large religious-affiliated development organizations such as Catholic Relief Services, World Vision, and Christian Aid achieved observer status with the Green Climate Fund. At a minimum, this meant some very experienced global religious actors were well connected to the emerging global financial system and stood to be in line for sizable grants to do actual mitigation and adaptation work in the developing world. They could also exert indirect if not direct influence on the culture of the large financial institutions that would be funding global work where it was most needed. We made a modest contribution to helping religious communities know about this arena. There is still a lot of room for religious community input into this emerging system.

But just as important are the questions religious communities should be asking about their own institutions and policies. Depending on who you ask, there are somewhere between 300,000 and 400,000 houses of worship in the United States alone. With very few exceptions, these buildings are ecological disasters. Likewise, there are over seven thousand religiously affiliated colleges and universities with physical plants that are similarly fraught with very large carbon footprints. When you begin to add the number of hospitals, orphanages, and other social-service providers, to say nothing of the fossil-fuel-consuming vehicles owned, religious communities, many of which have strong advocacy stands, are terrible greenhouse gas emitters. Add to this the billions of dollars invested in clergy and employee pension funds that hold fossil-fuel equities, very little of which seems governed by green investment strategies or is actively invested in green projects, and a picture emerges in which actual environmental practice does not match the environmental advocacy of many of these religious traditions. I should be quick to add that none of us in the planetary North have clean hands when it comes to environmental lifestyles. But if religious actors had stronger records cleaning up their own houses, they might have a more impressive record of influencing popular behavior and political sentiment.

Where do we stand at the moment of this writing on the Paris Agreement goal of limiting planetary warning to not more than 1.5 degrees (C)? According to the Intergovernmental Panel on Climate Change (IPPC), the planet warmed .087 degrees C between 2006 and 2015. The special report issued by the IPCC went on to say, "If the current warming rate continues, the world would reach human-induced global warming of 1.5 degrees around 2040."[19] The upshot, if this data projection holds, is that the planet has less than two decades to act sufficiently to avoid the consequences attached to a temperature rise of about 1.5 degrees above the preindustrial rate. The special report also contains a wealth of background information on rising global temperatures. We have very little time to make the changes necessary to avoid the worst consequences. This alarming realization further illustrates the magnitude of the moral depravity of President Trump's move to have the United States leave the Paris Agreement. We went from being part of the solution to being the leader of making things worse.[20]

In closing this chapter I want to do two things. First, I will describe what the Biden administration has proposed to do to address climate change. And second, I will sketch what a renewed Office of Religion and Global Affairs might contribute to a renewed US government effort to combat climate change. Given the dire warning of the increasing warming of the planet, the early work by the Biden administration is heartening and a glimmer of hope that the United States is rejoining the global effort against climate change after the four years of neglect and reversal by President Trump. These lost years will haunt us for years to come because of the ground we have lost. Whatever the coming climate disasters entail, historians will always point to the malfeasance of Trump and his enablers and wonder how it could have all been different. If the current emerging agenda had been started in 2017, we would have had much better odds at mitigating the coming climate madness that much sooner.

What did Biden propose and do in the first half of his first year as president? As of this writing in the early days of his administration, the Biden record is impressive on climate change and stands in radical contrast to the destruction of the Trump administration. I fully acknowledge that it is far too early to tell what the full policy story is going to be on climate change, but it is hard to imagine a better start. On the first day of his presidency, Biden had the United States rejoin the Paris Agreement, setting the stage for America to reclaim its role as one of the leading countries in the fight against climate change. Earlier, on December 18, 2020, Biden announced former director of the Environmental Protection Agency, Gina McCarthy, as the national climate adviser and head of the White House Office of Domestic Climate Policy and named former Secretary of State John Kerry as presidential special envoy for climate. They are two climate veterans with deep governmental experience who know how to get things done.[21]

McCarthy convened the National Climate Task Force several times in the early days of the administration. This is the policy forum where cabinet secretaries dealing with climate change routinely meet to design and implement climate policy. Examples of their work can be monitored in the Statements and Releases tab at whitehouse.gov.[22] For the first time, we have a whole-of-government approach to domestic climate issues.

On the international side of climate change, Biden convened forty world leaders to a Summit on Climate on April 22 and 23, 2021. After joining the Paris Agreement on January 20, 2021, and announcing his intention of reaching net-zero emissions economy-wide by no later than 2050, the president announced the new target for the United States to achieve a 50–52 percent reduction from 2005 levels in economy-wide net greenhouse gas pollution in 2030—which is the nationally determined emissions target for the United States as part of our commitment to the United Nations Framework Convention on Climate Change. These levels were the product of his National Climate Task Force. The United States is formally back in the global fight against climate change, and while Biden promised the task force will issue a national climate strategy later in 2021, by early 2022 the White House does not seem to have issued that strategy.[23]

The last piece of relevant news is on the climate-finance front. Biden issued the Executive Order on Tackling the Climate Crisis at Home and Abroad (EO 14008) on January 27, 2021, calling for the preparation of a Climate Finance Plan. The plan was published on April 27, 2021, as part of the Leaders Summit outcomes. A quick assessment of the top-line parts of this finance plan illuminates the pivot away from the failures of the Trump policy that the Biden administration envisions. The first and most important commitment is confronting the sharp drop in US international climate finances in the Trump era and in turn reestablishing US leadership in international climate diplomacy. The remedy proposed is to double, by 2024, the US annual public climate finance relative to the average level during the second half of the Obama-Biden administration. Part of that will include tripling the public funding of adaptation finance by 2024. The administration promises to have USAID release its new climate change strategy in November 2021 at the twenty-sixth Conference of the Parties (COP 26).

The plan also sets a goal to use public financing to leverage and mobilize more private finance through entities such as the Millennium Challenge Corporation and the Import-Export Bank of the United States. Scaling back public investment in carbon-intensive fossil-fuel-based energy and instead supporting the flow of capital toward investment opportunities that are consistent with low greenhouse gas emissions and climate-resilient pathways will be central parts of the new financial climate plan. Taken together, these policies represent a profound shift in US policy. As I mentioned earlier, I believe developing a sound financing apparatus is a key part of a successful global plan to address the goals of the Paris Agreement. These early financing plans of the Biden administration are encouraging.[24]

Taken together, the Biden policy aspirations in meeting climate change are impressive. But all political aspirations eventually have to meet domestic and international political realities, and that collision is only now beginning as I write. At this moment, the northwest United States is experiencing historic high temperatures. It is a powerful reminder that we are experiencing the horrible consequences of our own environmental malfeasance. And these consequences will not be delayed as we debate mitigation efforts. It is hard to push back on the nightmares of what an impeding environmental apocalypse looks like. Whatever effective responses we might have as a species, there is no avoiding the hard conclusion that the messy world of human politics will be a large part of the answer. This leads to the inescapable conclusion that if we are to stave off those apocalyptic scenarios, the time for action is upon us. That compels me to spend a moment describing what a renewed engagement effort by a rebuilt Office of Religion and Global Affairs might look like.

The first move would be to rebuild and expand the network of connections that the original public diplomacy team built among religious organizations, scholars, and activists. The number of such interested parties was large and has continued to grow since 2017. The collective work these entities do in educating, financing, and other forms of climate engagement is impossible to track and quantify because there are so many of them. But Todd Stern's observation still applies. If we are to successfully implement sufficient policies to respond effectively to climate change, religious actors are some of the key players.

It is important to remember that the necessary engagement has to go beyond hoping these communities will advocate for specific legislative initiatives. While helping to pass the Biden climate legislation is fundamental to any successful engagement on climate change, there are more ways religious communities can engage. As mentioned above, the financial investments of many religious traditions are immense. How do they act as financial actors? Do they remove their fossil fuels investments from their pension funds? Do they invite their adherents to act accordingly? What do they tell the boards of the corporations in which they invest their money? Do their colleges and universities adopt similar policies with their endowments? Do they model and commend reducing the carbon footprints of their adherents?

Similarly, do the large religiously affiliated development agencies seek out implementation partners in order to bring them into the emerging climate finance networks? A restarted S/RGA can point the giant-sized, medium-sized, and small religiously affiliated development agencies toward resources that will provide technical assistance to climate mitigation and adaptation efforts so that they can build out the path for more groups to expand the work against climate change. It is one thing to raise adequate funds for the work; it is another task to make sure that funding lands in the hands of organizations capable of doing the work in the countries that suffer the most from climate change itself. A new task that emerged in the Trump era is countering right-wing populist disinformation. Climate-change disinformation is one of the largest dark industries in the ultra-right in the United States, and the State Department public diplomacy efforts need to catch up. Climate disinformation is extremely well funded, and it is often linked to religious communities.[25] Climate-change denial seems increasingly to be part of the right-wing evangelical theological creed. I am not suggesting that the State Department needs to try and match these forces tweet for tweet. I do believe that the department can be a source for accurate information on US climate policy and state-of-the-art science information. The day has long passed when scientists can simply publish their research in scientific journals and be confident that their results will find their way into the mainstream public's awareness. More scientists will have to learn to communicate more effectively. Increasing the number of science fellows at the State Department has to take place if climate disinformation is to be engaged. That is why the two Jefferson Science Fellows we had were so crucial to our success. The public understanding of both religion and science is crucial to American diplomacy. Unfortunately, disinformation campaigns will remain a powerful political tool for the foreseeable future, and religious communities will be targets and carriers of this disinformation. The mountains of dark money flowing into these efforts, the networks that grow as a result of this cash flow, are now threatening the planet.

And finally, an office at State can help combat climate change by gaining a deeper understanding of the knowledge different religious communities produce that leads to action among their members. This is not done to manipulate religious groups into doing things they don't want to do. Rather, it is done to empower the State Department to understand how religious communities form and communicate their views of climate policy in order to increase the depth of mutual understanding in the democratic process of forming policy.

It was always interesting when we got occasional external criticism of our work in S/RGA that we were instrumentalizing religious communities when we spoke to them. The staff would occasionally quip that when religious groups came, it was the "instrumentalization of Shaun," in that religious groups were always critiquing our policy, requesting funding, or jockeying for influence within the Obama administration. They were not weak and passive victims who came volunteering to be manipulated by our office or the Obama administration, unlike the view of some critics who infantalized religious groups as weak victims of the US government who appeared at our door zombie-like waiting for abuse at our hands.

The lack of diplomatic literacy among these critics is palpable. Diplomacy is about talking in order to solve global problems. It is about trying to persuade people to embrace specific policies. It is not inherently problematic, nor is it inherently noble and good. But climate change threatens human existence and will require something of all humanity. In our work, I never asked any religious person, community, or network to do something I knew they would not or could not do because it violated their theological beliefs. And if they told me they could not do something I requested, I accepted that answer and moved on. Not all encounters were transactional. Many conversations allowed us to help American diplomacy be more informed, intelligent, and effective because we learned what life was like on the ground in countless spots around the world simply because we took the time to ask myriad religious actors what was going on in their worlds and how we might be able to do less harm and sometimes even act for the common good as they understood it. Diplomacy is at minimum a two-way conversation. The best diplomats know how to ask the right questions and pass along the answers. The fight against climate change requires nothing less than building the best mutual understandings in order to work more effectively against the global threat.

Chapter Six

THROUGH THE GOLDEN DOOR

I FOUND MYSELF IN A SMALL, hot, overcrowded room with twenty refugees from seven different countries who were waiting to meet me. I immediately read the atmosphere in the room and saw it was tense and heavy with a sort of pall hovering over everyone. The faces signaled the culture shock of having been in the United States only for a few months, the plight of leaving home under horrible, brutal conditions, and the tough landing site that was Jersey City, New Jersey, in winter. To add to their stress, staff at the refugee center run by Church World Service had asked them to meet with an unknown federal bureaucrat from Washington in a dark suit, with two of his colleagues to help him get a deeper understanding of their stories. Add the simultaneous translation of our conversation into many languages, and it all made for a very strange vibe in the room.[1]

Over the years I like to think I have developed a pretty decent ability to connect with people around the world through a combination of techniques in which I try to signal respect, humility, and genuine interest by asking lots of questions. Or so I thought. In many ways diplomacy is founded on the ability to ask the right questions and listen well. This might have been the hardest room I have ever worked. I began by talking a little bit about what our office did and why we were there. All I got back were stares of incomprehension. I was there to learn from them about their struggles, their successes, and their hopes. I wanted to know what worked in our refugee-resettlement process and what didn't. As I flailed around at the outset of our meeting, evoking stares of exhaustion and frowns, I struck a chord when I finally asked them what the hardest part of coming to America was. Their initial reticence evaporated, and the floodgates opened as I got an earful or travail. It was a very tough hour. Any illusions I might have had about how the actual refugee-resettlement process worked died that hour. This was not the stuff of future romance and family lore. These were tales of danger, pain, and disillusionment.

One young man described his work as an office painter that required him to take public transit all across the New York City metropolitan area. He was making $9 an hour, and his transit bill was over $300 dollars a month. He ran out of money before the month ended. There were nods across the room. The US refugee system stresses quick employment, and most of the refugee-resettlement centers I visited over the next twelve months were quite proud of their employment rates above 80 percent, but most of the jobs refugees find are low-wage jobs. Making it economically in New York is very hard on a miserly stipend and low-wage jobs.

An Iraqi couple—one spouse a lawyer and the other an engineer—was cleaning offices overnight and could not find work in their respective professional fields. Several refugees noted how the quality of their English-as-a-second-language classes was uneven and many of the teachers did not know the native languages of the class members. Housing costs were prohibitive, given the low-wage jobs they all had. And finally, one Syrian man spoke about his fear simply walking the streets of Jersey City. He had been routinely accosted verbally by random people on the street who suspected he was Syrian and therefore a terrorist. He feared for himself, his wife, and his ebullient two-year-old daughter, who seemed to be the only happy one in the entire room. I had no easy answers to their realistic but tough portraits of their lives as new refugees here.

While I am keenly, deeply proud of what the United States did in the Obama years in resettling hundreds of thousands of refugees and how the government has partnered with an amazing array of religious communities to do this work in a fair, nondiscriminatory fashion, make no mistake, it is hard to be a refugee here. Hard because to be recognized as a refugee by the United Nations, one has to prove that one was persecuted for a specific reason such as one's gender, religious affiliation, or membership in a specific political entity. Hard because one has to have crossed an international border fleeing persecution. Hard because, after arriving, it could take two years to be fully vetted for security purposes by the FBI and the Department of

Homeland Security. Hard because many of these refugees have fled some of the worst forms of persecution in modern times. And hard because many of them have lived for years, even decades, in cramped, dangerous, and poorly resourced refugee camps. But what I saw were forms of tenacity and resilience unlike anything I have ever seen in my life.

At some point in our hour I realized there were no simple, easy answers to the plight of these twenty people. I felt completely overwhelmed by their stories. The room was hot, my voice was failing, and the ennui in the room had colonized my brain. But as we were winding down, the wife of the Syrian man, and mother to the resplendent two-year-old girl, sensing my mood, had compassion on me and offered me words of comfort, saying, "Mr. Casey, despite how hard things are for us now, we all know we will be in a better place a year from now." And the room lit up. Everyone there seemed to affirm this statement of profound hope.

She was comforting me! I felt both ashamed of myself and convicted by her faith. The net result for me was that I resolved to always meet with refugees themselves on my subsequent resettlement center visits, and not just resettlement employees. In the next twelve months I met with over 120 refugees. This meant that whenever I spoke about the refugee experience in America, I could do more than simply recite cold US government statistics; I could tell stories that refugees had told me. So, when I would confront antirefugee zealots, which still happens to this day, I could counter their theoretical portraits about who and what refugees were with the testimony from actual refugees. Very rarely had any of the critics I met actually spoken to a refugee.

Many accounts of the global refugee crisis begin with descriptions of the unprecedented size of the global population on the move. Between formal refugees, internally displaced people, and so-called economic and climate-change refugees, the numbers are at record, almost unbelievable, levels. But in my experience, numerical approaches to this complex issue allow people to avert their eyes and move on quickly. Several websites run these rapidly growing numbers. I believe it is better to start with the human faces of those on the move, themselves. It is much harder for me to look the other way when I am in a room with people who are still in their first months in the country, after what can be a decades-long process to escape their old circumstances and build new lives elsewhere. The short verdict is that more people are on the move today than ever before, for an increasingly diverse set of causes, and the planet needs a better system filled with more resources to give these folks what they need and deserve in order to flourish as human beings. According to the United Nations, there are 82.4 million forcibly displaced people world-wide, including 48 million who are internally displaced in their own countries, 4.1 million who are asylum seekers, and 26.4 million who are refugees.[2]

This encounter in Jersey City was not my first foray into global-refugee politics, but it was my first deep dive into the lives of refugees who had been resettled in America. My baptism into refugee policy and politics took place many years before in 2002, in a conference room in Baltimore. The 1951 UN Convention on Refugees and the 1967 Protocol relating to the Status of Refugees built the legal and political scaffolding that has provided structure and justification for the global refugee system. In many ways, this document and its revision represent the pinnacle accomplishment of the UN system and aspirations. Its design, approval, and implementation demonstrated the world's ability to respond in short order to the great displacement of people in the aftermath of World War II.[3]

The convention sets out to address those people who have a well-founded fear of persecution for reasons of race, religion, nationality, or membership of a particular social group or political opinion, and are outside the country of their nationality and are unable or, owing to such fear, unwilling to avail themselves of the protection of that country; it also addresses those who, not having a nationality and being outside the country of their habitual residence as a result of persecution, are unable, or unwilling, to return to it. By 2002, the United Nations had not issued guidance on how to evaluate such claims for refugee status based on religion. To provide such guidance, the United Nations High Commissioner for Refugees (UNHCR) partnered with Church World Service, one of the larger religiously affiliated US-based refugee re-settlement services, to convene a group of religion scholars to discuss such standards, along with a number of US asylum legal employees. Somehow I was invited to the soiree in November 2003. Keep in mind that this meeting occurred when the US invasion of Iraq was still unfolding and the unantici-pated insurgency was beginning to haunt the Bush administration.

I don't remember a lot about the conference. But I do remember becom-ing enraged when an asylum judge gave a very condescending lecture on how he swiftly disposed of fraudulent applicants for asylum cases by asking just a few quick, factual questions on religion, based on his own Christian denominational catechetical and biblical knowledge. As I recall, my response was swift and not very temperate. (As a rule, I am not one to jump on top of tables in a rant, and I don't throw things in the air either.) A complicated and lively exchange was the result. Without going too deeply into the brawl, the outcome was actually not bad. The UNHCR issued a handbook of advice for legal staff who were charged with making these real-life decisions.[4] It was my first glimpse into the rickety system of evaluating claims by US government legal entities. I have since learned that of the handful of qualifying forms of persecution a potential refugee can invoke, the religious persecution criterion seems to be the least favorable path to choose. This was my first general lesson in my eventual realization that the intricacies and weaknesses of the global refugee system are legion. But even more pointedly, I learned religion was interwoven into the whole refugee process, from its possible legal warrant for creating a class of refugees to who administers the actual resettlement of refugees once they are moved to a new country, particularly the United States.

As I mentioned earlier, refugee resettlement was paid for and managed by the State Department. State funded nine implementing partners, six of them religiously affiliated agencies, to do the resettlement work. Given this religion angle, when the rise of ISIL and the subsequent global refugee crisis hit, I decided to travel around the country visiting six different refugee resettlement centers in 2016. With the souring politics of refugee resettlement nation-wide, I wanted to visit centers located in states where governors had said harsh things about refugees. I visited centers in Jersey City, Baltimore, Dallas, Phoenix, Des Moines, and Chicago, to see for myself what refugee resettlement looked like on the ground.

My first stop, mentioned above, was in Jersey City in January 2016, to visit a new center for refugee resettlement run by Church World Service (CWS), a global nonprofit supported by a number of Christian denominations, including the classic mainline Protestant denominations. Just before my visit, New Jersey governor Chris Christie had criticized President Obama for raising the ceiling on refugee admissions for fiscal year 2017 to 85,000, up from the previous year's goal of 70,000. The president also called for 10,000 Syrians to be part of this 85,000 refugee target, citing the particularly large number of Syrians entering the global refugee system who were fleeing the scourge of ISIS.

In retrospect, I am not sure what I was expecting to see at these centers. Whatever illusions I might have had about the plight of refugees who were fleeing persecution around the world, Jersey City was a reality check that would be confirmed by my subsequent visits. The CWS center was new and located in the recently revitalized Journal Square area around the historic old New Jersey Journal building. Just a stone's throw from Manhattan, this part of New Jersey manifested all the clashes and jars of contemporary urban life: decaying old buildings, new office construction, refurbished old buildings, a polyglot population, a thriving junior college serving a multiethnic student population, and a bustling street life.

When I arrived, along with two of my senior staffers, Liora Danan and Rachel Leslie, we met Mahmoud Mahmoud, a veteran of global refugee resettlement work who had processed refugees in North Africa and was now running this local resettlement center. Before my conversation with the refugees, we met in Mahmoud's office with an imam, a rabbi, and a Christian pastor! They were hardly the setup for a bad joke. Their three communities had come together to address the plight of refugees in New Jersey out of their most deeply held theological beliefs. In other words, they had found common cause with each other over the need to help resettle refugees, not out of some abstract notion of "interfaith dialogue." They each believed their particular theological beliefs and histories compelled them to serve the most vulnerable people they knew, and those people turned out to be refugees. I was fascinated and mesmerized as the leaders answered my question about why they were pushing back against the prevailing xenophobia and collaborating in ways their respective communities, Muslim, Christian, and Jewish, had not in the past. At the end of my yearlong visitations at these sorts of centers around the country, I realized that local religious communities were partnering in creative and new ways in response to the global refugee crisis. This was not interreligious work as theater. This was interreligious work as praxis. Only time will tell if this new form of work will grow and what its impact may be on the long arc of interreligious work. But it was fascinating to see it begin to unfold around the country. It is also worth noting that when President Trump drastically cut the number of refugees entering the United States at the outset of his presidency, he was directly attacking thousands of American faith communities on one of their central theological missions.[5]

Over the course of 2016 I visited five more refugee resettlement centers, and in those visits I was transformed. Rachel Leslie, the director of our public diplomacy team, scheduled the visits, making the arrangements and traveling with me. My guidance was twofold: let's visit states with governors who were saying stupid things about Muslim refugees, particularly Syrians, and let's see what the religiously affiliated organizations are doing. The trips were designed to help me tell the State Department's story better, to learn how the public/private partnership worked, and to get a sense of what people in the field thought could be improved. My operating hypothesis was that the state-level political hate rhetoric made the work of the resettlement centers harder to do. At the end of the tour I had to modify my hypothesis.

In December 2015 the Bureau of Population, Refugees, and Migration (PRM) held its Eleventh Annual Refugee Admissions Workshop in Washington. This was a gathering where State Department personnel met with all sorts of people from the nine implementing partner organizations who received federal funding for refugee resettlement to address a wide range of issues, including sharing best practices. Deputy Assistant Secretary Anne Richard kindly invited me to attend and set up a time for staff from the religiously affiliated resettlement partners to join me in a pull-aside meet-and-greet session. At the end of a main session, they announced that I would be meeting with any interested partners in the break time before the next main session. I was swamped before I could leave my seat and head to the designated room. Representatives of all the religiously affiliated partners surrounded me, and forty-five minutes later I had still made no progress to the announced room. By the end of our impromptu scrum, I had invitations to visit centers all across the country.

PRM under Ann's leadership had a sterling reputation among our partners. The Obama administration expanded the volume of refugees entering the United States dramatically, and it was Ann's team that managed that dramatic increase with grace, professionalism, and passion. The faith-based partners were all pleased to see that our office took an interest in the work, knowing that we had Kerry's ear and that I was available to help magnify any news that came from their activities. They were eager to have me visit their sites to see the amazing work going on. In short order Rachel put together a series of visits to diverse centers across the country. I was about to get a hands-on education on just what policy looked like when it was implemented on the ground.

One of our first visits was to a center run by Catholic Charities in Dallas. Having misspent four years of my youth in Texas trying to get an education,

I was not particularly excited about the Dallas visit. I suspected there were strong antirefugee sentiments in all directions in the Metroplex based on my time in Texas thirty-five years earlier. I was prepared for a lot of hard stories. But I soon learned that my prejudices about prejudice needed some revision. I followed the model set by our Jersey City visit: first I met with the center director, then with a group of around twenty refugees, and then with a cross section of staff. In every case I had lots of questions, and in time my questions got better and more focused. So much of diplomacy is learning the right questions to ask and then reflecting on what you hear so that the next time you can ask even better questions. I asked the director if the bigotry of the current governor toward refugees made his work harder. As I recall, he smiled and said, "Not really." This was not the answer I anticipated! I asked him what he meant by that. He elaborated that when politicians made outrageous statements, his phone began to ring from a wide variety of religious communities, Christian, Jewish, and Muslim, all saying, "We want to help the people you serve who are in desperate need. Our theology calls us to help those who are oppressed the most, and out governor does not speak for our faith."

He was quick to add that he did not like the toxic public ethos established by ignorant politicians, but he saw a significant grassroots repudiation of the hate. He knew that the people he served felt the uneasy cultural schizophrenia of central Texas, but they also saw the compassionate antidote to the clown class, too. He was wary of the politicians but thankful for the response of the faithful. He and his staff took great joy and satisfaction in seeing the refugees take their first steps into American culture despite the winds that were blowing against them. It was a much more nuanced reality than my college days, ancient as they were, had led me to anticipate. I began to see the need to modify my view.

I remember two highlights from my conversation with the refugees I met that day. The first came from a conversation with a man who had spent over a decade at a refugee camp in Eritrea. When I asked my stock question about what the group had found to be the hardest parts of living in America, one man replied, rejecting my thesis out of hand, "Dallas is the greatest city in the world!" That did not comport with my memories of Dallas, but I tried not to betray my dissent as I asked him what he meant by that. He said that for the first time in fifteen years he was able to work with his hands, and as a result he could support his family. He took multiple buses to get to work and back, but his job as a mechanic had literally transformed his life and future. Compared to the constraints of camp life, existence in Dallas was liberating in just about every imaginable way for him. His sense of dignity and agency had been restored. His kids were in school, his wife and he had both found employment, and that mitigated the complexities of adapting to Texas culture.

His story sparked another question that soon entered my stock of questions at future center visits: "How are the schools your kids are attending?" Again, I was pleasantly surprised when he said his kids loved their classes and heads started nodding across the room. One woman said that the positive reception her children were getting at school was the key ingredient to their transition to America. The schools were used to welcoming students from a multiplicity of countries in recent years, and that experience was paying dividends for the children of these refugees. I asked them to tell me more about that. They mentioned an array of services for the students, ranging from age-appropriate English tutoring, to administrators being directly responsible for supporting refugee children and their varying academic needs, to resources for parents to understand the unique characteristics of American public education norms and processes. Happy refugee children in school went a long way in helping new refugee families adjust to American life.

I was pleased to hear this anecdotal evidence. But as a former academic colleague of mine once told me, "The plural of anecdote is not data." I want to be careful not to overgeneralize here, but I was impressed that many mid-sized and large public school districts are doing a lot to address the unique pedagogical challenges refugee children face in American classrooms. I know from experience that teaching is hard work. But in addition to hard work, teaching in a classroom filled with many students from many cultures and languages of origin requires special skills and training. It struck me that a high level of academic prowess and preparedness on the part of public school teachers has to be one of the crucial factors for success in resettling refugees.

Two of the remaining sites I visited merit deeper comment. The first was the center run by Lutheran Immigration and Refugee Services in Phoenix, and the second was a center in Des Moines. In Phoenix, I saw a mature social service agency that had refugee resettlement down to a science, but with plenty of openness for innovation. This was a common trait across the centers we saw. Almost all of them had feedback loops that routinely evaluated what they were doing and how they might improve services. Rachel and I were invited to sit in on an Iraqi family's orientation to the public schools that described to the parents and their elementary-school-aged daughter what to expect in the Phoenix public school system. As we were waiting in a child-friendly free-play area, Rachel struck up a conversation with the daughter as she was drawing with crayons and quietly talking to her parents. The parents looked tired, but the daughter radiated a calm, wide-eyed engagement with her environment. The daughter and Rachel conversed easily in Arabic, much to the parents' surprise and delight!

Once the staffer had moved us all into a comfortable room, she outlined all the services and routines the family should expect in their daughter's new school. The daughter was bursting with joy and anticipation at the thought of being in a real classroom with children her age. It was my distinct impression that their lives had been badly disrupted in Iraq for quite some time and that she longed to learn in a normal and routine school environment. Her enthusiasm was contagious and impressive. It was clear that the center and the school system had thought long and hard about how to welcome refugee children into the classroom and to prepare them for success. Again, my natural fear that we were in for a session filled with fear and mutual misunderstanding was misbegotten. I was beginning to see that despite the incalculable complexities of introducing refugee families into the complexity of American society, there were people and organizations that knew how to do this far better than I would have guessed.

As we toured the rest of the center, I was impressed by how many of the staff had been refugees themselves. Of course, this makes sense at so many levels: it met the huge linguistic demands of the diverse refugee population they were serving; it provided a multicultural capacity that is fundamental to introducing refugees to American life and institutions; and it sent a powerful signal to newly arriving people that they were not alone on their hard journeys. The director echoed the sentiments of the Dallas center director, saying that when local politicians said crude things about refugees, their phones started ringing from an array of religious communities asking how they could help. These centers matched the paltry federal stipends many times over, and they provided necessary services to their people long after the federal money ran out. It became clear to me that becoming an American citizen was a long and hard process, and without the nonprofit partners, the process would be far more chaotic and heartbreaking than it already is.

The other piece I began to see in Phoenix that proved to be common to all the centers was their deep engagement with diaspora groups. It makes sense that one aspect of historic American life, the formation of civic associations based on countries of origin, would continue in an era of increased immigration, but perhaps with different ends than in the American past. What I saw in Phoenix were multiple associations who saw helping new refugees from their home countries become acquainted with American life as part to their mission. The center had a large network with dozens of diaspora groups who served as mediators of the new country for the new Americans who were arriving. These mediating institutions had resources that the US government did not have and that the resettlement centers may have possessed only in limited quantities.

Des Moines continued my education. Our visit there centered on learning how an urban school district had creatively addressed the complexities of handling a dizzying array of refugees from all over the world. By the end of our conversation, Des Moines Public Schools Superintendent Thomas Ahart struck me as a force of nature. But at the outset when he warmly greeted us, he had a look I recognized. It said, "Somehow a State Department bureaucrat from DC got on my daily schedule, and I have no freaking idea how that happened. And please don't waste my time." When I explained to him who I was and that I was visiting cities that managed large numbers of refugees, particularly those doing innovative work, he instantly got why I wanted to see him. He knew the State Department funded the first few months of a refugee's life in the United States, and he also knew the vital role religiously affiliated refugee-resettlement agencies played in that process.

I asked him what they did in Des Moines Public Schools (DMPS) to serve the needs of their refugee students, and we were off to the races. He was clearly proud of what they were doing, and his passion for their innovative work soaked every sentence. English-language learners (ELL) constituted around 20 percent of the school district's thirty-two thousand students. Over one hundred languages are spoken in households that make up the student population of DMPS! That fact alone, to say nothing of the cultural, religious, and social issues attached to that linguistic diversity, has to be mind-bending to teachers and administrators. Since 1990, the number of English-language learners had grown by 700 percent, while the overall number of students in the district had remained stable.

Ahart told me that he was not satisfied with the state of Iowa's metrics for judging success and failure of student learning. He told us the story of a young Burmese woman with no formal education who showed up at one of their high schools on opening day of classes in the fall. Based on their battery of assessments, her educational attainment was several years below her age cohort. By the end of that academic year, the woman had progressed four years but remained a year or two below her age cohort. While her teachers, school administrators, and ELL staff were celebrating a miraculous performance by this woman, by the learning standards of the state of Iowa she was a failure, as were her teachers and her school! The teachers and school saw four years of growth in one year as nothing remotely close to failure. Ahart declared this unacceptable and was driven to help the state legislature develop more sophisticated metrics to parse the complexities of educating new students from beyond the United States.

Superintendent Ahart introduced us to Vinh Nguyen, the ELL assessment and accountability specialist for the district, who came himself as a Laotian refugee to Des Moines in the 1970s. Nguyen explained to us how they tried to meet the challenges of their evolving student body's learning needs. It was clear to me after an hour of conversation that the senior leadership of the school district felt not only a legal responsibility to do their best by every one of the thirty-two thousand students in their charge, they also felt a moral and civic duty to prove that public education was up to the task of educating all their students to the best of their abilities. They would not be deterred by complexity, criticism, or lack of interest on the part of some in society. Slowly I began to see that serving the needs of refugees and children of refugees, while hard, was possible given a whole-of-society approach. With the rise of populism in our country, sustaining the necessary collaboration was becoming much harder, but Superintendent Ahart was living proof that it could be done.

Other visits in Des Moines only helped me see this revelation more clearly. We sat down with Carly Ross, director of a resettlement center run by the US Committee for Refugees and Immigrants, another one of the formal partners of the State Department for resettling refugees. Carly walked us through the various programs they run to help refugees find employment, navigate American culture, and gain access to a variety of social services. As I saw in other centers, there was a strong sense of civil, moral, and social duty attached to this work. All the centers I ended up visiting had a vibe that spoke of deep knowledge, compassion for those who were on a very difficult journey, and a deep sense that this work could be done for the benefit both of the refugees and of the country as a whole.

The police department had liaisons to various Asian and Hispanic communities and immigrant groups. Our conversation with one officer at a community center was utterly fascinating, as he described his complex role as a community liaison. He was well known on the street and had earned the respect of community leaders as well as his police and city government peers. Meeting with Mayor Frank Cownie and members of his senior staff reinforced to us that the increasing ethnic and religious diversity of the refugees required a whole-of-government approach. And city governments were on the forefront of that effort. I got the distinct impression that the mayor and his team were proud of what they were doing but not heady or complacent. There is no manual that city leaders can pull off the shelf to tell them how to welcome these new Americans, and I got the distinct impression federal government leaders were not everyday visitors either. As I would learn later, mayors and county leaders are the ones on the cutting edge of innovation when it comes to welcoming refugees, and they tend to learn more from each other than from state and federal employees. From my limited vantage point, it is hard to render a national judgment on where the most innovation is coming from, but anecdotally, the most impressive work I saw was being done at the local level by local governments in partnership with private, often religiously affiliated, agencies.

When it came to religious communities, we saw some interesting dynamics at work in Des Moines. Rachel and I had a fascinating lunch discussion with a large group from the Des Moines Area Religious Council. The religious diversity of the area is breathtaking, although on further reflection, such pluralism is becoming more and more the American norm. We talked at length of the collective work of this nonprofit in interfaith engagement, not just interfaith conversation. I think this is a key distinction. An earlier iteration of interfaith dialogue in the United States was more along the lines of getting to know each other. There have been at least two major evolutions in interfaith interaction since the early days in the last centuries. First, there was a very tentative round of discussions on the beliefs of religious groups, which led to calls for mutual toleration. Let me be clear that I am all for religious toleration and conversation! But the last phase, which is where I think Des Moines and many other American cities are heading today, is forms of engagement around pressing political and social issues such as the welcoming of new Americans in the form of the increased number of refugees welcomed in the Obama years. It is likely that a majority of refugees welcomed here post-9/11 were settled by religiously affiliated agencies and by millions of dollars and hours of labor contributed by local houses of worship. New interreligious relationships have been formed in America in the last decade by this public-private partnership centered on refugee work. And the civic good this produces has not been fully documented or understood. But I saw a roomful of people from Des Moines at that lunch who embodied this latest iteration of interreligious collaboration.

The last stop worth mentioning was our visit to Chicago. Our first stop was at the Muslim Women Resource Center. We found a bustling organization that started in 2001 as the only resource center in Illinois specifically for Muslim women. Over the years their work expanded to help immigrants and refugees without regard to gender, religious identity, race, ethnicity, or age. It was an amazing organization. We met with a small group of women from all across the globe. What united them was their respective pilgrimages to Chicago that led them to the center to find resources for themselves and their families. Here was a small center that was in its second decade, having grown significantly to serve a burgeoning population. Their work was people centered, concentrating on skills they found necessary for refugees to succeed in Chicago. This was an organic nonprofit organization that sprang up in the aftermath of 9/11 to deal with the specific needs of Muslim immigrants and refugees. Over time their success led them to expand their client base. These sorts of organizations meet a growing demand for what social scientists in an earlier era called mediating institutions. As such, they help bridge the gap in civil society between individuals or households and government by providing training and connections to public services such as schools and other government entities, all in the name of helping people orient to their new environments. Needless to say, in 2001 Muslim women who were immigrants and refugees were under tremendous stress in the United States.

Our next meeting was with Refugee One, a unique organization in the dazzling array of refugee service providers. Malineh Kano, the director of Refugee One, was our host, and she assembled all the resettlement agency directors in Chicago as well as the Illinois state refugee coordinator to meet with us. Refugee One was the Illinois affiliate of Church World Service, Episcopal Migration Ministries, and Lutheran Immigration and Refugee Services. At that point, Chicago was welcoming roughly 1,700 refugees each year. What we saw in Chicago was a coordinated network of resettlement agencies, mutual assistance associations, and yet again, contributions of volunteer hours and financial support from individual houses of worship. The whole-of-society approach was staring me in the face as we sat down to talk in the Refugee One conference room.

All parties introduced themselves and their organizations. As is often the case, my mind was racing and I had questions for them to test my impressions, observations, and theories. Again, I have come to see diplomacy more and more as the pursuit of asking the right questions and listening hard for the answers. Three things struck me as we talked. First, these organizations were very good at what they did. They knew how to welcome people from all over the world and how to help them navigate the complexities of the inevitable weirdness of American culture. They had a confidence that was born out of experience. Second, they were passionate about work that led to practices of collegiality and not arrogance. I think they all knew that with tens of millions of people on the move around the world, there was little room for competition among agencies. These people seemed comfortable working together toward a common goal. This is not always the case when addressing such large and intractable issues as refugee resettlement. I did not detect the usual preening, competing, and not-so-subtle signs of attempted dominance I often see in Washington-based meetings with multiple partners. I don't mean to be naïve here, but in twenty years in Washington public life, I haven't seen as much ego disarmament as I saw in my travels around the country nosing around organizations helping refugees.

And third, they spoke with one voice in asserting that the entire global system for dealing with refugees was teetering on collapse. While they were busy bailing water out of the boat, so to speak, they warily noticed that the waterline was creeping up to the gunwales of the boat. And I got an earful as the State Department guy. Melinah, herself a refugee, an Armenian from Iran, who was resettled by Refugee One in 1984, had assembled a very impressive lineup of veterans of the refugee business, and cumulatively they made an impressive case that the global system needed rethinking and deeper resourcing. The current global system as well as the American system were not sustainable in their view. They impressed upon me that the need was growing globally and that the United States could take many more refugees, but both systems were on overload. Here there is a double challenge, which is typical for foreign policy issues. On the one hand, there is a set of emergencies to be addressed with the pressure of here and now. On the other hand, the so-called liberal international order, made up of a maze of institutions, often designed in the years after World War II, is decrepit, underfunded, and no longer sufficient for the long-term issues plaguing the world. To use a hackneyed metaphor, we have to rebuild the airplane while we are flying it. We have engineers to design new planes and pilots to fly them. But we don't seem to have many people who can do all the work simultaneously. More about this in a moment.

One last stop in Chicago proved to be something of a capstone for my refugee education. We met with Ivo Daalder, the president of the Chicago Council on World Affairs. He was a veteran diplomat and academic whose work I had admired for a long time, but I had never had the privilege of meeting him. Back in 2010 the council had issued a very important study, "Engaging Religious Communities Abroad: A New Imperative for US Foreign Policy." This meant they were predisposed to be interested in our work. He served as US permanent representative to NATO from 2009 to 2013. He was also on the advisory committee for the Secretary of State's Strategic Dialogue with Civil Society, which had germinated the idea of launching a religion-advisory office. I was particularly interested in learning about an initiative he was launching on global cities. It was becoming clear to me that cities were where the real innovation was going on in the refugee-resettlement space. While a Republican-led Congress was clearly irritated with the Obama administration's progressive increase in the annual target for refugees to be settled here, the gathering storm clouds in Washington signaled that Republicans were increasingly seeing xenophobia as a winning electoral strategy. At this point no one saw Donald Trump as a serious presidential candidate, nor did anyone see the dramatic rise in antirefugee sentiment as a successful electoral strategy along with the rise in populism.

Daalder struck me as something of a prophetic voice, and I wanted to pick his brain. He made a very compelling case that cities, and in particular mayors, are now in the foreign policy business. If downtown Hampton, Virginia, is flooding on an annual basis due to sea level rise, the mayor cannot say, "Don't blame me, we're waiting on Congress to act." A mayor has to develop a plan to mitigate the flooding. If 1,700 refugees are landing in your city every year, you have to address that. If the percentage of English-language learners in your public schools increases 700 percent in twenty years, you have to change in order to enable your school system to teach to that new student cohort. And the sad reality is, the US Department of State is not exactly ahead of this global curve. Most mayors around the world have not had to think too much about international policy issues until now. There are signs this deficit is being wrestled with by both sides, but there are huge gaps in understanding and resourcing on both sides of the divide. But with tens of millions of people on the move now, and no end to that growing number in sight, it is past time to think hard on these issues. Daalder and his tribe need to grow.

Revisiting my 2016 tour through the prism of the xenophobic Trump approach to refugees, a cruelty-based white Christian nationalism political strategy designed to amplify the basest forms of religious bigotry and hatred, has been a sobering process. On the one hand, with President Biden's election and early policy moves to restore refugee resettlement by setting an annual goal of 62,500 in 2021, there is hope to restore a good measure of the progress made during the Obama administration. On the other hand, Republicans seem bent on continuing to stoke the fires of fascist antirefugee sentiment going forward.

In the country's struggle against this right-wing populist tide, I now would frame the discussion as revolving around two key terms, "proximity" and "agency." I think one of the key factors in welcoming new Americans is whether or not a wider swath of Americans can develop relationships, or proximity in its deepest sense, with refugees coming to America. There is interesting data suggesting that knowing a Muslim has a profound impact on one's antipathy or receptivity to Muslims in America.[6] This seems to be self-evident, but it needs stating clearly. Many white Christian Americans do not know refugees personally. There is no better antidote in addressing bias and hatred than face-to-face relationship building. In our deeply divided country, the less proximity across our various divides only deepens the hatred driving our divisions and prejudices. Without proximity, there can be no kinship, no neighboring, no trust between peoples. Public schools, soccer fields, and local political activism are laboratories for creating the proximity necessary to create community.

Agency is important too. If I were honest, I would admit that a lot of my earlier thinking was more than tinged with paternalism, with a touch of rescue, when it came to thinking about America's duties toward refugees seeking shelter in new places. I have come to see that refugees have dignity and agency. And I learned this by actually talking to refugees. I now see them as ordinary people, who, with great tenacity in their encounter with harrowing persecution, navigated a fragile, complex, and bewildering process in order to seek out better lives. Acknowledging their active and innate power is an important step in designing a better, more humane resettlement system.

Listening to their stories, both in person and through reading, has led me to this conclusion. Writer and friend Jessica Goudeau has helped me see this point more clearly in an afterword to her award-winning book *After the Last Border: Two Families and the Story of Refuge in America*. She quotes Viet Than Nguyen in his introduction to *The Displaced*: "True justice is creating a world of social, economic, cultural, and political opportunities" where refugees and displaced persons can "tell their stories and be heard, rather than be dependent on a writer or representative of some kind."[7]

More than four years after my year of travel, the fate of refugees has only gotten worse between the rise of more global populist regimes, including the Trump administration, and the attendant attack on refugees, the cascading impact of climate change triggering more refugees, a growing gap between actual funding and the increasing volume of refugees, and the slow-motion collapse of the global refugee system. What is the alternative? What different kind of world can we imagine that would address this complicated issue set, and how would we go about building it? I will spend the balance of the chapter trying to sort out these questions, which I take to be a combination of moral challenges as well as international policy challenges. In other words, what ought the world to be doing for the record numbers of people on the move, and what sorts of international political institutions will be required to address their needs? I'll take up the moral question first and then take up the political institutional question.

It would take a very long, complicated book to sort all the attempts to answer the moral question of why people should be concerned about the plight of refugees. I will not attempt to write that book in the remainder of this single chapter. But I will claim that an overlapping consensus can be anticipated and outlined, drawing on any number of philosophical and theological arguments. There is a nascent exploration of what that might look like going on among a large number of scholars representing a wide variety of traditions and orientations.[8] For the sake of brevity, I want to focus on one philosophical attempt to hold together the moral and the policy question, and I will also include a snapshot of some theologically informed arguments; after all, at least in the United States, a large portion, perhaps a majority, of refugees are resettled by religiously affiliated organizations. These religious groups do this work based on theological warrants from their respective religious traditions.

The single best comprehensive attempt I know of is advanced by Alexander Betts and Paul Collier in their book *Refuge: Rethinking Refugee Policy in a Changing World*. It is one of those rare books that takes up the moral and the descriptive and empirical tasks of describing a wickedly complex global problem: global refugees. They also advance a moral argument for why we have a duty to refugees and offer a sophisticated set of policy prescriptions to solve the problem. One need not embrace all their arguments and prescriptions, but it is jewel of a book that gets at the right questions and goes a long way toward some solutions.[9] I commend their work not because it has all the answers, but because it is a complex argument that recognizes the moral and political dimensions of this complex policy debate, and it presents a helpful attempt to frame the issues at stake.

In my view, one good starting point for both the moral and policy discussion is to see the moral and political claims made in the foundational moral and political document, which is, of course, the United Nations Universal Declaration of Human Rights. Articles 14 and 28 are the most relevant here. Article 14 states, "Everyone has the right to seek and enjoy in other countries asylum from persecution." Article 28 states, "Everyone is entitled to a social and international order in which the rights and freedoms set forth in this Declaration can be fully realized." Drawing on these norms, the 1951 Refugee Convention relating to the Status of Refugees is firmly anchored in the language of the UN Universal Declaration of Human Rights. The UN launched the global refugee system in the aftermath of World War II to manage the massive refugee flow.[10]

Of the several important aspects of the Refugee Convention, the most important is the definition of a refugee as "someone who is unable or unwilling to return to their country of origin owing to a well-founded fear of being persecuted for reasons of race, religion, nationality, membership of a particular social group, or political opinion."[11] While at first blush this seems to be an expansive definition, current global conditions suggest that many people are on the move for economic and climate-related reasons. And this definition does not address the vast number of people who are displaced within their own countries. The old definition is not sufficient to adequately address the plight of all the people on the move around the world. Simply put, the world today is far too complicated to be served by a definition from 1951.

The second observation is that while the convention embraces a doctrine of not returning people to their country of origin if they think their safety would be imperiled, this is not currently honored in many places, either for lack of political will by the receiving country, such as recent US attempts to send many people away without allowing them to file for asylee status, or lack of international capacity to move people out of refugee camps to another host country.

The final important observation is that the system established by the convention in 1951 is radically underfunded and the vast majority of Muslim-majority countries are not party to the convention, so that we do not have a global refugee system that is truly global or sufficiently funded. Currently 147 countries out of 195 around the world have acceded to the convention. Today millions of people are stranded in large camps where stays last, on average, longer than two decades. Clearly the system is not living up to the moral norms of the convention or the UN Universal Declaration of Human Rights.

As an ethicist and a theologian, I am habitually drawn to moral questions when trying to sort diabolically complex policy positions. It is very much to the credit of Betts and Collier that they see the need to sort the moral dimensions of the global refugee crisis as well as the policy side of the equation. I am not as sanguine as they are about innate human generosity in the face of global failure, but they raise a set of very interesting, even necessary, moral questions regarding if refugees have a right to haven and if all people have a duty to respond to those in deep need.

The global signals indicate that our collective moral will to address the refugee crisis is shrinking quickly. The European Union member states were not able to honor their original commitments to resettle refuges, and even Germany, one of the bright lights among European countries dealing with refugees, has scaled back its efforts in light of domestic politics and burgeoning costs. Given the speed with which the United States has effectively gutted its long-standing bipartisan commitment to resettling refugees, our own moral resolve has eroded significantly. I saw the seeds of this moral fatigue emerging in late 2015.

I have seen with my own eyes how many social scientists and policy wonks who work on the issue of refugees get impatient, even agitated, when moral and theological questions arise in policy discussions. I am convinced that without some sort of moral consensus emerging from a multitude of religious and moral traditions, maddeningly complex issues such as refugees and climate change will overwhelm our capacity to respond in what is now an increasingly anarchic global system. And we have to cobble together that overlapping consensus while the number of people on the move explodes into the hundreds of millions in fairly short order. Assuming enough political will emerges from a deeper moral case to do more to address the problem, we turn to what a more adequate system would look like.

In the fall of 2015, Undersecretary of State for Political Military Affairs Wendy Sherman and Deputy Secretary of State (now Secretary of State) Antony Blinken called a hurried meeting of senior staff to brainstorm possible policy responses to the burgeoning crisis. I tended to hold back in large meetings like this because I had a direct path to the most senior leaders through David Wade, the chief of staff. However, midway through the meeting, someone unknown to me offered an incoherent statement indicating that Pope Francis might be coming to Washington, and maybe we could get him to make some sort of pro-refugee statement. As the "religion guy," I was damned if I was going to let this moment pass without speaking up and proposing something better.

Blinken recognized me, and, completely on the fly, I acknowledged that Pope Francis was coming to address Congress in September 2015 to discuss his new encyclical on the environment, *Laudato Si*, but his itinerary was already set, and any additional agenda items were unlikely. I proposed that we ask the Vatican to cosponsor a summit with Kerry in Rome with other religious leaders and the Organization of Islamic Cooperation (OIC). Such a summit could pressure European Union members to fulfill their pledges of accepting more refugees, woo the Muslim-majority countries of the OIC to formally join the UN Refugee Convention, and significantly increase the funding of the global refugee system. After my quick intervention, there was a momentary silence—an unusual thing for such a meeting—and then Wendy Sherman responded and blessed the proposal, saying it was a very good idea. We now had a stake in the early refugee response, and I spent the next six months trying to make a deal with Rome.

Despite offering to pay for the summit, provide logistical support for the Vatican, and collaborate on media, we were not able to persuade the Vatican to host this meeting, despite Pope Francis's amazing emphasis on the need to show mercy and hospitality to refugees. The team in our embassy to the Holy See confirmed that the Vatican was not interested, but they were never able to get a straight answer for why. Later in 2016, on a trip through Rome, I met with a senior leader in their secretary of state's office, and I put the question to him. I wasn't seeking to embarrass anyone, but I thought we had a great idea and Kerry was very enthusiastic, so I wanted to know why we weren't able to make an agreement and whether we could have done something else to enhance the chances for reaching an agreement.

My interlocutor had three answers, one of which I should have known, and two that surprised me. He said that over the years many of the Muslim countries who made up the OIC had said very negative things about the Catholic Church. I took this to be an understatement, referring to historic grievances over a long arc of time of conflict in the Middle East. What he was saying was that, despite the pope's call for dialogue with the Muslim world, cohosting a meeting with the OIC trying to coax them formally into the UN Convention on Refugees was a very tough sell inside the Vatican. If I had been more diligent in my research, I could have figured that out and found a way to mitigate their heartburn.

What I failed to communicate was the high level of eagerness on the part of the OIC to come to the Vatican for this meeting. There were signs that the OIC could have brought more countries and funding into the UN refugee system.

The second thing I learned was just how small the diplomatic team in the Vatican really was. My conversation partner asked me how many staffers I had in the Office of Religion and Global Affairs. When I told him thirty-five or so, he paused, sighed after a few seconds, and said there were approximately seventy staffers in the secretary of state section that dealt with relations between states. They simply didn't have the capacity to run a large gathering of this sort. We had offered to do the logistical work and pay for the conference. So it could be that this was simply a way of saying that they were too busy with more important work.

And finally, perhaps most telling, he admitted that the pope could not ensure that the senior bishops of all the European countries would take the Vatican's line that each country in the European Union should honor its commitment to resettle 125,000 refugees. This meant the Catholic leaders of at least Hungary and Poland would not be willing to show up, agree with the pope, and then head home to pressure their national leaders to step up and do their duty with regard to refugees. This was one I should have seen coming. No pope is going to hold a press conference when he can't get his fellow cardinals to fall in line. Especially if the archbishop of Canterbury, the ecumenical patriarch, and the general-secretary of the World Council of Churches are all there in full support of the gathering between global Christian and Muslim leaders. "It would have been a good idea" is a common refrain in diplomatic life.

In late 2016 we had the opportunity to collate best refugee practices from the American experience and send staff to Europe to share these with a number of European countries. We were able to assemble what we had learned from our research and visits across America on the central role of faith-based institutions and local congregations and share that information with countries that were still dealing with the massive wave of refugees throughout Europe. The unique structure of the US system was not always directly translatable to contexts where both the political and the religious landscapes were different from ours; nevertheless, the feedback we got was positive.

What has transpired regarding refugees since January 2017? First, an initiative that the United States supported at the United Nations General Assembly meeting in September 2016 led to the issuance of the Global Compact on Refugees two years later in 2018. I'm sure the Obama administration assumed in the fall of 2016 that the compact was laying the groundwork for continued US leadership on resettling global refugees in the Hillary Clinton administration. But the compact simultaneously embodied the worst and the best of the United Nations while overlooking the possibility that Clinton might lose the upcoming election.

What do I mean by this? On the one hand, the compact document is a laundry list of policy recommendations and infrastructure designed to continue and expand the UN's work on refugee resettlement. It restates the various underlying UN documents that give moral and political warrants for this type of work. The whole effort is an implicit recognition that the current UN system faces a combination of international donor fatigue and growing political opposition from global populist governments and political parties that oppose refugees and immigrants of just about all types. It is a classic UN document in its architecture, systematic aspirations, technical rationality, and political naïvetè. It is naïve in that it is not a legally binding document but is dependent entirely on voluntary participation, and without any obligatory funding. It does not admit that rising political opposition to this sort of work is why more refugee work is necessary.

Here is a revealing paragraph: "The global compact is not legally binding. Yet it represents the political will and ambition of the international community as a whole for strengthened cooperation and solidarity with refugees and affected host countries. It will be operationalized through voluntary contributions to achieve collective outcomes and progress towards its objectives. . . . These contributions will be determined by each State and relevant stakeholder, taking into account their national realities, capacities and levels of development, and respecting national policies and priorities."[12]

The political vulnerability of this effort was made clear to the whole world when the Trump administration refused to support the compact in 2018, as it was in the middle of effectively shutting down its own refugee-resettlement program in the United States. The global refugee system is teetering in terms of both inadequate funding and evaporating participation of nation-states in the system. Agreements that are not legally binding on the member parties will not succeed in the current dark global political mood. And the United States Senate is unable to pass any UN treaty with the required sixty-seven votes, as we saw regarding the Disabilities Treaty. We seem stuck in a political limbo for the foreseeable future when it comes to expanding international platforms for addressing the growing refugee problem.

And yet there seems to be something in my DNA that refuses to take no for an answer. Multiple times in my time at State, no meant try a different path. What are the elements of a different approach? While it would take a book to set out a fully orbed policy reform plan for the global refugee system, I can set out a handful of principles and suggestions that might guide a transition to a new or renewed system. These observations are ad hoc and idiosyncratic on my part, but nonetheless they reflect my own experiences and observations.

First, the massive refugee camps around the world are a moral stain. Their proliferation represents massive failure. The best evidence I have at hand suggests that in 2018 there were over two million refugees in the ten largest refugee camps. The average length of stay is decades.[13] Theoretically, these camps were supposed to be temporary way stations to allow people either to return to their country of origin or to move to another country. Any serious effort to reform refugee resettlement has to address eliminating these human warehouses.

The 1951 UN Convention on Refugees needs to be replaced or superseded. As I have argued, this is a very tough sell in the current global and US domestic context. In four short years the Trump administration has succeeded in abandoning the previous bipartisan consensus that America not only needed refugees but had a moral duty to accept them. Restoring a moral and political commitment to the world's most vulnerable and oppressed people will not be easy. The same populist forces at work in the Trump assault are more powerful today globally than at any other time in recent memory.

There are two ways that these political hurdles might be mitigated, borrowing approaches related to the Paris Climate Accord. The first would be a step-by-step approach in which individual nation-states begin to negotiate bilateral agreements to address specific regional hot spots. The second step would be to apply the diplomatic theory embodied in the Paris Accord of common but differentiated responsibilities and respective capabilities. The distinctions here would be between rich countries and not-rich countries, between countries in proximity to the sources of refugee flows and those farther away, and between politically stable countries and those that might be destabilized or overwhelmed by huge flows of refugees. In other words, while all countries have some moral and political duties toward refugees, those duties are not the same. These distinctions are not reducible to algorithms, but they need to be taken into account in apportioning responsibilities and costs associated with refugee resettlement.

Relatedly, I think the accepted wisdom that the first hope for refugees is eventual return to their countries of origin is wise but obviously not always possible. I also believe the principle of non-refoulement is correct as well.

Refugees should not be forced to return to their country of origin if they have a plausible fear of more persecution or if there is not a reasonable chance of human flourishing there. Whatever system replaces the 1951 convention has to be legally binding and have sufficient funding to meet the growing demand of people on the move. Tougher calls have to do with expanding the definition of who is a refugee. As climate change may soon become the greatest driver of people on the move, the current legal definition of a refugee as someone in flight based on a reasonable fear of persecution due to gender, religion, political belief, etc., is too narrow. Economic dislocation is also a powerful driver. While we probably will never be able to grant an automatic unregulated right to migrate, the growing number of people on the move and the growth of large refugee camps illustrate that we need a more rational and sustainable system than we have today.

Where does this leave the Biden administration? I have five suggestions as I write in the early days of his presidency.

First, shore up the current system as envisioned in the 1951 convention and its additions by raising more money and bringing more countries into the convention, especially Muslim-majority countries.

Second, the United States should join the global compact, despite its weaknesses as a purely voluntary agreement.

Third, negotiate bilateral and multilateral agreements over specific cases, such as the plight of the Uighurs in China and the Rohingya, who were driven out of Myanmar and are now stranded primarily in Bangladesh, and the large flows of people from Central America who continue to arrive at our southern border.

Fourth, we need to lead the long and complicated process of negotiating a new, better, larger, and adequately funded successor convention in the United Nations that will address the flaws and weaknesses of the current system. Among other things, this would require more sustainable funding levels, include more countries, and promulgate a wider and more relevant set of categories for legal movement across borders to include internally displaced people, economic refugees, and climate refugees. At a minimum, the concept of a refugee must be expanded beyond the current relatively narrow lens of persecution within the limited set of specific reasons for persecution.

And finally, I believe the State Department should craft a strategy to enlist global religions and religious networks not only to expand their efforts at refugee settlement but also to lobby their governments to make and meet specific commitments to fund and build more robust efforts at refugee resettlement. I still believe our attempt to partner with the Vatican and the Organization of Islamic Cooperation makes sense. There are many such collaborations waiting to be struck.

This is the rare issue where some religious communities are deeply involved already in providing services to match their moral and theological critiques. There are times when governments can actually push religious communities to match their prophetic language with prophetic action. Sadly, at the time of this writing, it is fair to say that the campaign rhetoric of candidate Biden has not become incarnated in policy. The Biden administration's policy responses on several fronts related to people on the move have been chaotic, incoherent, and seemingly feckless. Only time will tell if this changes.

Chapter Seven

CONFLICT

J UST ABOUT EVERY OFFICE IN THE STATE Department believed that addressing conflict was one of its main missions. At times that made for very contentious relations across the vast diplomatic bureaucracy. Secretary Clinton established an Office of Conflict Stabilization Operations (CSO), but it suffered in part because a lot of other offices felt like it was trespassing on their territory. This chapter tells the story of how we brought our unique skill set to this fray, offering a pragmatic case-by-case approach in our analysis of religious dynamics in conflict areas. Here I will make a deeper case for how we were "foxes" who knew a lot regarding how religion played various roles in different conflicts, while others at State were "hedgehogs" who stubbornly held to one big idea regarding religion and conflict. We had to guard against constantly telling peers that "it was more complicated than you think" all the time when presented with the many hot spots around the globe. Adding valuable insights to otherwise "hedgehog" analysis required a form of internal diplomacy.

We found at least three common assumptions about religion and conflict or violence in the halls of Foggy Bottom. The first was that religion is inherently violent (or at least some religions are). The second was the reverse of the first, that religion is a source of global peace (or at least some religions are). And the third related common assumption was that religion could be reduced to simplistic stereotypes such as Christianity is good, Islam has five pillars, Buddhists are all pacifists, etc. Against that reductive and yet theory-rich space, as the new religion guy for the secretary, I found myself navigating a complex web of conflicting theories, historical understandings, and policy recommendations when it came to religion and conflict. For many State Department employees, religion and conflict was all they could imagine for the mission of the Office of Religion and Global Affairs. I was determined to subvert these stereotypes and, in their place, offer a capacity to understand each unique conflict and its religious dynamics with the best analysis we could muster, and not be hampered by any overly esoteric or expansive theories about religion and conflict. For us, thick analysis preceded thick theory. And religion dynamics were about more than just conflict.

Back in the 1970s the discipline of academic theology in America became increasingly obsessed by theological method. A sort of metadebate emerged and threatened to subsume the actual work of theology itself. Camps were formed, parties were defended, various scholars were pilloried or celebrated, tenure was granted and denied, and the discipline-wide sense of inferiority in the wider academy and on specific campuses became a standard feature of the study of religion. Fifty years later, that initial devolution spiraled into a similar partisanship related to various "methods" in the study of religion.[1] There is a similar diversity of theoretical approaches to religion and conflict. I will not attempt to map that diversity of theory. As I note throughout this book, I am not inclined to align myself with any particular school or movement, especially as a substitute for a pragmatic, multidimensional, and contextual approach to assessing conflict dynamics, and only then, if necessary, drawing any grander theoretical conclusions. And I built an office full of smart, well-trained people who were not aligned with a single theoretical approach to understanding religion and conflict.[2]

This chapter will examine three representative conflicts. First will be our contributions to our diplomacy on Israel/Palestine. Next will be our assessment of the Russian invasion of Ukraine in 2014 along with a few comments on the current full-blown invasion of Ukraine. And finally, we'll look at our advice on the conflict in Ethiopia. Our efforts were tailored to the unique configurations of each, as the nature of the conflicts varied widely. I will introduce the specifics of the issues we found, describe the teams that worked on each, and describe how religion was woven into each example.

This chapter will also introduce, in passing, the analytical capacity we built on the Muslim world. I hired Islamic studies scholars Peter Mandaville from George Mason University and Qamar-Ul Huda from the US Institute of Peace. Along with Shaarik Zafar, the special representative to Muslim communities, and Arsalan Suleman, the acting Special Envoy to the Organization of Islamic Cooperation, we had several working-level staff who had expertise in various aspects of the Islamic world. And the focus of their work was not sorting out bad Muslims and creating "moderate" Muslims. It was about pushing back on stereotypes and looking for a multitude of avenues for engagement with the remarkable diversity of global Islam. We ended up with more analytical capacity in the Islamic world than anyone in the executive branch of the government outside of the intelligence community. I believe we produced insights that proved useful to a wide array of diplomats that would have gone unnoticed had we not done this work. Our religion-in-context approach belied any one-size-fits-all analysis of a grand theory of religion and conflict.[3]

Our work with the Office of the Special Envoy for Israeli Palestinian Negotiations began in our early days, as I mentioned earlier. That we were invited in to provide support demonstrated Kerry's willingness to enlist our aid in one of his signature issues, Middle East peace. Ambassador Martin Indyk, the special envoy, had assembled his team to revive the peace process. David Wade convened a group of us to think about how to engage civil society, including religious actors, both here in the United States and in Israel and Palestine, to support their leaders in the negotiations. Indyk thought the United States had not done as much as it might have in the past to rally public support both here and there, among the three religions, Judaism, Islam, and Christianity, for the two negotiating parties to do the hard work of closing the negotiating gaps. As we were committed to aligning our work with Kerry's to the greatest extent possible, this was a golden opportunity for us to come alongside Indyk's impressive team and see if we could play an ancillary but potentially important role in the process. We began working with Laura Blumenfeld, a former *Washington Post* reporter, who was leading the civil-society engagement effort around the peace process. In addition, we got to know people like Hady Amr, Ilan Goldenberg, and Michael Yaffe who brought us up to speed.

Our staff lead on our work here was Liora Danan. Having lived and studied in the region, she was well positioned to be our liaison with Laura's efforts and to be my tutor and guide along the way as well as our point of contact with the consulate in Jerusalem as we began to prepare for our first visit to the region. Being our chief of staff was a full-time job for her, but I knew she would have much to contribute to this portfolio.

I knew enough about the history of these peace negotiations to know that I had a steep learning curve. During the next several months, we spent a lot of time engaging religious actors both in the United States and in the region. But it was a sign of how the department saw the importance of our work that Kerry suggested to Indyk that we could be useful on this, one of Kerry's priority issues. And it is a credit to Indyk that he saw a role for us to play. No one could say we were just window dressing.

What was the administration trying to do in the peace process? The basic premise was to narrow the range of possible agreement across the major issues that would be part of any future comprehensive peace agreement: security, borders, refugees, and the status of Jerusalem, including access to holy sites for the three religions. Even if a final agreement did not happen, as had been the case in the past, the state of the negotiations on the major issues when talks broke down was often the starting point for the next round of negotiations. It is also probably accurate to say that sorting out Jerusalem and its attendant issues was usually seen as the hardest puzzle to solve. Given that complexity, some wanted to push Jerusalem back on the timeline in hopes that it would be more solvable later. I'll return to this later in the chapter and make a case for why that is no longer a tenable strategy.[4]

It was Indyk's view that in the past when negotiations reached critical phases, civil-society support for continuing the negotiations had not been as robust as it could have been, and leaders felt politically isolated and vulnerable for lack of such support. His premise for our work was to rally public support from all three religions, Judaism, Islam, and Christianity, in the United States and in the region, and to encourage their leaders to continue to work, especially during the difficult moments that would inevitably arise. With that mandate, we developed courses of action domestically and in the region.

There was no shortage of domestic religious interlocutors who wanted to meet with us. In January 2014 we sponsored an off-the-record lunch meeting between national religious leaders and Secretary Kerry at Georgetown University. We quickly ran into two of the foundational truths of engaging with religious communities. The first one was general State Department angst about dealing with religious stakeholders: fear of lack of experience. Many of our colleagues looked at the prospect of equal numbers of Muslim, Jewish, and Christian leaders in a room quizzing the secretary on Middle East peace negotiations with very jaundiced eyes. They could only see potential disasters and not many helpful positive outcomes. This overlooked both Kerry's skill and his credibility within each constituency, and frankly, my team's ability to engage a set of religious leaders with whom we had previously established good personal working relationships extending back before our time at State. The second source of angst, far more probable than the first, was what I called the Noah's ark problem. (I experienced a version of this six years before on the Obama campaign.) This was all about the math. If you invite ten religious leaders, you risk offending one hundred who are not invited. Invite one hundred, and you risk offending one thousand. There is no easy cure for this dynamic, so we had to trust that advertising the opportunity to hear the secretary of state talk off the record on one of his signature issues would generate widespread interest. There is the related issue of professional Washington-based religious "leaders" who were professional self-promoters, in many cases with little or no real influence beyond the Beltway. And some of them would annoyingly refer to "Barack" and "John" in casual conversation just to show off.

Kerry gave a command performance detailing the state of the conversations and then took questions from the audience. In my experience with these sorts of interreligious gatherings, a general good vibe tends to prevail until someone has the wherewithal to ask the question many people want to hear answered but few are willing to actually ask. This time, we did not have to wait long.

An Orthodox rabbi raised his hand and asked Kerry how he could guarantee that the West Bank wouldn't turn into Gaza in his plan. And he added that his large synagogue would want him to ask Kerry this question, and without a convincing answer, they were not inclined to support his efforts. This was one of those moments when I knew Kerry's answer would determine the rest of the gathering's tone and outcome. Kerry's response did not disappoint. He began by saying that the security question was the fundamental question for Prime Minister Netanyahu in the peace process, and if he judged any proposal as threatening Israel's security, there was no reason to keep talking on any of the other issues. And he thanked the rabbi for getting the most important question asked at the outset. Kerry then went on to describe the role retired marine general John Allen was playing in working with Israeli security officials to design a plan to meet the security needs of Israel. Without sufficient assurance regarding Israel's security, there would be no deal. The rabbi thanked Kerry for his serious answer and said his answer would be eagerly heard by his congregants.

The consensus among the attendees across the three religions at the end of the event was uniformly positive. I thought we were off to a good start. But I soon came back down to earth as my personal engagement with different domestic religious constituencies expanded. One week typified my overall domestic engagement. During that week I gave essentially the same set of remarks in two different American religious contexts. The first talk was at a fairly large event with primarily liberal Protestants called Ecumenical Advocacy Days. After working systematically through my State Department talking points, I paused for questions. The very first question was something along the lines of "Why is the State Department historically so reflexively anti-Palestinian?" No response I could muster could have moved the audience off of its universal belief that the State Department was inherently pro-Israel and anti-Palestine.

A few days later, working with exactly the same talking points, I spoke to the board members of the Union of Orthodox Rabbis during a lunch at their periodic Washington, DC, meeting. The first question I fielded went along a different tack: "Why is the State Department inherently pro-Palestine and anti-Israel?" Again, my protestations to the contrary, my auditors would not be moved off of their assumptions. It was an important lesson for me, and in the long run it was very helpful. I believe each audience was committed to finding a peaceful solution, but neither was going leave any mistaken impression about their framework and historical understandings. If the United States is going to play a role in any political progress in the Middle East, it will have to be patient with a variety of what appear to be incommensurate basic assumptions. Informally, we called this playing the piñata. I would meet more than a few US diplomats who acted as if they had to defend all recent US foreign policy as mistake-free and argue with anyone who disagreed before the conversation could continue. I never found this to be a fruitful strategy.

In fact, when talking with countless Muslim leaders around the world, they frequently kick off a litany of US blunders in the Middle East with the 2003 invasion of Iraq. I recall one leader in Palestine on my first trip there who, after the initial greetings, launched into his list of grievances against the United States and paused after a few minutes to let me respond. I agreed with him on our invasion of Iraq and added that I thought it was the worst US foreign policy mistake since Vietnam; in fact, I told him, I had launched my public career in Washington a decade before, protesting and condemning the war. He was surprised, as was, I suspect, my escort from the US consulate. But once we got past his airing of grievances, I was able to ask the question I came to ask: How does your community view the current efforts at peace there?

I distinctly remember three types of reactions I got on my first trip. The first one, much to my relief, was gratitude that the United States was finally sending someone who had some understanding of religious communities. A quick Google search would reveal that I was a Christian, and I wondered just how that fact might land on the ears of folk who did not share my affiliation. It wasn't that our diplomatic personnel in the region did not care about religious communities; it was that there had not been much attention on the part of Washington-based diplomats when they came to the region. People cared that I understood and generally respected the work local religious communities were doing. The second reaction was also one of gratitude for Secretary Kerry's indefatigable work on behalf of peace. People were very happy he was working hard for peace and had sent someone to take their temperature on what was happening in the region. And the third reaction, despite all the gratitude, was that most people thought it wasn't going to work!

One scene from my first visit to the region typified our engagement there. On that trip I met with the Roman Catholic archbishop in Jerusalem, the Latin patriarch Fouad Twal. He rose from his chair to meet me and said, "Dr. Casey, it is so good to meet you. We've been waiting for you for forty years!" I told him that was the best opening line I had heard yet, and with that we dove into a fascinating conversation. Just about every religious community I met on my various trips to Israel and Palestine was happy that Washington had sent someone who understood the complex religious landscape there and who would interpret the conversations back to the senior leadership in the States. The archbishop had many concerns, not the least of which was a road being built by the Israelis that cut off access to the their Cremisan Monastery in the West Bank and expanded access to a Jewish settlement at the expense of the monastery's access to its own groves. The Vatican saw this as a fundamental issue in their relationship with the Israeli government. Even though we conveyed the archbishop's and the Vatican's dismay to Secretary Kerry, who raised it with the Israelis, the road was built. It really was an unnecessary and shoddy move on the Israelis' part, and they were either blind to the depth of irritation this caused the Vatican or they simply didn't care. But it was precisely the sort of unforced error that only reinforced diplomatic heartburn in Rome. Visiting the site only reinforced the frustration I had seen around the globe regarding how the Israeli government was treating the monastery. A senior leader at the US Conference of Catholic Bishops told me that frustration about the Israeli government's handling of the Cremisan Monastery fiasco was driving more European Catholic bishops toward supporting the international Boycott, Divest, and Sanctions (BDS) movement.

One vital key to our work in Israel and Palestine was the superb personnel at the embassy in Tel Aviv and in the consulate in Jerusalem. They understood our mission; connected us to the right people in the right religious communities, based on their extensive knowledge; and stayed in constant contact with us in Washington. The most consequential staff person proved to be Rachel Leslie, who handled the religion portfolio at the consulate. When Washington-based diplomats arrive at the airport for a visit, they are met at the bottom of the ramp by a control officer who accompanies them for the duration of the visit. I learned very quickly that control officers meet their Washington guests with a sense of anticipation that can range from dread to joy. The dread can stem from a visitor's reputation that is less than stellar; the joy, in seeing a repeat visitor friend or a former colleague from another post. I tried to put my control officer at ease that I was going to be a nice person to be around and not a pain in the ass.

Liora and I met Rachel Leslie at the end of our jetway when we landed at Ben Gurion Airport. We were to have a great visit. On our late-night trip into Jerusalem, I asked Rachel what her story was, and by the time we made it to the hotel in Jerusalem, I knew she was going to be the perfect match for our visit. It turned out Rachel had taken a year off from the Foreign Service to do an MA degree at the University of Chicago Divinity School, where she wrote a thesis on how the State Department should launch an office on global religion, if it ever got that smart! By the time we arrived at our hotel, I had asked her to email a copy of her thesis. By the time we left, I had told her that when she was applying for her next rotation site, she should consider joining S/RGA to run our as-yet-not-started public diplomacy team. In time, she arrived in Washington to do that very thing, and our public diplomacy team soon became a large factor in our office's mission. I'll have more to say about that later in the book. But Rachel's skill and performance typified the high caliber of other personnel, ranging from Ambassador Daniel Shapiro, whom I had met back in 2008 on the Obama campaign, to Consul General Michael Ratney; Yael Lempert, deputy chief of mission at the consulate; Richard Buangan, head of public diplomacy at the consulate; and our control officer on a later trip, Mimi Asnes. It was very nice to work with diplomatic staff who did not need to be convinced that diplomacy that included religious communities was important in their space.

Rachel's expertise allowed us to engage a wide variety of religious actors and organizations across Israel and in Palestine. Our basic task was to promote the idea in each context of encouraging communities to support the peace process in public and soliciting their input on it. Given the significant absence of people-to-people engagement across the political divide, it became paramount to resist easy stereotyping among the three major religions. But it was a very hard diplomatic sell. Several anecdotes will give a flavor of our work. Perhaps the place to begin was our interaction with the CRIHL, or Council of the Religious Institutions of the Holy Land.

The CRIHL was founded in 2005 by an interreligious group of leaders who came out of the earlier Alexandria Accord effort, which sought to end violence and promote respect for the integrity of the parties' historical and religious inheritance.[5] In many ways it is a classic case of a top-down interreligious leader-consultative group attempting to broker communication among the most important religious leaders, Israeli and Palestinian political leaders, and the bewildering landscape of international actors in the area. Its constitutive members represented the Chief Rabbinate of Israel, the heads of the local churches of the Holy Land, the minister of the Islamic Waqf at the Palestinian Authority, and the Islamic Sharia Court of the Palestinian Authority. I interacted with the membership of the CRIHL on several occasions, and with leadership of most of the member groups individually. Several internal rules such as having private conversations where all spoke freely and prohibiting public airing of differences led to frank exchanges, but perhaps less effective public engagement in tense times. The Norwegian government funded its activity, and veteran Norwegian diplomat Trond Bakkevig was the chief staff person who managed the CRIHL.

I came away from my interaction with a number of impressions. First, much to my surprise, I found a real sense of community from the constituent representatives of the three religions across the two peoples. They were all veterans of the troubled history of the neighborhood, but they had found a way not only to get along but also to forge bonds of apparent affections. Yet, they also had a sense of fatalism about the futility of the time. In a classic rookie diplomatic mistake, I asked them for their individual assessments of the current state of affairs. They dutifully mouthed their commitments to "the status quo" as we went around the table. About halfway through I asked them what they meant by that term. My query was met with ironic grins and chuckles that revealed no one should ask that question since everyone knew the term masked the diversity of opinion on just what that term should mean. They were clearly constrained by their political leadership on just how open and honest they could be with the shiny new religion guy from the United States. I should have anticipated that and found a more indirect line of questioning that might have led to a more fruitful exchange rather than asking a direct question at the outset that was beyond their comfort zone.

The CRIHL was born out of a moment of real passion on the part of a handful of religious leaders a decade earlier. But its bureaucratization by the respective governments and the intractable politics surrounding the Middle East peace process had drained the life and energy out of it by the time I arrived. I asked them to engage their communities to support their parties at the negotiating table, and they fell mute pretty fast. Likewise, they were loath to offer opinions on the issues under negotiation. What they wanted from me was a photo opportunity with Secretary Kerry to bolster their sagging credibility. I wasn't going to bother him with a request for a photo when he would not get anything in return from the CRIHL.[6] In the end, the CRIHL did not survive the Trump peace plan. What started out as a noble interreligious endeavor died as a weak pawn in the midst of the Trump Middle East grift and the political weakness of Benjamin Netanyahu and Mahmoud Abbas. If there is a lesson here, it may be that a degree of political independence and freedom to speak bluntly and publicly to one's political masters may be necessary for interreligious councils to have real political impact on intransigent governments. A corollary is that many times interreligious organizations harbor hidden and unspoken agendas that belie their boilerplate public-facing virtue signaling. They are sometimes riven with less noble personal agendas and self-aggrandizing impulses, as almost all human institutions are.

One of the most interesting conversations I had in Israel was with the Palestinian liberation theologian and Anglican priest Naim Ateek, who directs the organization Sabeel, a Palestinian center for liberation theology in Jerusalem. As a theologian, I was familiar with his work many years before I came to the State Department, and I was eager to meet him and, to be honest, a little nervous about our conversation. Eager because it wasn't often I got to meet an internationally renowned theologian, and nervous because I had no idea how he would respond to me as an American theologian-turned-diplomat. As I usually did before I met religious leaders around the globe, I did my homework. One item on his résumé struck me as very unusual, and that was his undergraduate degree from Hardin-Simmons University in Abilene, Texas— the same place Rick Warren had attended! Given my sojourn in Abilene at Abilene Christian University two decades after Ateek, I had to ask him about that at the beginning of our conversation. As a side note, I learned quickly that Google has colonized the world, and many of my interlocutors knew more about me than I did about them when we sat down to talk![7]

How a diplomatic conversation begins is always interesting, hard, and sometimes pivotal. Typically, you are booked for an hour, but if a meeting is fruitful, it can blow past any scheduled stopping point. But if you have a full day of meetings, going long early in the day can anger people you meet later in the day because you are running behind. Parties know what they want to say, or not say, and yet stilted formalities have to be observed many times. Too hot a start might derail a conversation. Too slow a start and the conversation might not ever take off. Tea, coffee, or, depending on the particular religious community serving as host, alcohol might be offered at the outset. I always had what the host would have to drink. One Jerusalem patriarch offered me a tray of shot glasses full of cognac at a 9:00 a.m. meeting. Despite my Irish heritage, or maybe because of it, consuming a high volume of alcohol early in the day does not render me smarter. I remember thinking, I hope I don't fall out of my chair dead-drunk over the course of the hour. The patriarch looked me dead in the eye, and with a very sly grin, said, "You and I are religious scholars, and we have both been praying and studying hard since 5:00 this morning. Would you like a drink?" I demurred, and thankfully he was not offended, and in fact, he did not drink any cognac either.

I took a gamble with Ateek, and, after our first greetings, I told him that, as a graduate of a religious college in Abilene, I had to ask him about his Hardin-Simmons connection. He was gobsmacked. A very nice smile broke out on his otherwise somber face, and our conversation took off. He told me that when he told the principal of his Anglican high school in Israel that he wanted to go to college in America, the principal refused to help him, telling him he wasn't smart enough for that, so he went to the principal of the local Baptist-run high school, who helped him enroll at the Baptist-affiliated Hardin-Simmons College. He also told me that in 1958 the best soccer game in Abilene was on Saturday afternoons at Abilene Christian. It scrambled my brain to image a Palestinian Anglican playing soccer there back in the day![8]

Ateek has been a global lightning rod over his long career, especially in the United States. So, I was braced for a harsh tone, but the conversation was anything but that. He expressed gratitude that I had chosen to meet with him. And he was happy, as was just about every religious leader I met with, that Kerry was sending me, someone who knew and respected them, to talk to religious leaders and communities. He laid out a vision of a two-state solution that was mainstream by anyone's standards. He was happy Kerry was reengaging on behalf of the Obama administration, but like most of my Arab conversation partners, he was not particularly optimistic about progress.

Another one of the most interesting people I met was Rabbi Michael Melchior. His biography is impressive: national rabbi of Norway, former Knesset member, former cabinet member, internationally renowned peacemaker, social activist, and indefatigable in his pursuit of peace between Israel and Palestine.[9] If the CRIHL represented a top-down approach by religious leaders pursuing peace, Rabbi Melchior represents a much more grassroots approach. The sheer breadth and depth of his engagement with Islamic leaders of an amazing range set him apart from most people working for peace between Israel and Palestine. It is his thesis that official peace processes by political leaders have paid only token heed at best to religious communities. At the same time, he argues that there will be no peace in Israel until religious leaders actually lead in the work for peace. He was pleased to see someone with my title showing up at his doorstep, but I think he thought it wasn't going to be enough to reach actual peace. I found him to be as engaging a figure as I was to meet in my entire work at the State Department.

Again, part of our rapport was based on asking him the right questions and listening hard to his answers. He was incredibly generous with his time and hospitality. The highlight for me came on our third and last visit to the region in 2016. The formal peace process had collapsed, but we made one last trip there to put a spotlight on religious-based violence against holy sites of all three religions. Rabbi Melchior invited our small delegation to Shabbat service at his synagogue and dinner at his apartment afterward. Our small band was comprised of me; Liora; Mimi Asnes, our control officer from the embassy; Sharik Zafar, the Special Representative for Muslim Communities; Ira Forman, the Special Envoy to Monitor and Combat Anti-Semitism; and Rustum Nyquist, our Near Eastern Affairs regional adviser. Three Jews, one Christian, and two Muslims. We probably were not the typical visitors to his synagogue, but we were welcomed warmly, and it was an honor to be there. Everywhere I traveled around the planet I was met with extraordinary and generous forms of food-based hospitality, even in places where the reputation of Americans was less than great. But I remember thinking that evening about the various powerful images in the Hebrew Bible and the Christian Bible of a messianic banquet.

We certainly weren't celebrating anything close to a messianic reign. But I was struck by the power of people of all three religions in the region meeting around a common table working and hoping for peace. We ate, we sang (my a cappella singing upbringing helped me limp through the songs), and we talked late into the night. This sort of people-to-people mundane exchange is very rare across the security line that separates Israelis and Palestinians. And that absence produces consequences that reduce the chance of peace to emerge there. But the good rabbi was modeling in his own home what he was preaching to anyone who would listen. If all three religions could produce a cadre of Melchiors who had the ear of their respective political leaders and street cred in their respective political units, the place would be different.

I had various engagements with parties associated with the Waqf, the organization overseen by King Abdullah of Jordan that is responsible for the administration of the Haram al Sharif, where the Dome of the Rock and the Al Aqsa mosque are located, and the Sharia courts. I was given a tour of the Dome of the Rock after an incident in 2014 where Israeli Defense Forces chased Muslim youths after a rock-throwing incident. One sensed the utter unsustainability of the security arrangements there. In one meeting with Sheik Azzam Al-Khatib, the director general of the Waqf, I was accompanied by Yael Lempert, the deputy chief of mission at the US consulate in Jerusalem. He told us about an impending speech in the Israeli Knesset that the leaders of the Waqf feared might incite violence on the Esplanade if it were to take place. Lempert notified officials in the Netanyahu government, and the speaker was prevented from giving or persuaded not to give the speech. Again, the randomness of my visit coinciding with this information received by the Waqf illustrated the fragility of the whole system. The avenues open to many sources to disrupt the so-called status quo cast doubt on the sustainability of the security system there.

I also witnessed the erosion of the historic prohibition against Jews praying on the Temple Mount, given the biblical prohibition against Jews praying in the holy of holies in the temple. The argument goes that since it is no longer possible to know the precise location of the now-destroyed temple, praying in the area represents the possibility of violating this prohibition. During another Shabbat dinner with an Orthodox rabbi and his family, we witnessed a tense disagreement between the rabbi and his adult son, who articulated a perfect parody of an American fundamentalist Christian argument that religious freedom was an absolute right and no chief rabbi could or should tell him he couldn't pray anywhere he wanted to pray on the Temple Mount. The father was flummoxed by his son's argument, to put it mildly.

These are just a few of the dozens of conversations we had across all three religions in both political spaces. I am in no way offering a comprehensive description of the religious dynamics of contemporary Israel and Palestine. But the conversations I do relate are representative of some of the complexities surrounding US diplomacy there. We engaged with Rabbis for Human Rights in their response to "price tag" attacks. On our last trip, we met with leaders of the three major religions to shine a light on the ongoing desecration of holy sites and of churches, synagogues, and mosques. I did a virtual college classroom visit with a Gazan international relations class and met with students and faculty at Bethlehem University and Bethlehem Bible College. We met with environmental NGOs comprised of Palestinian and Israeli constituents. We also met with various Israeli and Palestinian political and policy-making offices.[10]

Two tasks remain for me in this section: to assess what we can anticipate from the new Biden administration, and to describe how renewed strategies of engaging with religious actors there might open up fruitful lines of diplomacy over time.

The spate of violence in Gaza and Israel in the summer of 2021 shows the failure of the Trump policy attempt to resolve the conflict between Israel and Palestine. The occupation continues and hopes for any two-state solution seem as remote as ever. The new Israeli government has replaced the Netanyahu government, but the new coalition probably has even less political room to maneuver in the Knesset than the previous government. The Palestinian Authority also suffers from very weak popular support. Palestinian antinormalization attitudes haven't lessened any over recent years. Perhaps the most disturbing development of all is the increasing attempts to normalize Jewish prayer on the Temple Mount (followed closely by the continuing expansion of Jewish settlements). This is an explicit rejection of the admittedly porous definition of the status quo. It hardly seems like a formula for a comprehensive peace agreement anytime soon.

Despite closing the US consulate in Jerusalem, which managed the US relationship with Palestinians, and moving the US embassy to Jerusalem to great fanfare, peace did not come. The increased pressure on the Palestinian Authority through cutting aid funding and negotiating the so-called Abraham Accords did not result in the political embrace of Israel at the expense of Arab abandonment of Palestine. What the Trump administration did accomplish was to deepen American fundamentalist support for the administration at the expense of peace in the region. Yet that constant political wooing of the increasingly bizarre cast of evangelical Christian kooks, crooks, and charlatans was not enough to reelect Trump.

The eruption of violence in Gaza drew the Biden administration back into a significant diplomatic engagement, probably at an earlier time and with more resources than it had hoped to do. It is too early to tell what the combination of the failure of the Trump policy, the violence in Gaza, and the new Israeli government will mean for any ongoing peace efforts. And I am in no mood or position to make predictions. At the moment, the Biden administration is still putting together its team, and the early signs point toward a veteran team heading to the Middle East. I suspect they will reopen the consulate in Jerusalem, which will go a long way in restoring balance to our diplomacy there after four years of the Trump debacle.

The Gaza-based attacks on Israel and the Israeli military response in the middle of 2021 marked the failure of the Trump strategy to crush the two-state solution and demonstrated that the Abraham Accords were not a panacea. I think it is prudent to take a closer look at Secretary Kerry's final speech on Middle East peace delivered on December 28, 2016, and see what strands might be eventually picked up by US policy makers. At that point the Obama/Kerry efforts had failed. Trump had won the US presidential election and was signaling a very different, pro-Israel, anti-Palestinian policy in the Middle East. The speech is important for several reasons. It describes in specific detail what the US strategy was during the Kerry years. It is a blunt assessment of the threats to any two-state solution posed by the Israelis and Palestinians at the time. And most important for my purposes, it outlines the principles that formed the Kerry strategy; I believe Kerry thought these principles could serve as a beginning point for thinking about any efforts by a future administration attempting to negotiate a two-state solution. The speech also can serve as a jumping-off point for an analysis of how a renewed S/RGA effort might make contributions to future peace efforts on the part of the United States.[11]

I was in the Dean Acheson Auditorium at the State Department on December 28, 2016, in the waning days of the Obama administration when Kerry gave the speech. News of the speech passed quickly on the seventh floor, and many of us dropped what we were doing and hustled downstairs to hear Kerry speak. The mood in the building was very dark as hundreds of us who were political appointees were scrambling to pack up and tie up any loose ends in our work. The professional staff was bracing for Hurricane Trump, and they knew hard times were coming. The landing team from the Trump transition had taken a long time to come to State, and the stories coming from their temporary offices on the first floor had been grim. Some of the religious-freedom people were trying to sue for peace with the transition staff in hopes of saving their jobs. Ambassador David Saperstein was lobbying to keep his job, much to my chagrin, but in the end, he failed to persuade the new administration.[12] Knox Thames, a senior adviser to Saperstein, did manage to keep his job, despite the promised Muslim-ban proposal and the anti-Muslim tone that pervaded Trump's campaigning. I angled a meeting with the Trump transition person on religion just before I left, and she told me she heard S/RGA was too obsessed with gay rights and too isolated from various internal State bureaus and offices. I knew this was disinformation from inside the building, but I was helpless to knock it down.

Despite the dark mood, there was an odd electricity in Acheson that day, as those of us who had worked on Israel and Palestine were eager to hear what Kerry had to say. I won't rehearse the whole, long speech. But near the end Kerry listed six principles that guided the Obama administration's approach. I had the distinct feeling he knew the rough outlines of the very different Trump policy to come on the Middle East, so he was laying down historical markers for the diplomats to come after the Trump failure. Turns out he was right about that.

Kerry was blunt at the outset and continued that tone throughout: "the two-state solution is the only way to achieve a just and lasting peace between Israelis and Palestinians. It is the only way to ensure Israel's future as a Jewish and democratic state, living in peace and security with its neighbors. It is the only way to ensure a future of freedom and dignity for the Palestinian people. And it is an important way of advancing United States interests in the region." He quickly noted that despite our best efforts, the two-state solution was now in serious jeopardy. If the choice is one state, Israel can be either Jewish or democratic, not both. And it would never be in peace. The Palestinians would never fully realize their potential with a one-state solution.

In the final third of the speech, Kerry turned toward the future. After reciting the history of the conflict from 1948; to the United Nations General Assembly Resolution 181, which called for two states for two peoples, one Arab, one Jewish; to the Six-Day War and Resolution 242, which called for the withdrawal of Israeli troops from the territory it occupied in 1967 in exchange for peace and secure borders, as the basis for ending the conflict; down to the Oslo Accords and the Arab Peace Initiative, Kerry described the nine months of his work.

> Finally, some 15 years ago, King Abdullah of Saudi Arabia came out with the historic Arab Peace Initiative, which offered fully normalized relations with Israel when it made peace—an enormous opportunity then and now, which has never been embraced.

That history was critical to our approach to trying to find a way to resolve the conflict. And based on my experience with both sides over the last four years, including the nine months of formal negotiations, the core issues can be resolved if there is leadership on both sides committed to finding a solution.

In the end, I believe the negotiations did not fail because the gaps were too wide, but because the level of trust was too low. Both sides were concerned that any concessions would not be reciprocated and would come at too great a political cost. And the deep public skepticism only made it more difficult for them to be able to take risks.

In the countless hours that we spent working on a detailed framework, we worked through numerous formulations and developed specific bridging proposals, and we came away with a clear understanding of the fundamental needs of both sides. In the past two and a half years, I have tested ideas with regional and international stakeholders, including our Quartet partners. And I believe what has emerged from all of that is a broad consensus on balanced principles that would satisfy the core needs of both sides.

Kerry's observation that the role deep public skepticism on both sides of the conflict played in undermining the confidence of the two negotiating parties can be read two ways. It could mean that public engagement such as what our office did was futile and should not be tried again. Or it could mean that if there is a next time, a more robust set of engagements, including engaging religious communities, should be included in any US approach. I don't believe our work hampered the negotiations; instead, I think more such engagement is called for.

Kerry then proceeded to list six principles. First, provide for secure and recognized international borders between Israel and a viable and contiguous Palestine, negotiated based on the 1967 lines with mutually agreed equivalent swaps.

Second, fulfill the vision of the UN General Assembly Resolution 181 of two states for two peoples, one Jewish and one Arab, with mutual recognition and full equal rights for all their respective citizens.

Third, provide for a just, agreed, fair, and realistic solution to the Palestinian refugee issue, with international assistance, that includes compensation, options and assistance in finding permanent homes, acknowledgment of suffering and other measures necessary for a comprehensive resolution consistent with two states for two peoples.

Fourth, provide an agreed resolution for Jerusalem as the internationally recognized capital of the two states, and protect and assure freedom of access to the holy sites consistent with the established status quo.

Fifth, satisfy Israel's security needs and bring a full end to the occupation, while ensuring that Israel can defend itself effectively and that Palestine can provide security for its people in a sovereign and nonmilitarized state.

Sixth, end the conflict and all outstanding claims, enabling normalized relations and enhanced regional security for all as envisaged by the Arab Peace Initiative.

By now I think it should be clear that Kerry believes pursuing a comprehensive agreement has to take place within this principled, elaborated framework.[13] I agree with his understanding, and I want to wrap up this section of the chapter by thinking about how engaging some of the religious dynamics of this framework might be taken up anew by an American diplomatic effort.

Another way to put the question is to ask, In the future, how might engaging with religious communities and assessing the religious dimensions of the search for peace be a part of US diplomacy in Israel-Palestine? In contrast to the Trump administration tactic of isolating Palestinians, both Muslim and Christian, what would a more inclusive and balanced engagement look like? If the pan-religious CRIHL could not be sustained in the current era, is there a better model for religious communities to organize?

One counterintuitive approach might be to engage more directly the fourth principle, regarding access to holy sites in Jerusalem according to the so-called status quo. This is counterintuitive because many observers believe access to holy sites for the three religions is so complex that it is best to sort out all the other issues first, hoping that some form of diplomatic solution appears out of the ether many years hence to resolve the issue. It is also the case that there are now disruptors on both the Israeli and Palestinian sides who know they can scuttle a larger agreement on the remaining major issues at the last moment of an apparent comprehensive agreement.

There have been a couple of mild attempts to sort out the access and security issues around the holy sites.[14] But in my experience, many people pay lip service to the "status quo" while consciously avoiding defining the term, while various provocations on the Temple Mount keep leading to violence. It may seem crazy, but if there is an issue that can destroy an otherwise comprehensive agreement at the last minute for a range of individual actors, isn't that a reason to remove that spoiler issue? Also, given the fact that the Abrahamic Accords negotiated by the Trump administration should increase the number of Muslims visiting Haram al Sharif, the security protocols will need be strengthened even more. The other reason to address this issue earlier rather than later is that the question of secure access to holy sites is not dependent on either a one-state or a two-state solution. Providing maximum access and strengthened security will be needed regardless of anyone's opinion on all the other issues in play.

If there is a model process for what this might ultimately look like, it might be the security plan drawn up by General John Allen as part of the Kerry initiative. As far as I can tell, there is no publicly available account of the security issues General Allen sorted. But we do know it was an iterative process that included the political and security institutions of the various parties. I am interested in the iterative process, not the specific terms they came up with. At a minimum, any process, led by the United States or any other mediating entity, would have to navigate an equally complex network of political, military, security, and religious stakeholders. The task would be to maximize security while simultaneously maximizing access to the major holy sites of Jerusalem. Only a diplomatic effort that had expertise on religion and security could ever draft a plan to the satisfaction of all parties, including, obviously, the Jordanians, who administer the space on the Esplanade at the moment.

The value of a stand-alone agreement now, before a comprehensive agreement is reached, is obvious. If the former held and Jews, Muslims, and Christians could find a way to an agreement on access to holy sites, it could be the source of reduced violence, lowered tension, and in itself prove that modest confidence-building measures could help the parties make progress on the other major issues. Such an iterative process would require diplomatic actors with more than a little knowledge and understanding of the religious history and yearnings of the three religions; hence there would be a need for scholarly religious knowledge at the heart of the enterprise. It might be so volatile and difficult to negotiate as to require a nonstate international team in order to pull it off.

If a full peace process ever restarts with a modicum of seriousness, I believe religious leaders will insist on being consulted on many issues, especially those around access to holy sites in Jerusalem, because we established the position of including them. Given the perennial state of theoretical support for a two-state solution coupled with deep pessimism over the chance of it ever happening, winning the public support of the various religious communities will be an essential diplomatic task to accompany the actual negotiations. I believe such an effort by a Washington-based S/RGA-like office can augment the work of our embassy and consulate on-site.

The next case study in conflict and religion began inauspiciously enough. Very early in my tenure at State, when I literally had no staff, I received an email from the woman who ran the State Department's Russia desk. She introduced herself to me and told me she had received a request from the Russian embassy to send a staffer to meet with me. Somewhat flummoxed when I asked her why they would want to do that, she replied that she had no idea. I told her to set up the meeting, and we would find out together.

When the time arrived for the meeting, a young woman arrived straight out of central casting. A young, tall, striking blond woman entered the office, introduced herself, and promptly drew out a long yellow legal pad and began asking me a long series of written questions. For the first fifty-five minutes or so of the interrogation, the questions were quite banal and frankly puzzling. Several times I glanced over at our Russia desk person, and her face indicated that she was as puzzled as I was. But for the final question my Russian visitor asked, "Does your office have a strategy to engage the Russian Orthodox Church?" This was the money question, and I only managed to blurt out something like "No, not at this time." Little did I know that only a few months later President Vladimir Putin would seize Crimea and invade eastern Ukraine, setting off a cascading set of global events in which the Russian Orthodox Church would become a full partner in the impressive Russian international propaganda machine. The question looms far more ominously in my mind today than it did on that day in the summer of 2013. In retrospect, it is both chilling and impressive that the Russian embassy was already watching the State Department and trying to anticipate what the US response to Putin's aggression would be months before it actually happened.

In 2015, after Russia had seized Crimea and invaded eastern Ukraine, Ambassador Gregory Pyatt invited me to Ukraine to engage a diverse range of religious communities, primarily, but not exclusively, related to the internal struggle in the Orthodox Christian nexus. Assistant Secretary for Europe and European Affairs Victoria Nuland also had a keen interest in countering Vladimir Putin's power moves against Ukraine, and she naturally understood the crucial role the Orthodox Church played as part of Putin's expansionist program. Here, as in Israel, senior leaders in the State Department saw the value of assessing the religious dynamics of a country as part of the administration's diplomatic efforts in a key global hot spot, and they turned to us to help sharpen their analysis.

The presenting question was twofold in Ukraine, in terms of what our office might contribute to the analysis of the political and diplomatic strategy in Ukraine. First, to what extent was Putin using the Russian Orthodox Church as a force in his propaganda arsenal? And second, a potentially far more dangerous question: Might Putin resort to military force to block any attempt by the Ecumenical Patriarch in Istanbul to declare the Orthodox Church in Ukraine autocephalous, or independent from the Russian Orthodox Church?

As the Russian Orthodox Church has increasingly sought to displace the Ecumenical Patriarch in Istanbul as the spiritual leader of the Orthodox world, its struggle has been increasingly apparent in the geopolitics of Ukraine. Traditionally, the Ecumenical Patriarch has had the authority to grant national churches independent status, or autocephaly. In 2014, there were three different Orthodox churches in Ukraine: one related to the Moscow Patriarchate, one loyal to the Kyivan Patriarchate, and a small Orthodox church known confusingly to outside observers as the Autocephalous Orthodox Church. Ecumenical Patriarch Bartholomew was mulling a proposal to unite all three branches into a new consolidated Ukrainian Orthodox Church. Such a move would potentially result in the loss of thousands of parishes from the Moscow-related Orthodox church to the new united Ukrainian Orthodox Church, to say nothing of the property, and would represent a huge symbolic loss to Putin's pursuit of a renewed Russia. The stakes were high, and the tiny resources of Patriarch Bartholomew, living under a sort of modified house arrest in Istanbul, looked vastly overmatched compared to the resources of the Kremlin and the wealth of the Russian Orthodox Church.

The answer to the first question was obvious. Putin had struck a mutually beneficial understanding with Russian Orthodox patriarch Kirill that united the church and the state in a deep and intertwined fashion. To be Russian meant to be Orthodox, and to be Orthodox meant being loyal to the Russian state. I argued repeatedly inside the State Department that the US government should have no official opinion on the ecclesiastical question owing to its lack of competency to sort theological questions, either domestically or internationally, and a general sense of noninterference in ecclesiastical matters. The Russian propaganda machine constantly labeled Bartholomew as a CIA puppet, so it was important for the United States to be discreet about its interests there without creating false signs that Bartholomew was an American puppet. But as a diplomatic matter, if certain ecclesiastical decisions led to violence, the United States should not be caught off guard if religion-infused mass violence were in the offing, or in the worst case, an expanded invasion by Russia. Putin was volatile and unpredictable. We did not need to be in the business of creating false impressions that might provide cover, no matter how far-fetched, for Putin to act rashly in the name of countering alleged US interference in internal Orthodox religious matters.[15]

The second question was more complex and needed a calibrated approach. Our role was to take that approach and to provide analysis that could help make our diplomacy smarter. This was especially true since a large part of the Putin-Kirill platform was that the United States was exporting global secular decadence in the form of anti-Christian propaganda. Anything that looked like Western "interference" in Ukraine was easy fodder for the Russian propaganda machine. Luckily for us, Ambassador Pyatt; former ambassador to Ukraine John Tefft, who was by then our ambassador to Russia; and Assistant Secretary Nuland all knew that religious dynamics were woven throughout the Russia-Ukraine issue set, and we were able to chart a course through the political, religious, and diplomatic thicket here.

Before answering Ambassador Pyatt's invitation to come to Ukraine, I had to consume a lot of information about the religious dynamics there. Despite occasional sniping from a small circle of scholars about our work, the overwhelming reaction among American religion scholars to our work was positive. Sadly, the study of Orthodox thought and institutions in the West has not prospered in recent decades. I'm embarrassed to say that modern Orthodox thought is not a routine part of most American graduate theological education. In my case, I had a rare good education in early Christian thought, a period long before the Great Schism between eastern and western Christianity in 1054 CE, beginning in my undergraduate days at Abilene Christian through my first stint at Harvard Divinity School. Yet in my contemporary study of religion, Orthodox thought was not a robust part of the training. So, I had some catching up to do.

In addition to a wealth of resources from research offices in the State Department and in the intelligence community on the contemporary religious and political dynamics of the Orthodox world, I was able to turn to a number of current religion scholars for some tutoring. Will Storrar, director of the Center for Theological Inquiry in Princeton, New Jersey, put together an all-day seminar for me and a staff member on contemporary Orthodox thought and international politics that was immensely helpful. Scholars such as Aristotle Papanikolaou, Vera Shevzov, John Burgess, Robin Lovin, Nadieszda Kizenko, and others jump-started my immersion into the intricacies of contemporary religious dynamics of Ukraine.[16]

My trip to Ukraine in many ways was a sort of template for how we tried to generate an analysis of how complex religious dynamics were woven into a vexing diplomatic problem where the consequences could be catastrophic. A full-blown Russian invasion, beyond Crimea and the Donbass region in the east, could have spun into a global conflagration. Our lengthy preparation was led by our European regional adviser, Jennifer Wistrand. Our consultation with and invitation from Ambassador Pyatt ensured that we would see and talk to as many religious actors on the ground as possible in the kaleidoscopic religious landscape of Ukraine. At a minimum, we hoped that our contribution would stave off any unforced error stemming from ignorance of just how volatile the Orthodox dynamics were.

We spent an exhausting week in Ukraine visiting dozens of parties. Suffice it to say that while Orthodoxy is the dominant religious community in Ukraine, the country as a whole has a very pluralistic collage of religions. And I tried to meet most of them. To its credit, the country has a national religious council, independent of the government, with a leadership that rotates among the religions. This is fairly rare in many parts of the world. The two major branches of Orthodoxy are represented on the council, making it the rare enterprise where they collaborate. Ukraine has the opportunity to build on this religious pluralism, to remain officially independent from any single ecclesiastical domination of the state, and to try and find a unique path in that part of the world.

My major concern was the rift between the Moscow Patriarchate, led by Metropolitan Onuphrius, and the Kyivan Patriarchate, led by Metropolitan Filaret. My meetings with the leadership of each were not boring encounters. I had met Filaret's representative in my office at State some months before. Sporting an impressive flaming-red beard, the priest was a moose of a man. I am not exactly small, but in his flowing black robe and large black hat, he overwhelmed me with his bulk. When he met our black embassy van at the street curb, he bear-hugged me when I stepped out of the vehicle, lifting me off the ground like I was a rag doll, and kissed both of my cheeks. I think he was glad to see me. Metropolitan Filaret had a flair for the dramatic like many national religious figures sometimes do, and he regaled me with stories and general showmanship. He clearly enjoyed the role of entertaining US government officials from Washington. And I got the distinct impression he thought Patriarch Bartholomew was going to unite the disparate Orthodox churches and that he, Filaret, would end up leading that united church.

My meeting with the representative of the Moscow Patriarchate was even more interesting. Metropolitan Onuphrius was in Moscow at the time, so I had to meet with his second while he was out of the country. In contrast to my meeting with the gregarious Filaret, my meeting at the Moscow Patriarchate Church was stiff, formal, and orchestrated. I was led into a formal room with a large table, with at least twenty Orthodox priests on one side and just me on the other side. Normally these sorts of formal meetings start with introductions by both parties and then a short welcome by the host. The surrogate's welcome was quite long, read from a stack of papers at least two inches thick. It soon began to look like he would be reading for our entire hour. At the fifteen-minute mark, or so, one of the priests at one end of the table coughed quite conspicuously and frowned at the host, who quickly shut up. I was startled by this, because in American meetings people at the table are arranged in descending order of importance, so to me it looked like one of the corporals was making rude gestures at the general.

I decided to throw the surrogate a curveball. Since it was clear this opening soliloquy was supposed to be some sort of signal of my lack of importance, I decided to take a pastoral approach. The host's hands had starting shaking as he had read his printed remarks. For whatever reason, he seemed to be under tremendous stress. It occurred to me that since he was subbing for his boss, who was in Moscow, the phalanx of priests was probably closer to the boss than he was, and they were there to monitor him as much as they were there to give me the cold shoulder. I began by saying I understood how the current political climate presented a huge set of pastoral issues for Metropolitan Onuphrius and their whole community. He had recently committed a public faux pas when he did not stand for the playing of a song remembering the Ukrainian soldiers who had died fighting the Russian invaders in the Donbass region. This was widely interpreted to signal his support for the Russian invasion. Orthodox churches affiliated with Moscow were reported to be losing significant members to churches affiliated with the Kyivan Patriarchate. And if Patriarch Bartholomew declared a new Ukrainian Orthodox Church, Moscow would lose churches and money.

I went on to say that I had sympathy for his political and ecclesiastical conundrums, given the bad choices that had been made. I asked him what he thought was going to happen regarding the Orthodox Church. At that point the surrogate got back to his talking points on why the Russian Orthodox was the true Orthodox church in Ukraine. But I was able to see firsthand just how anxious the Russian Patriarchate Church in Ukraine was about what Bartholomew might be doing, the implications of Putin's invasion in driving people away from the Moscow Patriarchate churches, as well as their recognition that the United States was aware of their anxiety.

Later, in June 2016, I had two opportunities to meet one on one with Patriarch Bartholomew to get his assessment of what was going on in Ukraine. The first encounter was in Crete at the Pan-Orthodox Council called by the ecumenical patriarch. The formal title of the gathering was the Holy and Great Council of the Orthodox Church, and it was a historic assembly of representative bishops of the autocephalous churches of Eastern Orthodox Christianity. The Russian Orthodox Church decided not to attend the synod in protest against Bartholomew. I was invited as an informal observer, and I had a private audience with Bartholomew after the conclusion of the council. When I met Bartholomew, he was exhausted but ebullient. Despite the last-minute refusal by the Russians to attend, he had successfully demonstrated his leadership and authority across the Orthodox world and had beaten the Russian attempt to undermine his official status and had resisted Russian efforts to prevent him from having the authority to declare a single Ukrainian Orthodox Church.

We had a warm conversation in which the very tired patriarch beamed with satisfaction that the synod had held the Orthodox Church together and that a path toward unity in Ukraine was still viable. When I asked him how he would make the decision regarding uniting the three Orthodox churches in Ukraine, he said his sole criterion was how to best preserve the unity of the church. And by that I took him to mean the unity of the church in Ukraine and globally. In other words, he wanted the Moscow Patriarchate Church to unite with the Kyivan Patriarchate into one church, and he wanted the Russian Orthodox Church not to interfere. He was very careful not to give me any sense of his timeline, which I understood and respected. But I knew the crude last-minute boycott of the Russians was an attempt to render the synod and Bartholomew politically weakened and any attempt on his part to declare autocephaly impossible. Their ploy clearly failed, and Bartholomew was now in a strong position politically and ecclesiastically to keep moving forward.

Shortly after the synod, Bartholomew was nearly a victim of a political event he could not have anticipated. On July 15, 2016, there was a coup attempt in Turkey designed to depose Turkey's prime minister, Recep Tayyip Erdogan. Unfortunately, the patriarch had flown out of Istanbul for a long-standing vacation trip to western Europe on the evening of the failed coup. Bartholomew had to extend his vacation in fear that the Erdogan government would arrest him upon his return for allegedly being a part of the coup and fleeing when he saw it was failing. This charge was untrue, but it did raise concern in the Department of State that Bartholomew might suffer unacceptable consequences. As part of the US government's response to the Erdogan postcoup crackdown, I was one of a series of senior Washington-based diplomats who traveled to Turkey to show the government we were concerned about the country-wide crackdowns. I met with Bartholomew in Istanbul to see how he was faring under Erdogan's wrath and to send a not-so-subtle signal to the government that we cared a lot about the ecumenical patriarch's status.

I was very happy to see a well-rested friend. He assured me that he was not under any new pressure in the aftermath of the failed coup. I also was able to visit the famous Halki Orthodox Seminary, which the Turks had long since shut down as an active seminary as part of their anti-Greek policies. It was a good time for me to consolidate my thoughts about what was going on in Ukraine. First, after the two conversations with the ecumenical patriarch, I became convinced he was on a path to declare autocephaly for a united Ukrainian Orthodox Church, but he probably wasn't clear in his own mind when he was going to do that. I was proven correct when he made this move on January 5, 2019. My second conclusion, which I had come to a bit earlier, was that the United States had to be prepared for Putin to respond in anger at any such declaration. I think it was one of our signal policy successes to raise the possibility that Putin might react very poorly if this decision had been made on Obama's watch. It was precisely the sort of issue that might appear so esoteric to White House foreign policy staff, who might not be attuned to the significance of this seemingly intramural religious spat, that they would miss it and walk into a blunder. Luckily, between our ambassadors in Ukraine and Russia, Assistant Secretary for European and Eurasian Affairs Victoria Nuland, and our staff, we were able to make sure the issue got the scrutiny it deserved at the State Department and the White House.

This is not the place nor do I have the time to comment extensively on Putin's 2022 invasion of Ukraine. But it is important to note that in many of Putin's statements of grievances before the invasion he has argued that the separation of Russia and Ukraine reflects a rupture in the unity of Russian Orthodoxy. For him, restoring greater Russia includes erasing any separate Orthodox Churches in Ukraine and uniting them with the Russian Orthodox Church. We now know that is part of his web of arguments used to justify the invasion.[17]

The last case to look at in our work at the intersection of religion and conflict goes back to my very earliest days at State. I mentioned earlier that the same month I started, July 2013, the National Security Council Directorate for Global Engagement released a document entitled "National Strategy for Integrating Religious Leader and Religious Community Engagement into U.S. Foreign Policy." The directorate, under the guidance of Shaarik Zafar, had been working on this document for several months through an interagency group called, in the elegant jargon of the National Security Council, the Interagency Policy Council, or an IPC for short. I knew nothing about this effort before landing at State and made no material contribution to its production. But I soon discovered that everyone involved with its writing, as well as everyone on the secretary's Civil Society Working Group working on religion and diplomacy, assumed I would be the primary holder and driver of this policy. This was a role I was happy to play.

The advantage of having a White House–produced strategy is obvious. I could refer to the document whenever I got resistance from anyone in the executive branch. I was also free to interpret the document in pretty much any fashion that served the interests of the Office of Religion and Global Affairs. Add to this the all-points document, called an ALDAC, that Secretary Kerry sent out to all US State Department embassies and posts around the globe, describing our mission and asking everyone to take our calls and play nicely with us, and we were launched with as strong a set of mandates and permissions as any office in the State Department. I didn't have to do much persuading to get an audience across the administration or beyond it. What I had not planned on was a codicil in the strategy that called for doing a series of three religious-engagement country studies at the outset of the strategy. There was no money designated for these studies, and I had no staff! I had to scramble quickly. In one of the early IPC meetings among about twenty different agencies and offices across the national security apparatus, I left the meeting with a legal pad with a list of forty-five suggested countries for the three-religion country studies! This was my introduction to the interagency process! No money or staff, and forty-two too many countries to survey and study! After some frank discussions, I chose Ethiopia as our first test case and proceeded to beg, borrow, and steal resources to put together a team and hit the road.

Two of the rites of passage in my childhood were learning to read a road map and then, in a more advanced skill, learning to read a topographical map and navigating a path from one point to another with a compass. These skills were taught such that one day on a family trip Dad would toss the map into your lap and say, "What's the best route to St. Louis?" And suddenly you are the navigator. It never occurred to me to ask who made the maps. As a diplomat, I was now in the map-making business. The map making wasn't about physical topography; it was now about crafting landscapes of religious communities. Ethiopia would prove to be an excellent training ground. One of the work products we commended to posts was a country religious landscape. This was a document that outlined the major and minor religious communities, including brief histories, who their leaders were, how to contact them, and a running record of how often embassy staff interacted with them. As embassies routinely engage as many political parties and civil society organizations as possible, and on an ongoing basis, it makes sense to maintain such networks among religious communities, not only in case of national emergencies but also for a deeper understanding of the myriad ways these communities influence the whole of society and raise diplomatic issues over time. In Ethiopia, such an understanding might have better prepared our diplomats to anticipate the unrest in certain sectors of the Muslim community and might have prepared them to offer better counsel to the Ethiopian government sooner.

Likewise, not to jump too far ahead, if the embassy in Addis Ababa had expanded on the network we helped them build and develop, it might have had a stronger grasp of the influence of a Pentecostal version of the prosperity gospel embraced by the current prime minister, Abiy Ahmed (and his Prosperity Party), and how that particular tradition might have fed his thirst for committing possible atrocities.[18]

During the months we were preparing for a ten-day visit to Ethiopia, several fortuitous things happened. First, I met a senior minister in the Ethiopian government, Shiferaw Teklemariam, who was visiting some senior leaders in the Bureau of Conflict Stabilization Operations at State. Deputy Assistant Secretaries Patricia Haslach and Jerry White served as hosts for the small gathering. Pat would soon be named ambassador to Ethiopia, and she would be our host and partner once we made our trip. The focus of the discussion was on the recent controversy in Ethiopia in which several thousand Muslims had peacefully demonstrated against the government's harsh treatment and scrutiny of their mosques and leaders across the country.

Despite their constitution's talk of freedom of assembly and religion, the on-the-ground reality was much different. Imams were appointed and sermons were regulated by the state. The state ran an official national board of Muslim leaders and kept them under close watch. These events were close enough in time to the Arab Spring to make the national government nervous, especially since it was dominated by Orthodox Christians, not Muslims. Add to this a lot of US-based rhetoric on countering violent extremism in Muslim countries, and you suddenly had a nervous government, used to exercising complete political control, creating an atmosphere of possible government miscalculation. The government responded to the demonstrations by arresting many Muslim leaders and holding them in prison for an extended time. Eventually many were convicted and imprisoned as terrorists while most were released. The rule of law appeared to many Muslims to be nowhere in sight. In the course of the meeting, Minister Shiferaw officially invited me to come to Ethiopia to assess the government's response to the protesters and offer my advice to him. I was pleasantly surprised by his offer, and it helped to cement the embassy's commitment to making our visit a success.

Second, we developed a process of preparation for these sorts of visits that usually entailed a checklist of tasks like the following.

Surveying the State Department views and cables. It is hard to overstate the volume of papers being constantly produced by embassies and posts, to say nothing of the multitude of other State Department offices. A single Washington-based diplomat has hours of instantly available analysis to consume in preparation for a visit. It is very easy to get a feel for the current views within the executive branch on any given issue in any given space around the world. There is a reason academics who join the State Department tend not to write very much during their diplomatic tenures. And that is because there is too much internally produced material to read to do your job well. Doing your homework Stateside is hard work. If events are happening quickly on-site, a diplomat can struggle to digest all the information being generated.

Establishing points of contact with the embassy or consulate. Building strong staff ties to the host embassy is just as important as learning all you can learn. I once visited an embassy on a one-day, single-mission trip, the purpose of which I can't talk about. Out and back in a little over twenty-four hours. It was a sensitive trip on a sensitive issue, and the ambassador did not want me to come and made that quite clear. When I landed, my control officer told me the ambassador was out of the country and I had to meet with the deputy chief of mission before I had my single appointment outside the embassy. When I was led back to the senior offices on the secure side of the security doors, I passed the cell phone grid box where staffers had to leave their cell phones before they entered. Often, the upper-left-hand slot was reserved for the ambassador's cell phone. If his or her phone was in the box, it meant he or she was in the building. As I passed the box, I saw the ambassador's phone in the specially labeled slot. The ambassador was in the building! But the ambassador clearly didn't want to see me.

The deputy chief of mission (DCM) gave me a stern talking to and reminded me my control officer would be in my meeting and would take copious notes. I assured the DCM I would stick to my script and would not go off the reservation. I complied, had a short, fruitful discussion, and got back on the plane to the States. I hasten to add that this was a very unusual occurrence. We always worked hard with staff on the ground weeks ahead of time if possible, in order to leverage the amazing talent in our embassies. If we had clarity of mission and a strong day-to-day schedule worked out in advance with posts, we were almost always successful in our missions. Most ambassadors went with us because we often got meetings they had a hard time getting, and they got to meet a range of religious actors they often had not met themselves.

Engaging religion scholars. This was routine. In the Ethiopian case, I knew the work of Terje Ostebo, a professor at the University of Florida. He graciously came to Washington to meet with me and gave me an extraordinary briefing on his years of work in Ethiopia and in the Horn of Africa. We also met with a group of Africa scholars from the Washington, DC, area. I want to make clear that they in no way were endorsing any particular US policy; rather, they were trying to make us smarter, perhaps less error-prone, and to point us to the best analysis of religious and political dynamics of our destination. I tried to make it clear that I did not assume their willingness to talk to us meant they were endorsing any policies of the Obama administration.

Engaging other interested parties before we traveled. Talking with NGOs was incredibly helpful because it allowed us to learn what sorts of work was going on in the country, and it allowed the NGOs to comment on the religious dynamics in the country based on their experience. In similar fashion, we spoke with the various offices represented at the Interagency Policy Council to get an understanding of how they worked in the country and what lessons they had learned. We also spoke to religious leaders we knew in the United States or other countries to glean their perspectives on the religious dynamics of the country being studied.

We gathered other information, including how religious communities related to the relevant country, regional, and domestic history and what the policies of various US government entities were, especially the White House, Congress, and the rest of the State Department. When possible, we met with diaspora groups here in the United States. We learned quickly that diasporas were often quite active politically with regard to their countries of origin and were rarely united in their views of both US policy and domestic politics in their home country.

The ultimate goal of embassy visits was to demonstrate how to engage as wide a menu of religious communities as possible, and in doing that, expand the number of relationships embassies could build with these communities. Most people do not realize that while embassies attempt to represent the United States to their host countries, embassies also interpret and explain the host country back to the US government. If religion is a powerful force in the life and politics of a country, the US government needs to understand those dynamics in order to relate to that country. Embassies that "don't do religion" in countries where religion is a significant part of social and political life are bound not to fully understand what is going on there. At its worst, this sort of ignorance may have a body count attached to it.

Once we got to Ethiopia, we spent two weeks on a whirlwind trip across the country, with dozens of meetings with a kaleidoscope of people. Three visits stand out in my memory now. We met with members of the government-sponsored Muslim council. It was a warm meeting, and they were keen to display a stance of comity with the government. I knew they had to be under significant duress from the government in light of the public demonstrations and subsequent crackdown. At the end of our meeting, I asked them whether I could meet leaders at the mosque in Addis Ababa, where the demonstrations seemed to be the largest and most visible. A lot of pained glances were exchanged by hosts. I had clearly touched a nerve, as one of their delegation whipped out a cell phone and left the room. After several minutes of private discussion, they said I could visit the mosque and they would call me later with a time. They called back later to say that the meeting could not be arranged.

I was not surprised by this. I don't want to overinterpret this, but it was clear the wounds from the unrest two years before had not healed and the government was too nervous to let me meet with some of the leaders of the protests.

The second memorable meeting came on an overnight trip we took outside Addis, accompanied by Ambassador Haslach. In this city we met the mayor and a number of religious leaders to get a perspective beyond the capital. We had a casual coffee at an outdoor café with two citizens who had made State Department–sponsored tours in the United States. Back in that day, some eighty thousand international visitors came to the United States for a two-week visit to see and learn about American society every year. It is one of the best programs the State Department runs. Over the decades, the number of international visitors who go on to be political leaders in their own countries after being on these trips is phenomenal. We routinely met alumni of these programs when we were abroad. In the middle of our very interesting conversation, one of the alumni shifted topics on a dime, away from his account of what he thought was going on in Ethiopia. The rest of the conversation was dramatically more mundane. He called our control officer later in the day to apologize to the ambassador. It turns out he noted two men at the table next to us whom he recognized as government agents. It seems the government took a keen interest in our presence. It was a disturbing but instructive moment for me to realize this. Most Foreign Service officers I suspect have had multiple experiences when they knew they were being monitored by host governments and took it in stride to be careful and not to be too upset by it. My rookie status, my Western academic privilege, and my lingering small-town naïveté combined to leave me shocked. I was also worried that my conversation partners might face negative repercussions from the Ethiopian government.

The third meeting was with embassy staff. Most Americans do not realize that the largest contingent of staff in most US embassies is locally employed, that is, citizens of the host country. I had a long, deeply informative conversation with a large number of them in our embassy. These conversations represent a chance to get a more ground-level view of religious and political dynamics than just relying on the opinions of religious leaders, who are overwhelmingly male, represent the official views of religious communities, and are often, frankly, at some remove from the lived religious experiences of the majority of adherents. In my experience, there is almost always some distance between the official version of religious leaders and the version on the ground, and for diplomatic purposes, the word on the street may carry far more interesting insights.

Near the end of our time in Ethiopia, I went with Ambassador Haslach to meet with Minister Shiferaw to discuss my preliminary assessment. I had three simple recommendations. First, abide by the rights your constitution purports to embrace regarding freedom of assembly and freedom of religion. If you discriminate against Muslims, that only creates more friction between Orthodox Christianity and Islam. Second, practice the rule of law. Rounding up public dissenters and holding them without charging them violates your commitment to the rule of law and risks making you a pariah state. And finally, these sorts of behaviors only contribute to the pressures you most fear. Injustice is not a long-term strategy. It only creates more political unrest. The growing religious pluralism, to say nothing of its dizzying ethnic pluralism, can be a great national asset, and should not be treated as a political threat.

As I recall, Shiferaw listened intently, didn't offer much commentary, and thanked me for my time and suggestions. In the end, I never expected that our trip would somehow convince the government to change its behavior dramatically; that is rarely how diplomacy works. But I think there were several positive outcomes. We showed a smart embassy team how to expand their knowledge of Ethiopia's religious landscape and deepen their understanding of the complex and powerful religious voices there. I believe these relationships yielded actionable knowledge for the embassy. We also helped our ambassador strengthen her ties to senior government officials and national religious leaders. And we showed a significant number of civil society actors that the embassy was genuinely interested in establishing long-term relationships with them.

Our trip to Ethiopia allowed us to begin to craft our means of researching a country, hone our methods of engagement while in country, and think about concrete products we could produce for interested parties in the US government. I knew we had to find ways to share our knowledge with policy makers domestically if our work was to have impact beyond the embassy or post level. Inside the department, this meant sending summary notes of findings to the senior leaders and functional offices that dealt with cross-cutting issues. We often held posttrip debriefings with any interested parties across the department, but also with the National Security Council, the Pentagon, the CIA, and USAID. This helped build out our relationships across the many people interested in the diplomatic implications of religion. And sometimes what we learned was important to pass on to Secretary Kerry.

I intended this chapter to do a number of things. I want to make clear that we were not exclusively the "Religion and Conflict Office," as some thought we were or might be. We did not traffic in farcical stereotypes of good religion and bad religion or nostrums about peaceful religions and violent religions. Instead, as I have shown in these three cases, the role of religion in conflicts was always complex, irreducible to shallow prebaked theories, and woven into all sorts of social, political, and historical forces. The list of places of conflict we worked to varying degrees is long and includes Myanmar, Northern Ireland, Sri Lanka, El Salvador, Cyprus, Kazakhstan, China, Nigeria, Benin, Turkey, Iraq, Syria, and Yemen. I often get what I have come to call the "burning building" question: "Did you ever save any lives?" I find that an odd question, but the short answer is yes, but I can't talk about them. But that was not our normal work.

The next chapter is similar to this one in that it tells of three different lines of work on cross-cutting issues: anticorruption in Nigeria, helping to reestablish ties with Cuba, and working with the Vatican. I have shown how we addressed the global cross-cutting issues of refugee resettlement and global climate change, religion and conflict in three specific settings. Now I will turn to case studies of opportunities that emerged after the start of Obama's second term that, frankly, I did not anticipate at the outset of my tenure at State.

Chapter Eight

RESPONDING TO THE UNIVERSE

E VERY PRESIDENT AND EVERY SECRETARY of state attempts to develop a set of foreign policy priorities at the outset of each term. It is perhaps the first and last time any US foreign policy leader has any semblance of control over world affairs. History has a way of shredding even the wisest and most prudential plans. This chapter could have borne the title "Surprises," in that each of the three topics I will cover, the Vatican, Cuba, and Nigeria, was, to some degree, not on the radar when I was offered the job at State in late winter 2013. The resignation of Pope Benedict XVI on February 20, 2013, and the election of Pope Francis on March 12, 2013, galvanized the world. And on May 29, 2015, when Mohammadu Buhari was elected president of Nigeria, the international community was similarly shocked. President Obama's restoration of diplomatic relations with Cuba on July 20, 2015, capped a period of secret conversations that also took the world by surprise. Each of these events opened opportunities for us in the Office of Religion and Global Affairs to swiftly leverage our expertise and make significant contributions to our diplomacy. Only the installation of Pope Francis dealt overtly with religion, yet religious dynamics were at play in all three areas when it came to US diplomacy. I hope to display some of the nimbleness we had to add value to issues that from the outset did not appear to be fruitful lines of engagement for us, yet in time we were able to make significant contributions.

Pope Francis's election occurred in the interregnum between my being hired at State and my waiting for security clearance to come through in May. My mind was a million miles away from Vatican political intrigue in that period. I noted his election, which surprised many observers, but was distracted by completing the spring semester teaching at Wesley. I didn't have much of a sense of the change in tone that was about to emerge when Francis was installed. My knowledge of Pope Benedict's diplomatic efforts was limited to the controversy he created in a speech with some negative remarks about Islam. My knowledge about his papacy tended to be limited to liberal Catholic outrage at his attempts to corral alleged heterodox theologians.

That all changed for me once I landed at State. Very early in my days there, I was visited by Steve Colecchi, director of the Office of International Justice and Peace of the US Conference of Catholic Bishops. He was the chief foreign policy expert for the bishops and a good friend. I was a bit anxious to see him in my official capacity because this was precisely the moment when the bishops were locked in a complex fight with the White House over the contraception mandate. I was afraid he was coming to tell me his bosses would not meet with me due to the White House imbroglio. Much to my relief, he told me the conference wanted to work with Kerry whenever and wherever they could. They would be able to bracket out their vexation with the White House while working with us. I was quite pleased, and so was Kerry. Steve proved to be helpful on several important policy issues.

I also paid a personal call to Cardinal Wuerl, the archbishop of Washington, who gave me a very warm welcome. I should also say that I crossed paths with Cardinal McCarrick a handful of times, almost always when I was on the road attending various public meetings. He was incredibly kind to me, in small and large meetings. He was always complimentary. It was pretty clear in time that he was something of an independent actor in the church and around the world, contrary to my childhood low-church Protestant assumption that the Roman Catholic Church was so hierarchical that everyone had a direct supervisor and the chain of command went from the Vatican all the way to the pew, no matter how remote the location of the pew. What we now know he did was outrageous, and the harm he inflicted on his victims was unspeakable. And how he was able to elude supervision and accountability is still incomprehensible to me.

In my first days at State, in early August, when Kerry held a public rollout event for me, I met Ken Hackett, our Vatican ambassador nominee. Ken had served for decades for Catholic Relief Services (CRS), capping his career as president of CRS. Obama could not have named a better ambassador, as he had decades of providing humanitarian relief and walking the hallways of the Vatican. We hit it off instantly, and I learned something from Ken in every conversation we had. He would prove to be a strong advocate for our work.

As mentioned earlier, my first trip to the Vatican while accompanying Kerry to meet Parolin was to be the first of several interactions with the Vatican over the course of S/RGA's life. By choosing a veteran of the Vatican diplomatic corps, Archbishop Pietro Parolin, to be his secretary of state, Francis made it clear he wanted to revive the moribund Vatican diplomatic apparatus. Parolin's predecessor, Cardinal Bertone, was part of the Vatican Bank scandal and was widely seen as a weak secretary of state. Parolin was a breath of fresh air and has been a strong partner in implementing the pope's early global reforms. Victoria Nuland, the assistant secretary of Europe and Eurasian affairs, was in the meeting, too, and she saw the new possibilities of a deeper relationship with the Vatican.

I have already mentioned my ill-fated attempt to set up a global event on refugees with the Vatican and the Organization of Islamic Cooperation.

Over the years I think US diplomacy has struggled to know how to view and how to engage the Vatican. This is due, in part, to the changing global context, changing secretaries of state, changing popes, and changing presidents. But the stars were aligned in my time at State. I should hasten to add that in our suite, Amy Lillis monitored the daily relationship between S/RGA and our embassy to the Holy See. Having a career diplomat of her stature minding the relationship was of incalculable value. Among many other things, she developed ties to our embassy staff and to working staff across the complex bureaucracy of the Vatican.

Over the course of my travels, I had the opportunity to meet with many powerful cardinals, or archbishops who later became cardinals. I made a quick trip to Honduras to meet with Cardinal Rodriguez, who had been president of Caritas Internationalis, the global Catholic charity, to discuss possible funding for relocating former Guantanamo Bay detainees. I met with Archbishop Souraphiel (now a cardinal) in Addis Ababa, while on my Ethiopia trip, where we talked about the influential role the Catholic Church played in several leading institutions around the country. Later, when Ethiopia exploded into a civil war in early November 2020, Souraphiel was in a position to help mediate between the warring parties, but I do not think our embassy there nor the Trump foreign policy apparatus had the knowledge or the relationships to see whether he might have been helpful. I represented the United States at the beatification of Oscar Romero, the martyred archbishop in El Salvador. During the Mass, I sat on the altar with Representative Jim McGovern of Massachusetts and witnessed a crowd of several hundred thousand, most of whom had traveled there by foot to remember their national hero. McGovern had been traveling to El Salvador since the '80s when he was a staffer for Representative Joe Moakley. Before the Mass started, we stood at the edge of the altar looking out on the VIPs, some of whom probably participated in the machinations to kill Romero, and also looking out at the exuberant crowd. I asked him if he could have ever imagined this day when Romero's path to sainthood would happen. And he told me never in his wildest dreams.

Whenever I passed through Rome, I tried to tack on an extra day to check in with our embassy and do some door-to-door diplomacy in the Vatican. One of my favorite stops was with Archbishop Silvano Tomasi, who was the permanent observer of the Holy See to the United Nations Office and other international organizations in Geneva from 2003 to 2016. After his service at the UN, Pope Francis brought him back to Rome to begin consolidating several Vatican departments into one large entity, the Dicastery for Promoting Integral Human Development.[1] This reorganization of the Curia consolidated a number of smaller units, including one related to refugees, whose effectiveness had apparently been assessed as inadequate for the emerging global needs. Pope Francis appointed Cardinal Peter Turkson of Ghana to lead the discastery, but Tomasi was to consolidate the existing departments into one larger unit. Prior to his diplomatic work, he was the founding director of the Center for Migration Studies in New York and also served as the director of pastoral care of migrants and refugees at the US Conference of Catholic Bishops in Washington.

I always found Cardinal Tomasi to be warm, open, honest, and direct. That is not always the case with international diplomatic veterans! I loved Tomasi's low-key candor and impishness. The fact that he gave great answers only whetted my appetite for asking him more direct questions. He managed to tell me that Pope Francis had asked him to organize the new dicastery but told him he couldn't fire anyone from the four offices that were being united! A few years later I asked him in a meeting at Georgetown University how he would characterize the pope's progress on his dialogue with the

Muslim world. He smiled at me and said, "Shaun, you always ask me the complicated questions!" His answers always reflected the studiousness of his Fordham PhD as well as his years of service as a Vatican diplomat in Africa and in Geneva. I also sensed great satisfaction on his part that the Vatican was consolidating and expanding its resources in addressing the growing refugee crisis, his signature scholarly and ecclesiastical issue. Pope Francis has been described as a pope in a hurry, and that is supported by the diplomatic resurgence and strong leadership he has elevated among the Curia. In all my interaction with the Vatican, I had the strong counsel of Ambassador Hackett and my former doctoral adviser at Harvard, Fr. Bryan Hehir, answering my questions and giving me sage advice. Hehir would figure in my story about Cuba, which I will get to later.

On my last trip to Rome with Kerry in December 2016, I had two unusual encounters. The whole visit was unusual on the face of it. The Vatican had requested Kerry to come for a private meeting with the pope. The embassy staff told me they had no record of the pope meeting with a foreign minister of any country alone, without the head of state being present as well. I rode with Kerry from the hotel to the Vatican. There wasn't time to write any kind of memo, so Secretary Kerry quizzed me on the ride over what I thought was on the pope's mind. Having worked my information networks, I thought it was pretty clear the pope wanted an unvarnished view of the president-elect. Kerry then asked me if it would just be the two of them alone. I answered that was my understanding, but there might be a priest present to help with any translation issues. Kerry said, "Good." I obviously was not in that meeting, nor have I ever had the chance to ask him about it. I did get to meet the pope immediately after the meeting. Usually on the rare occasions I have met global leaders of any type, I try to think a lot about what I will say ahead of time. I have to confess, when I met Pope Francis my mind went absolutely blank! I am sure I babbled something nonembarrassing (I hope), but to be honest, I really don't know. After the short moment, Kerry went his way to more Rome meetings and I headed back to our embassy.

In my time at the embassy I got to have a final conversation with Ambassador Hackett, and also one with a senior embassy staffer who asked me a very interesting question: Would I convey a question back to the Trump administration on behalf of the Vatican, via a US Catholic leader? I was stunned, to put it mildly. Why would the Vatican choose me as the courier of a question to the nascent Trump administration via a US Catholic leader? I'm still puzzled. I suspect the answer was that they trusted me since I was so closely associated with Kerry. But they had to know I was hardly a neutral party. The Vatican wanted to convey their desire to have a career diplomat appointed by the Trump administration to the Holy See and not the usual political appointee. This was apparently not the first time such a request was made by the Vatican. For them it would be a sign that the United States saw the Holy See as worthy of the stature of having a career diplomat and not a political appointee. I was skeptical about being the alleged courier of the Vatican's request. Nevertheless, when I got back to the State Department, I met with Ambassador Thomas Shannon, the undersecretary of political affairs, the senior Foreign Service officer at State. Tom listened carefully, as he always did. After telling him the tale, I asked whether I should contact a friend at the US Conference of Catholic Bishops and see if he would ask the Trump camp to relay the Vatican request to the president-elect himself. Tom said he saw no harm in me approaching my friend.

I called my friend, who in turn asked a senior American cardinal who knew Trump, if he would relay the message to Trump personally. The account I got back was that the senior cleric made the call to the president-elect and was told, thanks, but no thanks, they already had a nominee in mind! As most people know, that pick was Callista Gingrich, wife of Newt Gingrich, the former Speaker of the US House of Representatives. This was as political a choice as any political ambassador would have been. Suffice it to say, the Vatican's hopes were not met in this selection. I will not rehearse the entirety of her term but focus on her emphasis on religious freedom, particularly on an episode near the end of Trump's presidency. This story is important because it reveals the extent to which electoral politics colonized US diplomacy in the Trump era, and it demonstrates the deep repair chore the Biden administration faced at the beginning of its time in office.

As I have written about earlier, one of the central grifts among Trump's many grifts was the public campaign by Trump to exploit the theme of supporting religious freedom while simultaneously actively limiting the religious freedom of millions of people around the world. This was all done to cement even deeper ties with his most loyal voter base in the United States, white evangelical Christians. In the end, this political strategy failed, for despite robust support from these Christian fundamentalists, he still lost the popular vote and the Electoral College vote. The embassy to the Holy See was caught up in promoting the religious freedom political strategy in very dramatic and public fashion near the very end of the Trump presidency.

In the middle of the 2020 presidential race, Secretary of State Mike Pompeo published an article on the website of an obscure right-wing anti-Francis Catholic publication, *First Things*, titled "China's Catholics and the Church's Moral Witness."[2] The short piece essentially accuses the Vatican of failing its mission to promote religious freedom before the repressive Chinese government and instead capitulating to the increasingly aggressive moves of the Chinese Communist Party against all religious groups, including the Catholic Church. The source of Pompeo's wrath was the announcement that the Vatican was meeting soon to negotiate the renewal of a 2018 private agreement between the Vatican and Beijing regarding the appointment of Catholic bishops in China. Pompeo opined that the earlier agreement, the details of which were never made public, had failed to stop the march of religious oppression in China against Catholics and others.

This was as stunning an intentional break in international diplomacy among allies as I can recall. Pompeo was calling Francis a failure on religious freedom and a coward in the face of Chinese repression. He was doing this in public less than two weeks before he was to headline a conference on international religious freedom in Rome, sponsored by the US embassy to the Holy See and where senior Vatican officials were to speak. If Pompeo really believed the Vatican needed a reprimand, he should have delivered it face-to-face privately. But the real purpose, and this is doubly astonishing, was to curry political favor with disaffected American critics of Pope Francis in the upcoming presidential race. Veteran Vatican observer and journalist John Allen, while downplaying the long-term impact of Pompeo's overtly political stunt, admitted that the move was unusual.[3]

That Pompeo would risk insulting the Vatican in order to score cheap political points based on a dubious gamble that American Catholics who were disgruntled about Pope Francis shows not only that he is a poor diplomat, but that he is even a worse politician because he believed such a move made any political sense. Only days after the *First Things* article appeared, Pompeo delivered a set of remarks in Rome where Cardinal Parolin and Archbishop Gallagher were present, essentially repeating the gist of the article, just in case the Vatican had not read his earlier piece. In later meetings, Pompeo revealed he pressed the Vatican to take a stronger stand against Chinese repression of religious groups. Press reports conveyed the Vatican's heartburn over Pompeo's boorish behavior and also denied Pompeo's request for a papal audience.[4]

To sum up, there are multiple problems with this episode. Besides the obvious violation of diplomatic decorum with an ally, the overt politicization of international religious freedom just confirms the fact that the Trump administration used the issue almost exclusively to curry domestic political favor. The human rights policy staffers in the administration had to be in on the grift. In contrast, the Vatican strategy is not based on US election cycles but rather on a long game with China. Their strategy is one of incremental change that has a decades-long time line. The State Department knows this even if Pompeo didn't. One can, of course, question that strategy, but it was clear Pompeo had no interest in learning what the Vatican strategy was. And the Vatican saw this. As an aside, my own conversations with Vatican diplomats about the Trump administration revealed that they were very clear-eyed about what to expect from Pompeo and Trump on religious freedom. They wanted the relationship to last beyond that administration, so they bit their tongues to the extent they could and were willing to wait them out.

Finally, as we now know, thanks to John Bolton's book on Trump, the president told Chinese president, Xi Jinping, on more than one occasion to build the concentration camps for Uyghurs. Even Trump staffers knew the occasional religious freedom action on the part of the Trump administration was a façade. I can confirm that the Vatican has access to Google, so they know their early suspicions about the political agenda around international religious freedom was duplicitous. There is really only one direction for US-Vatican relations to go in the future, and that is up.[5] To this day I am puzzled at the ability of many international religious freedom advocates to give Trump a pass here. Is it because they still fear Trump? Is it because they want to preserve the stranglehold that the Republican Party has on the issue set and criticizing Trump's hypocrisy would undermine that perception? I think it has to be a combination of factors.

The next episode is Vatican-related but merits attention on its own. My engagement with Cuba started quite by accident and almost ended my diplomatic career prematurely. One day in 2015 I was sitting at my desk, and I got a call from Fr. Bryan Hehir, who chaired my dissertation at Harvard

Divinity School and was also working for Cardinal O'Malley, in the office of the Archdiocese of Boston. O'Malley has a long history of interest and work in Cuba, so I was not too surprised when Bryan told me an interesting story. He said that he heard a rumor that Cuban Cardinal Ortega had been seen at the White House, and Bryan wanted to know if I knew anything about that. I told Bryan I didn't have a clue about the rumor, but that I would call a friend at the White House and ask.[6]

I hung up with Bryan and dialed my friend, who, like me, didn't know the answer but said he would make a call to see if anyone could give an answer. I said thanks and didn't think any more about it. Just a few seconds later, the friend called back and said I needed "to stand down immediately!" Apparently, my friend called someone directly involved in what were secret conversations going on between the cardinal, the Vatican, and the White House about Cuba. That person hung up on my friend, appeared at my friend's desk moments later, and wanted to know how I knew about Ortega. The brief conversation ended with my friend being told to call me back and tell me to stand down. I was more than a little unnerved.

I immediately emailed David Wade, Kerry's chief of staff, and told him I had a troubling interaction with the White House and I needed to talk to him in person as soon as he had a free ten minutes. A few minutes later I was in his office offering my confession about how I stumbled into a hornet's nest. In his preternatural calm, he smirked at my tale and told me not to worry. He didn't know what was going on, but he was pretty sure the boss, Kerry, was involved and aware of something in that general area. He told me to stand down as instructed and not to worry about it. These were new waters for me, and the prospect of somehow blowing the cover on something that would prove to be very important was not something I enjoyed contemplating.

And then there was the question of what to do about calling Bryan Hehir back! Bryan, as I noted earlier, was a mentor, friend, and someone I wanted to do well by. I decided that as a priest, he would understand if I didn't get back to him immediately, if ever, if confidentiality was required. After my tenure at State and after the story of how the United States reestablished diplomatic relations was revealed, I finally told Bryan the story years later, and he completely understood why I didn't call him back. But if nothing else, I kept my eyes open for the public splash if and when the story broke. I wanted to go to Cuba if diplomatic relations were going to be restored.

I didn't have to wait long. But before news broke about President Obama's restoration of diplomatic relations with Cuba, I had two interesting episodes related to Cuba. The first took place in the early days of the office when our staff was small and our regional advisers were not all onboard. I got an invitation to attend a meeting between some staff from the Bureau of Western Hemisphere Affairs (WHA) and a delegation from the Cuban Council of Churches, which was being hosted in the United States by the National Council of Churches. I was to learn later that the Cuban Council of Churches was seen by some inside Main State as Castro lackeys, and not vocal enough in criticizing the Castro regime. Later, when I met with them in Cuba, they chafed at that description. It is true that different religious communities in Cuba had developed different strategies of getting by with respect to the government, and even within the same communities, different actors chose different paths. To me this was a classic example of how some diplomats hang a label or stereotype on an entire religious group in complete ignorance of the fact that many, even most, religious communities are internally plural. When it comes to a national coalition like a council of churches, it should be a given that in any delegation there are going to be distinct differences in theology and politics.

At any rate, someone in WHA invited me to attend the meeting, since I was the new religion guy. As was far more common than I care to admit in the early days, I was late to the meeting, as I often got lost in the mammoth Main State building. My mantra was usually "on time is late," but this time I walked into the crowded meeting room and was hurriedly introduced as the discussion unfolded. Very quickly a State employee took a pretty aggressive line, attacking Fidel's legacy on human rights. This struck me as a very bad move, and it hardly enriched the discussion. After this unhospitable contribution, the leader of the Cuban delegation bristled and reminded the interrogator that Fidel stepped down as president in 2008 and was no longer their leader. The meeting was beginning to careen out of control. In a moment of desperation, the convener of the meeting turned to me and asked me if I wanted to say something.

I wasn't particularly happy to be thrown into an emerging fight, but I was, after all, the secretary's religion guy, so I was supposed to be up for these moments. I took a deep breath and began by thanking them for what their communities were doing to help the Cuban people. I had seen the list of visitors, and they were mainly from what we'd call mainline Protestant churches here in the United States. They were well educated and canny clergy who had learned how to deal with the gyrations of Cuban politics over the decades. I knew that they had survived, and at times even prospered as religious communities, under a quixotic set of changing repressive political conditions over the years. But they were actually doing good work feeding people, training clergy, and working for human rights in an environment with very little breathing room. They were not there to be beaten up rhetorically by nameless American diplomats. As I spoke I sensed their relief that at least one American in the room had a modicum of understanding of their work. Likewise, I picked up a little heat from my brother diplomats. As I was to come to learn in greater depth later, some old Cuba hands in the State Department only knew one stance on Cuba, and that was the party line of economic boycott, narrowing the political and economic apertures, and maintaining the orthodox party line going back decades.

I had a good exchange with several of the delegates as the temperature in the room went down a few degrees. I thought they were signaling a desire for a possible thaw in our bilateral relations. At least I helped avoid an unproductive hourlong food fight. It was a good lesson for me because I knew, early on, that working on Cuba policy meant there would be internal critics, to say nothing of external critics when the policy changed.

The other encounter came as a result of fighting a different part of the State bureaucracy. My onboarding at State was managed by a remarkable human relations veteran, Pat Carter. She helped me through the complicated wickets of State Department human relations onboarding: seemingly hundreds of papers to sign, background checks, and file completion that was unlike anything I had ever encountered. She had been at State for a while and had seen it all. She was so professional, kind, and supportive, I could not help but be impressed. Once settled in, and with Liora as my chief of staff, we hit a major roadblock in trying to navigate the arcane, decentralized human resources employee onboarding process. Even though we were in the "S," or Secretary's Bureau, I incorrectly assumed bringing people to our staff would be easy. I met with Pat and asked her if there was a staff person who could advise us on how to master the hiring process. She mentioned another woman to me, Laterica Curtis, who was working in HR but who was thinking about joining the Foreign Service. Liora and I met with Laterica and found out for ourselves what a wizard Laterica was on the HR labyrinth. Along the way I asked if it was true she was interested in changing lanes at State. She affirmed she was interested in exploring joining the Foreign Service, and she also mentioned her interest in the Bureau of Western Hemisphere Affairs. Before long we made a deal with her in which she would help us complete the recruitment and onboarding of our staff, and then she would become our WHA adviser. It was one of the smartest decisions we made. And when she formally took over the regional adviser position, I told her she had one major job: get us to Cuba! And she did that very thing.

Laterica was as diligent and effective as our Western Hemisphere adviser as she was a personnel wizard. She set up an active relationship with the Cuban Affairs office and began laying the groundwork for our eventual visit. I knew it would be a long and slow process, since it seemed everyone wanted to visit Cuba. But I knew she was up to the task.

I knew from my earlier near disaster that something was afoot between the Obama administration and the Cuban government, but I was still surprised at how fast the conversation evolved. Obama's announcement on December 17, 2014, caught a lot of people off guard. A senior Christian cleric in Florida, who had been an active supporter of better relations with Cuba, told me that the Republican-elected establishment in Florida knew that eventually we would restore diplomatic relations with Cuba, but they were surprised by Obama's speed. He told me that one leading Republican elected official told him that when the day of changing the Cuba policy came, he would stick to his old-line talking points against any change in relations with Cuba for a couple of weeks, and then tear them up and accept the inevitable change. But that did not prove to be the case, as I was soon to learn.

Obama's remarks announcing the new Cuba policy were vintage Obama. He pointed out that engaging with our adversaries is not a bad thing. In fact, refusing to talk to those with whom we disagree makes far less sense than talking to them. Talking does not represent capitulation. Forty years of policies that have not led to progress needed to be rethought and changed if there are better routes worth trying. Before progress could be made, however, Cuba and the United States needed to resolve the status of two Americans held by Cuba, Alan Gross, a USAID subcontractor held for five years, and an intelligence asset who had been held for over two decades; also needing resolution was the status of three Cuban agents held in the United

States. Pope Francis had appealed to both Obama and Raul Castro to resolve the Alan Gross case and the release of three Cuban agents who had been held in the United States for over fifteen years. The intervention and mediation of the Vatican were crucial throughout the whole process of reestablishing diplomatic ties between the countries.[7]

Obama instructed Secretary Kerry, first, to immediately begin discussions with Cuba to reestablish diplomatic relations that were severed in January 1961. He pledged to reestablish and staff the embassy in Havana, and send high-ranking US officials to visit Cuba. He believed there were many common issues we could collaborate on, such as health issues, migration, counterterrorism, drug trafficking, and disaster response. And on issues where we disagreed, such as democracy and human rights, we would continue to engage them, and in so doing we could do more to support the Cuban people and promote our values through such engagement.

Second, he promised to have Kerry review Cuba's designation as a state sponsor of terrorism. And third, Obama said he was taking steps to increase travel, commerce, and the flow of information to and from Cuba. This was based on his belief in freedom and openness, and the power of people-to-people engagement. This work included making travel to Cuba easier, increasing the amount to money that could be sent to Cuba, removing limits on remittances that support humanitarian projects as well as the Cuban private sector. Likewise, the administration was working to increase authorized financial transactions between the countries, so that US exporters would have an easier time selling goods in Cuba. He also promised steps to increase telecommunications with Cuba. All these changes were within the power of the president to implement. The embargo that had been imposed was codified in legislation, and the president promised to engage Congress in an honest and serious debate about lifting the embargo. He concluded by saying, "Today, America chooses to cut loose the shackles of the past so as to reach for a better future—for the Cuban people, for the American people, for our entire hemisphere, and for the world."

One of the first things the White House did after the announcement was to convene a series of technical briefings with various domestic constituencies about how the new Cuba policy would change their work for the better. S/RGA sponsored one such opportunity for American faith-based groups who did humanitarian relief and development in Cuba to meet with White

House and Department of Treasury officials about the new opportunities the change in policy meant for them. As it turns out, our briefing had the largest attendance of any of the White House briefings on Cuba, which in turn elevated our chances of doing more in this space. It wasn't an accident that we drew the large crowd. Between our public diplomacy team led by Rachel Leslie, which had built an impressive set of relationships with domestic faith-based development organizations, and Laterica's relationship building inside the State Department and other government offices doing work related to Cuba, we were well positioned to get the word out to organizations who wanted to know how the policy changes were going to increase their chances of doing more work in Cuba.

The Cuba desk at State also noticed the success of our meeting, and Laterica continued to build that relationship. They were in charge of putting together a roster of Washington-based diplomats to head to Cuba, and before long we were in the queue to head to Havana. In the meantime, we continued to research religious communities in Cuba, their connections to the United States, and talked to as many US-based organizations as we could find with work in and ties to Cuba. As it turns out, a personal friend of mine, Aldo Gonzales, had been leading US United Methodist church groups on trips to Cuba to assist Methodist churches in Cuba for years. In particular, Aldo had built a strong working relationship with Caridad Diego, the chief of the Office of Religious Affairs in the Cuban government. This office was in charge of regulating the interaction of international groups who worked with Cuban religious communities. Aldo had successfully navigated the complex wickets of the Cuban bureaucracy for years, and his relationship with Diego was central to his success. His counsel would prove invaluable. Over the course of my tenure, the serendipitous encounters proved to be the key to various diplomatic successes, and I never took that for granted. My networks were always surprising to me, in a good way.

In the year and a half between Obama's announcement at the end of 2014 and our visit to Havana in July 2016, we spent time researching the religious landscape of Cuba, dealing with some internal politics inside the government, and beginning to interact with our embassy in Havana. The internal politics took two forms. The first form related to Senator Marco Rubio's office. At some point Rubio wrote a letter to the State Department protesting the fact that I was being sent to Cuba and not the Ambassador at Large for International Freedom. And on a much more ominous note, it complained that I was planning only to engage members of the Cuban Council of Churches. What was so disturbing about that? First, it meant someone inside the State Department had sent false information to Senator Rubio's staff about my upcoming trip. I was planning on seeing as many different religious communities as possible, within the time the Cuban government would allot me for my visit. And that list went well beyond the Cuban Council of Churches. It was true the embassy did not want the international religious freedom ambassador to come, because the major policy tool he had was "name and shame," and that hardened diplomatic stance did not fit the tone the embassy was trying to set. And at any rate, the embassy routinely communicated religious freedom violations annually for the yearly International Religious Freedom Report. They felt like there was nothing new to be gained in that arena. And embassies carry tremendous clout when it comes to allowing and planning for Washington-based diplomatic visitors.

I do not know who passed this incorrect information along to the senator. I don't believe it came from the International Religious Freedom staff. In all likelihood, it came from someone in the wider Bureau of Democracy, Human Rights, and Labor, where the International Religious Freedom Office was housed, and where some older career human rights folks probably did not support Obama's new engagement. The Office of Cuba Affairs took responsibility for replying to Rubio's complaint, and that was the last I heard of that. But it was just another sad episode illustrating how threatened the whole Washington international religious freedom sector was by our work.

As it turned out, the Cuban government granted us thirty-six hours in Havana! And we were determined to cram as many visits as possible into that narrow window. Based upon our research, I crafted four basic questions I would try to ask all the communities we encountered. These were: How is the government treating you in comparison to the past? Where do you see the bilateral relationship in ten years? Has the new US policy improved the lives of ordinary Cubans? And finally, does your community support lifting the economic blockade of Cuba? This would allow me to collect comparative data that the embassy could assess as it continued to implement the new Cuba policy. Jeffrey DeLaurentis was appointed chief of the US Interests Section when the embassy was reopened in mid-2014, and his support was crucial for the success of our trip. He and his team agreed to this framing, and they were eager to have us.[8]

Once in Havana, we hit the ground running. Our first visit was with the auxiliary bishop of Havana, Msgr. Juan de Dios Hernandez. The newly installed archbishop, who succeeded Cardinal Ortega, was visiting the Vatican, so we met with the veteran Hernandez, who served as auxiliary bishop from 2005 through 2019. Since the Catholic Church had played a vital role in the effort to restore diplomatic relations between the United States and Cuba, it made sense to start our visit at the Conference of Cuban Catholic Bishops. The bishop painted a hopeful picture of the future of relations between the two countries. On the one hand, he was deeply schooled in the repressive nature of the Cuban government toward religious communities, while on the other hand, he knew the dynamics were changing. He told me that the increased engagement of the Obama administration was seen almost universally by Cubans as a good thing.

Our next stop was to see Imam Pedro Yahya, the leader of a growing mosque near the center of Old Town Havana. By the end of our lightning trip we would glimpse the religious diversity of the country, which is primarily Catholic, but here we saw a vibrant community that appeared to be bustling and growing. The imam was relaxed and quite happy to tell his story and show us the growth of Islam on the island. Old Havana was a remarkable neighborhood, and this particular community stood out for its energy and sense of vitality. The arrival of a small delegation of American diplomats was cause for much curiosity, and we were welcomed warmly.

The imam painted what would be a constant refrain. They were accepted by the government, and they did not experience major harassment. They stuck to their work and did not venture to establish a critical public voice against the government, and they were left alone. And that seemed to be fine with them. From the mosque we went to a restaurant where we met with over a dozen people representing several traditions, including Presbyterians, Assemblies of God, Nazarenes, and Mormons. While we had a private room, our presence could be seen by many of the regular diners. Our guests were happy to see us, and they shared their unvarnished commentary on the lives of their religious communities. Some human rights organizations criticized us after the trip for meeting with religious leaders in a public setting. But no one had coerced these people to join us, and if they were at any political risk, they did not betray their anxiety to us. It was a lively discussion, and they indicated they had all found ways to do their ecclesiastical work and not draw the ire of the Cuban authorities. They, like our other interlocutors, welcomed the restarting of diplomatic relations with America, and they thought it boded well for the country and the future of their work.

Our other conversations included meetings with Buddhists, the Cuban Council of Churches, the Jehovah's Witnesses, representatives of the Matanzas Seminary, and Beth Shalom Synagogue. The synagogue director, Adela Dworin, was used to American visitors and was an amazing host. She told us of the history of Jews coming to Cuba while fleeing persecution in Europe. Dworin told us how many American tourists come to Cuba, and only after arriving do they learn of the existence of a synagogue and insist on visiting. She told a story about one American family that came to the synagogue. The dad was wearing cutoffs and a ratty T-shirt with a sports logo on it, but was nonetheless quite interested in the history of the community. As they were touring they came upon a trash can that was catching water dripping from a leak in the ceiling. The dad inquired about what it would cost to repair the roof, and Adela answered words to the effect of, more than you can afford. The dad said try me, and Adela named a figure, and the dad wrote a five-figure check on the spot. Turns out, he was one of the owners of the sports team whose T-shirt he was sporting. Adela said dryly after that, that she never judges a potential donor by his T-shirt.

But this points to a larger point: almost all religious communities in Cuba depend on their US-based coreligionists for financial and spiritual support. The Obama reforms meant more funds, pilgrims, and visitors would come to Cuban religious communities. While it is undeniable that the Cuban government represses religious freedom, the cost of America's embargo has been to constrict the resources of Cuba's religious communities. It makes sense to try a strategy of more robust engagement to enlist rank-and-file Cubans to work for more liberal policies from their government. As one person told me, everyone in Cuba has at least an American cousin. "We love them, and we want to have greater access to American people and goods."

Adela also said the synagogue has a history of directly engaging the Castros. That set them a bit apart from many religious communities in Cuba. Fidel had attended services there. She believed that reminding the government of the long presence of Jews in Cuba was to their advantage, and the decades-long strategy seems to have worked. Since there are no rabbis living in Cuba, Beth Shalom has survived against long odds. And engagement both with the Cuban government and with Jews around the world has been a key to survival. She was very pleased with the new strategy of engagement on the part of the Obama administration. I think it is important to see that different religious communities in Cuba have developed different strategies of engagement with the government. The sense I developed, and it was admittedly a small day-and-a-half sample, was that there had been a mild but noticeable sea change in recent years, and most communities were having an easier time with less overt repression and more relative calm from the government.

My last meeting with a religious community was with a gathering of twenty-four evangelical house-church pastors, and it was quite interesting. We met in a house church, which, as the name implies, is simply a house that looks identical to all the houses on the same block, only this one belonged to a clergy couple, as I recall, and served as a worship space for a small congregation. One floor had an open design, and perhaps thirty to fifty people could fit in for a worship service. The proliferation of these sorts of churches made it virtually impossible for the Cuban government to register all of them as separate churches and to conduct any sort of real inspection or surveillance of their activities. It is impossible to know just how many of these house churches existed, and, given their free church polity, no one single leadership structure controlled them or accounted for the total membership. But from a government regulation perspective, they presented a much too complicated existence for the government to control. Obviously, there were informal networks between pastors and individual house churches, but their loose structure and alliances were perfect for subverting a government bent on monitoring and controlling ecclesiastical activities.

As an aside, I should note that I am not a big fan of efforts by governments, particularly repressive ones, to register religious groups. I could never see a positive outcome to that work. Time and time again I saw governments crack down on religious groups for nefarious reasons, and registration laws were very useful smoke screens. In some contexts, such as in Kazakhstan, groups like the Jehovah's Witnesses were harassed for their unwillingness to be registered. Likewise, some religious groups that did not register were attacked under a government policy of countering violent extremism, on the supposition that resisting registration was de facto an act of subverting the government. I never got much traction in the department for my views. I did hear the argument from some NGOs that such registration laws were not all alike, and working to make them less bad was worth the effort if the state in question was determined to institute them. But at the end of the day, in my view such laws were inevitably manipulated to state ends at the expense of disfavored religious groups.

I remember several aspects of my conversation with the evangelical group. Many of them had passed through different stages in their relationship with the government. Street preaching is a common global technique in the evangelical world. I can remember an era in Boston in the 1980s when Spanish-speaking street preachers could routinely be heard on the Boston Common. Apparently, that resembled political agitation to the Cuban government, so they were not exactly kind and hospitable to evangelical street preachers in Havana. Evangelical preachers are nothing if not adaptive in their methods, so moving indoors was an easier alternative to public proclamation. House churches were a natural evolution in the volatile political ethos of Havana.

Another interesting dynamic was the deep relationship most of these pastors had to supportive megachurches back in the United States, particularly in Florida and Texas. It was clear that they had deep ties to spiritual partners there who supplied money, volunteers, and ecclesiastical energy to the growing movement of small house churches. I noted to myself the deep irony that most of these American churches were allied, or at least attracted to, conservative American Republican-affiliated politicians, who were working at cross purposes with the work of the Cuban house churches they supported. That is, these politicians supported the stark economic boycott of Cuba and policies that limited remittances to Cubans from Americans and limited the money US churches could send to their Cuban religious cousins.

And the last thing I recall is that their answers to my stock questions paralleled the answers I had been getting my whole trip. They supported Obama's normalization of diplomatic relations between the countries; they saw their relationship with the government as being better than before, and, as a result, they were optimistic about the future improvement of life in Cuba; and they saw lifting the US economic boycott as a move that would greatly benefit their churches.

The last vignette to relay is my visit to the Office of Religious Affairs (ORA) to meet with the director, Caridad Diego. This was the first time a

Washington-based US diplomat had met with the Office of Religious Affairs. The ORA is housed within the Ministry of Justice, and the office was located in the Palace of the Revolution. My first few moments projected a feeling of déjà vu, as if I had suddenly been transported into a le Carré novel. By this point in my career I had developed a sense that all national government buildings were the same. But that evaporated very soon once inside the Palace. As I entered our meeting room, Caridad rose from behind a very large conference table and moved to greet us. She stuck out her hand and moved, not toward me but toward my control officer, and when she shook his hand, she called him by name, telling him it was good to meet him. He told me later that this shook him because it was her signal to him that the Cuban government knew the names of all the embassy staffers, meaning that the government was routinely surveilling all of them. Only after greeting him did she turn to me and welcome me.

The room was quite large. She led us to the conference table, where she sat on one side, with me directly opposite her on the other side. And she sat just below a wall adorned with three massive black and white photos, one of a very young Fidel, another of a very young Raoul Castro, and one of a very young Che Guevara, all striking revolutionary poses and looking like they were in their early twenties. The symbolism of asserted revolutionary power was simultaneously dramatic and over the top. There I was, a bald late-middle-aged US diplomat up against a demonstration of a nostalgic Communist, but more than a little threadbare, vanguard of the revolution.

Caridad was straight out of Hollywood central casting. Short, powerfully built, and efficiently and subtly radiating the glory of Cuba past, and possessor of a PhD in Leninist philosophy from the University of Leningrad, she fit the part well. And she was also nervous. I noticed, as I had earlier of the representative of the Moscow Patriarchate in Kyiv, Ukraine, her hands were shaking as she read her lengthy introduction and welcome to me, immediately after we sat down. I suspected she expected me to hector her about Cuba's miserable record on religious freedom, and her manner was a bit of a preemptive signal that she could withstand any incoming fire I might be bringing. But I was determined not to fall for that trap.

Instead, I chose to follow Obama's line of celebrating the new policy of diplomatic engagement and to look toward the future. In due course, our International Religious Freedom Report would come out with its usual list of the government's bad behavior. I was hearing a different message from religious communities on the ground, and I wanted to build on that. I began by relaying my friend Aldo Gonzalez's greetings and to say that I was there to begin the new era between our countries. I was there to build a new relationship between our two offices as well. My strategy was to try and point to a better future between the coreligionists in our countries. My memory is that she was caught off guard by my approach. And she softened a bit in her demeanor.

We had a very interesting exchange as a result. She acknowledged the strong historical ties between American and Cuban religious communities, and she said the government saw that as a good thing. Many of those American groups brought not only volunteers but also hard US currency that supported the burgeoning tourist industry in Cuba; but beyond that, these American visitors helped build housing, expand farms, and in some cases built roads and other necessary infrastructure around Cuba. In the middle of the conversation, I asked her if she had ever been to the United States. As it turns out, she had been to New York City once, as part of the official Cuban delegation to the opening week of the UN General Assembly, years ago. But she had been busy with official duties and had not had much of an opportunity to really see the city, or any of the country beyond. She seemed genuinely touched by the invitation.

My thinking was, it would be fascinating for her to come to the States and begin to get a sense of American religious pluralism and to be able to visit several cities to get a sense of how greater freedom for religious communities might look in real life. And I also thought it would be good for her to get a feel for how popular normalizing diplomatic relations with Cuba was among American religious communities. I have to confess I had not cleared that idea with anyone back at Main State. But I had met with dozens of interreligious delegations from all across the globe that were brought to the United States by our Bureau of Educational and Cultural Affairs, so I knew this was one aspect of relating to global religion that the State Department actually did very well. None of the embassy staff blinked an eyelash later when I mentioned this part of my discussion.

While we invested a lot of time and energy in attempting to aid the Obama administration's new policy of engagement with Cuba, and ultimately most of that was undone by several factors, including Trump's reversal of Obama's policy, the beginning of the "Havana Syndrome" attacks on US embassy staff in Havana, and the impact of COVID-19, we made a major contribution to a new policy. The impact of our work is remembered both here in the States and in Cuba, and our work can serve as a model for the eventual renewal of the diplomatic and economic ties between our countries. Such a rapprochement between Cuba and the United States makes sense economically, culturally, and politically. Deeper official ties there will also unlock many doors throughout Central and South America. The role the Catholic Church played there also was something of an object lesson for many US diplomats in showing that the Vatican can play a salutary role in advancing American diplomatic success all around the planet. Instead of being simply an enigma, the Vatican can be a strong partner in many diplomatic cases. As it happened this time, the Vatican was overstocked with powerful diplomatic players with a keen interest in Latin America in general, and Cuba in particular. And their role in this story was crucial to success. In the case of S/RGA, we had or acquired expertise in both the Vatican and Cuba, so we were able to strengthen our diplomatic hand. I do not believe any other office in the US government was capable of saying that.

The final example is our work fighting corruption in Nigeria. This case emerged in no small part because one of our regional advisers, Rebecca Linder Blachly, saw an opportunity based on a chance meeting in Benin, and immediately saw its relevance in its much larger neighbor to the east, Nigeria. I originally met Rebecca several years before, when she, like Liora, was working at the Center for Strategic and International Studies (CSIS) back in the middle of the decade 2000–2009. Liora, in fact, recruited Rebecca to join us in S/RGA. Rebecca had all the skills and attributes we were looking for in a regional adviser, and then some. She went on to work at the Pentagon and helped the military stand up its new Africa Command (AFRICOM) in 2007 in Stuttgart, Germany, and then went to Harvard Divinity School to earn a degree concentrating in African religion.

Rebecca and I traveled to Benin in West Africa in May 2015 to attend a government-sponsored pan-African conference in Cotonou, with support from the African Union, the Economic Community of West African States, and the National Commission for the United Nations Educational, Scientific, and Cultural Organization. The theme of the conference was "African Initiative on Education for Peace and Development through Inter-religious and Intercultural Dialogue." Several hundred participants came from all over the continent. These sorts of conferences are fairly common all over the world, and they serve many purposes, not the least of which is the chance to meet lots of interesting people on the sides of the formal meetings, and this trip was no exception. I made brief remarks as one of the few attendees from beyond Africa.[9]

The most noteworthy conversations came after the conference when we traveled around the country for several days under the skilled workmanship of our control officer at the embassy. Along the way I managed to get a preliminary commitment from the government to accept a Guantanamo Bay detainee, and I met with the new Millennium Challenge Corporation leadership, who were reforming their financial control practices to recover their eligibility for more funding after losing those privileges for past corrupt financial practices. I also met with a number of religious leaders, some with unique views. A senior Christian cleric asked me if it was true that only gay applicants received USAID grants. I assured him that was not true. A Muslim leader told me Benin was 25 percent Muslim, 25 percent Christian, and 80 percent voodoo! The Western view of religious affiliation as singular and mutually exclusive clearly was not embraced in Benin.

But for my purposes here, the most interesting meeting took place in the embassy with a set of religious radio station directors. These stations had received $2,000 grants each from the embassy for programming to educate listeners on religious violence, tolerance, and anticorruption. These six radio stations constituted major sources of news across the whole country. The protective umbrella of modest US government funding provided the reporters from these stations protection from harassment and violence in their coverage of public corruption. All the reporters felt protected by their ability to meet regularly inside the US embassy. It had never occurred to me that US funding would have such a direct impact on the security of reporters who were doing the dangerous work of reporting stories of government corruption. A modest affiliation with the US embassy sent a powerful signal to any parties who were corrupt, such that they were more reluctant to harass or harm the reporters. The station managers were unequivocal in their belief that this was the case.

This trip coincided with the inauguration of President Buhari next door in Nigeria. Once in office, he announced that three of his priorities would be defeating Boko Haram, improving the national economy, and addressing rampant public corruption. Rebecca drew the connection from Benin, where religious communities were tackling public corruption through their news outlets, to Nigeria by asking what role religious communities in Nigeria might play in the Buhari era. It was a natural question, but it would not have happened had we not spent a very interesting couple of hours with the journalists in Benin. This was a classic example where our experience in a region led us to think harder about an issue that actually had a religious dimension, but not one that was visible from Washington.

Rebecca went to work to investigate corruption in Nigeria and to see if religious leaders, Muslim and Christian, could leverage their resources together to contribute to anticorruption efforts. In short order, she put together a bold idea, along with the support of Amy Lillis, who did her first tour as a Foreign Service office in Lagos, Nigeria. A few months later we were convening a two-day conference in Lagos, in collaboration with our consulate there, one day for Christian leaders and one day for Muslim leaders on the broad topic of how religious communities could help push back on public corruption in Nigeria.

During the planning phase a question arose with the staff of the US consulate in Lagos over whether to hold a single meeting with both Christian and Muslim leaders, or separate meetings. This is a perennial question for US posts regarding religion, and the almost universal impulse is to go with what I called the Noah's ark routine. Which means, pack the room with delegates from every imaginable religious group. And often that impulse is the safest route. But as I learned a very long time ago, if you invite one religious group, you risk alienating a hundred. If you invite ten, you risk the wrath of a thousand, and so on. But in this case I held out for separate meetings because our research suggested Christian communities in Nigeria had a much larger set of corruption issues internally than the Muslim communities did. To put it succinctly, the Christian prosperity gospel was quite prevalent in Nigeria, and any analogues among the Muslims were not as significant. I thought it would be much more likely for the Christian churches to engage in blunt talk about their unique problems without the Muslim leaders at the same table. As Ambassador Linda Thomas-Greenfield, the assistant secretary for African affairs, semi-jokingly put it to me, "Good luck finding an uncorrupt Christian clergy there." After a lot of back-and-forth negotiating with post staff, they agreed to separate meetings.

We structured the conversations around a series of objectives. We wanted an honest conversation, but we did not want to come off as just the latest version of the "white man's burden" by telling them what they were doing wrong and how to fix "their" problem. We also didn't want to simply throw a pile of cash at them for a one-off event; we wanted them to make a difference over the long haul. We also believed an interreligious effort would ultimately have the greatest chance for long-term impact in Nigeria—after all, Nigeria is the only country that is on the top-ten list in both Christian population *and* Muslim population. If the Buhari government was going to be successful in addressing public corruption, it would need to persuade all of Nigeria, not just one of the larger religious communities.

We addressed these questions by designing a process where the United States used its convening power to gather representatives of the two major religions, tried to leverage the expertise of indigenous African organizations with chops in fighting corruption, and tried to tie the work to a long-term effort grounded in Buhari's call for fighting corruption to be led by Nigerians, and not simply a US-owned and US-operated line of work like so much of the International Religious Freedom–funded efforts had been over the years. The list of religious communities in attendance included Ansar ud-Deen Society of Nigeria, Qareeb Islamic Society, the Nigerian Supreme Council for Islamic Affairs, the Islamic Platform, the Nasrul-Lahi-L-Fatih Society, the Redeemed Christian Church of God, House of the Rock Church, Daystar Christian Center, the Cherubim and Seraphim Movement, and the Baptist, Methodist, Catholic, and Apostolic Churches of Nigeria. The consulate estimated that over 1 million adherents were represented by these leaders.

We enlisted the aid of a couple of religion scholars, Georgetown's Katherine Marshall and Harvard Divinity School's Jacob Olupona, to lead parts of the workshop, and we also found some African-based anticorruption organizations to present on their work with religious communities. We also invited representatives of three African organizations, the Centre for the Rule of Law, the African Council for Accreditation and Accountability, and an organization called BudgIT, to present their work and how it could help the religious communities at the workshop develop their own corruption-fighting tools.

Serendipitously, Nigeria celebrates Martin Luther King Jr. Day much as the United States does, and that coincided with the date of our visit. Rebecca caught this unique time frame early on in our planning, and it was a key insight. This enabled me to set a tone of modesty and humility for the exercise at the outset of each day's conversation. I wanted to avoid at all costs any hint of the US government parachuting into Lagos with a ten-step plan to "fix" Nigeria's public corruption "problems." By introducing King as a powerful reformer of America's Jim Crow laws, I was able to decenter any possible interpretations of our alleged virtue when it came to corrupt laws and practices. They all knew of King and admired his work for social justice and against corruption in the United States. I spoke of my time as a leader in a religious community and how I had trained American clergy to parse and digest the lessons and nonviolent techniques King had promoted. Rebecca's insight that King could be a powerful bridge in both the Christian and Muslim communities proved crucial to our success.

Katherine Marshall described how religious leaders were working all over the world to address multiple facets of corruption. She encouraged the leaders not only to address Nigerian corruption but also to think about attending an upcoming international anticorruption conference in Panama in 2016. She noted how the loss of public trust in the integrity of national governments due to corruption was a destabilizing factor in many countries around the world.

The next presenter was a world-renowned expert on African religions, Jacob Olupona. Olupona was the son of a famous Nigerian Anglican bishop, and was something of a legend among all the attendees. He gave an account of several of the common justifications of corruption, including the endemic and deep-rooted nature of corruption, low salaries that encourage bribe taking, and a generation for whom corruption is normalized. He argued that these challenges should not discourage religious leaders from taking actionable steps and developing systems that minimize corruption. After each of these presentations, vigorous discussions ensued. Any initial anxiety I might have had was quickly allayed. In both workshops the question arose regarding why the two sets of religious leaders had separate sessions. I gave a straight answer that the constellation of issues internal to each community were unique, and yet we hoped in the end that they could come together and work with consulate staff. Both groups embraced that logic, and in the end, they did pledge to work together.

As I recall, the Christian leaders spoke bluntly across the table that different denominations had varying degrees of culpability for both their own internal practices and the public embrace of corrupt politicians by some churches. There was a clear sentiment that such practices needed to stop. During a break

I mentioned to one pastor that I had read somewhere that there were more Christian pastors in Nigeria with private jets than in the United States. He grinned slyly and told me that was because their road system was not as good as America's! In the end I was impressed with the candor and the relative lack of defensiveness across some of the community boundaries where one might expect tension. Both Marshall and Olupona were powerful presenters, and each gave remarks that catalyzed the following discussions.

The three African-based anticorruption groups gave electric presentations. BudgIT, in particular, gave an impressive account of their work. This group was a small coterie of young programmers who had developed a cell phone app that empowered ordinary citizens to challenge their elected representatives in the country's parliament. Users could enter their addresses into the app, which in turn sent them a list of capital investment projects and their addresses that the parliament had funded in recent legislative sessions in their area. The citizen could then go to that location and take a photo of what was or was not actually transpiring at that site. Apparently, it was standard practice for parties to siphon off such funding without embarking upon construction. App users could send a photo directly to the email addresses of their representatives and inquire why projects were not built.

At the end of the BudgIt team's presentation each day, the assembled religious leaders were stunned. On the first day there was a period of silence, and then one attendee asked the presenter how large their security detail was when they made public presentations around the country. The leader said they had no security, which prompted visceral surprise. The leaders were amazed at their bravery and wanted to know if the organization could provide their members training, which, of course, they could. One participant expressed amazement at their courage and said, "When you fight corruption, corruption fights back." Both workshops ended with a brainstorming session on possible responses by religious communities and possible lines of collective effort, led by Rebecca. This was where we would see if the concept of the workshop would have any legs. The religious leaders did not disappoint. As I frequently saw happen, these men and women could talk when given space and freedom to speak their minds. Seven themes emerged over the course of the brainstorming about next steps. Let me run the list.[10]

First, they suggested they should empower their congregants by building their capacity to engage civic leaders by developing specific tools and training. Based on tools offered by the three NGOs, they could train their people to read and understand national and state budgets, report progress on infrastructure projects, and submit freedom-of-information requests. They also expressed interest in developing media and social-media campaigns with a focus on anticorruption.

Second, they expressed a desire to engage government leaders. "If all religious leaders begin to hold government accountable, there will be major change," said one pastor. They pledged to develop a "transformation theology" that would underwrite creating a sense of needed reform in their communities. More direct engagement with federal, state, and local officials as well as active participation in the legislative process and with the judiciary would magnify their moral message on anticorruption. They recognized that they possessed moral authority, but ultimately the government had political responsibility for the state of Nigeria.

Third, they believed that churches and mosques needed to do a better job leading in developing educational materials to promote integrity from a moral standpoint, especially for youth. Both communities had helped develop previous teaching materials on anticorruption, but they noted that many in the workshops had never heard of these resources, so they committed to putting them online.

Fourth, Christian participants, in particular, discussed the need to eradicate in-house corruption by improving internal recordkeeping and financial transparency to legitimate their leaders' efforts to engage on this topic. One pastor said, "What bothers me most is that religious leaders are involved in corruption. . . . They romance with corrupt government leaders, and accept stolen money." The presentation by the African Council for Accreditation and Accountability presented a model for how churches can demonstrate good financial management and undergo an accreditation process. They also noted that religious communities need to anticipate a backlash to their anticorruption efforts while cleaning up their own finances. Clean hands gave them credibility in engaging corrupt officials. Some leaders made it clear they did not want government regulation of their communities because that could empower backlash against them.

There was some dissent among the leaders about reporting any corruption they saw. Some argued for keeping those conversations within the communities themselves, given that the clergy-parishioner relationship was based on trust. One pastor suggested establishing internal standards and controls to detect fraud and corruption within churches. This distinction before spiritual formation of community members and public shaming was a common theme. Certainly, any attempt on the part of civil society to colonize law enforcement efforts is problematic at so many levels. But the power of moral suasion and forming of a democratic citizenry have long been one of the functions of religious communities.

Fifth, and related to the last point, participants suggested communities should develop formal mentoring programs for public officials and religious leaders to promote anticorruption principles in government and religious communities.

Sixth, a theme of uniting for power and protection was named. Both Christian and Muslim participants emphasized the importance of uniting behind a shared anticorruption platform. After BudgIT's presentation on both days, attendees questioned how the speaker avoided retribution for exposing political corruption, saying, "When you fight corruption, it fights back." In light of the possibility of possible backlash, the participants advocated fighting corruption as a group, which they believed would make a much more elusive target than a lone activist.

Finally, there was a universal call for preaching anticorruption values. Leaders in both workshops expressed frustration with some religious figures who focused their attention and preaching on gaining material wealth instead of moral values. Critiquing the "prosperity gospel," participants called on fellow religious leaders not to celebrate the corrupt, but rather to praise good stewards of the public trust. Some suggested using their influence to "redefine the moral compass of society." One minister, however, said that preaching would not be enough: "We've been preaching and corruption never stopped." Actions such as public antibribery pledges were discussed as a concrete step to help change widespread cultural acceptance of corruption.

We got very good news at the end of our workshops when the attendees formed a working group to continue their work together; Muslim and Christian leaders pledged to carry on their newfound collaboration. Later in 2016 Kerry made a visit to Nigeria with Ambassador Linda Thomas-Greenfield, and they met with a subcommittee of the working group. One morning I was sitting at my desk, and Ambassador Thomas-Greenfield called me to tell me that the meeting they had was one of the best conversations she had ever had with a civil society group in Africa. That was high praise, and it confirmed to me that this sort of engagement with religious leaders could pay dividends, if planned right and if it empowered indigenous religious communities and was not premised on US overreach.

The usual US approach to fighting corruption in places like Nigeria has a distinctly law-enforcement tinge to it. When we did our briefing back at Main State, as we frequently did after a significant trip or initiative, a representative of the Bureau of International Narcotics and Law Enforcement Affairs attended and confessed that he was unaware civil society actors such as members of religious communities could make a major difference against a culture of corruption. Indeed, as former US ambassador to Nigeria John Campbell has noted, the US approach to corruption in Nigeria has historically concentrated primarily on recovering large sums of stolen public monies. It has not developed a comprehensive approach that includes civil society.[11]

Campbell's provocative account of a new kind of diplomacy in Nigeria supports the type of US embassy engagement with religious communities very similar to what we promoted all around the globe. He is a veteran diplomat who has thought long and hard on reforming US diplomacy in a manner that includes paying attention to engagement with religious dynamics in a fashion that is congruent with the mission of the Office of Religion and Global Affairs and the earlier intuitions of Madeleine Albright and John Kerry. I'll have more to say in the concluding chapter about the future of this sort of diplomacy.

In the past few chapters I have given examples of how we did our work on issues that directly tracked with Secretary Kerry's priorities, such as combating climate change, addressing the global refugee crisis, and mitigating violence in conflicts and conflict-prone areas. And in this chapter I related an example of where our talented regional advisers discovered contexts where we were able to address opportunities that appeared along the way during our three and a half years in the Obama administration. What remains is to resolve a number of lines in our story and to take a clear-eyed look at what the future might hold for a mission like ours.

Chapter Nine

THE DEVIL?

T O BE INVITED BY THE SECRETARY of state to launch a new office on religion and global affairs, in the Secretary's Bureau, and then to be able to design, build, and lead that office for almost four years was the opportunity of a lifetime. It is impossible to fully convey the challenges and joys of that task in this book. I have told a fraction of the stories I could tell. The team we built, the places we went, and the people we engaged along the way were truly remarkable. And to be able to do that against the background of an increasingly unstable international order made the work all the more important and interesting. As I argued at the outset, religions are powerful forces in global diplomacy, and the United States has paid a high price for its reticence, ineptitude, and unsophisticated dealings with religions throughout its history. We began to model a different approach to religion based on Secretary Kerry's realization that we would continue to pay a high price for mistakes and missed diplomatic opportunities without a better capacity to interpret religion. As I write these words, the future of the work we did in S/RGA for American diplomacy is unknown. I believe that without such an institutional capacity, the US government will not be able to help the world answer major global issues such as forced mass migration, burgeoning climate change, the effort to inoculate the planet against COVID, and the securing of full human rights for women and girls, to name a few issues where religious communities are simultaneously part of the problem and part of the solution. If the human race is to meet these and other challenges successfully, the energy, wealth, and collaboration of religious communities are essential.

I began to think about writing this book almost from the moment Donald Trump won the election in 2016. In the weeks leading up to the election, I had a very good feeling about what we had accomplished. In September 2016 we put on a conference on religion and diplomacy, which we called RadCon, to great fanfare with hundreds of our partners and supporters from around the world. White House Chief of Staff Denis McDonough gave the keynote address, and we accomplished our goal of reminding friends and a few foes of what we had accomplished in our short life. We helped advance US strategic priorities in dozens of countries, on issues related to sustainable development, mitigating conflict, and promoting a roster of human rights, to name only a few issues. We built an analytical power to help our diplomats assess religious dynamics, we engaged thousands of religious actors, we brought deeper scholarship to bear on US policy, and we built a global network of thousands of partners. The conference was a time for us to remind people what we had done and to celebrate our success.

I was exhausted, and I had decided to go back to academia. I had even managed to secure an informal commitment from a senior Clinton presidential transition official to let me name my successor as special representative for religion and global affairs. I was feeling pretty good about what we had done. I would choose someone who knew the history of our office; possessed the necessary skills, energy, and brains; and would help solidify S/RGA's future as a permanent part of US diplomacy. I kept an anxious eye on Hillary Clinton's sliding poll numbers over the course of the summer and fall, but I had faith she would win. Obviously, I am not as smart as I thought I was.

I had always made two assumptions about the durability of S/RGA. First, it would take at least two consecutive presidential terms for the office to become a permanent feature of American diplomacy. Change does not come quickly to the State Department, and I knew it would take time to win a sufficient number of hearts and minds of the career staff. And second, if the work were to be truly successful, we would eventually put ourselves out of work. By that I mean, if we were persuasive, the missions we promoted would be woven into the standard diplomatic DNA, and there would no longer be a need for a single office dedicated to keep the secretary apprised of the religious dynamics in American diplomacy, to train embassies to understand and engage the religious landscapes of their host countries, and to provide a point of entry for interested parties so they would have routine access to the offices and bureaus at State that dealt with their issues.

With the advent of the Trump administration, all of that vision was destroyed. I went to bed in the wee hours of the morning as Election Day bled into the next day. But as I struggled to go to sleep, I knew all we had done was soon to go up in flames. I even awoke from a nightmare a few hours later in which I dreamed the FBI came to Main State and arrested us all for building a religiously diverse staff and for trying to undermine an exclusively Christian State Department. My subconscious anxiety was telling me the obvious: the Trump administration could never tolerate what we had been trying to do in S/RGA. The book idea was the best way of resisting what the new administration was going to do that I could think of. In short order the new regime at State closed our office, eliminated the position of special representative for religion and global affairs, and set up a small group of four or five staffers to attempt to replicate our mission within the Office on International Religious Freedom. But that was all window dressing. Our mission was defunct.

I did have one surreal interaction with a senior member of the Office of Policy Planning on Secretary Pompeo's staff in the summer of 2017. I had a conversation with an old friend in the State Department who was serving as the deputy chief of mission (DCM) at an American embassy. The DCM reached out to me and encouraged me to talk to a senior member of the Policy Planning staff about S/RGA's work, as Secretary Pompeo had replaced Secretary Rex Tillerson, and Pompeo had decided to rethink Tillerson's decision to close our office. The DCM suggested that there was a window of opportunity for me to persuade Pompeo to keep S/RGA alive. I was skeptical of the whole idea, to say the least. At one level I thought putting our mission into a Trumpian State Department where it could be completely co-opted by an allegiance to white Christian nationalism would permanently taint the whole S/RGA concept. Maybe shutting it down was the best option for the long-term survival of the concept. I also found it very hard to believe someone on Pompeo's staff would ever reach out to me to talk. But to my surprise, the DCM contacted the staffer, and the staffer reached out to me. In the summer of 2017 I found myself back on the seventh floor, in the office next door to our old office, trying to explain what our mission had been!

Again, to my surprise, I had a very interesting conversation. The staffer began by saying there were three criticisms of S/RGA she had heard.

I thought, only three? That's surprising. I also had a strong suspicion I knew the source of the critique. It was probably one of the few people I knew who was hired in the Obama era in the international religious freedom space who survived the orthodoxy tests of the incoming Trump folk. At any rate, I was told, first, that S/RGA was the tip of the spear for Obama's global gay marriage campaign; second, that we did not work with the regional bureaus; and third, that we refused to engage with domestic religious groups. Upon hearing this list, I knew it was compiled by someone with an ax to grind against us.

We did do a very modest amount of work regarding LGBT rights. Early on in my tenure I was asked to join a department working group on LGBT rights, which I was more than happy to do. This came about mainly because of my early work on the Disabilities Treaty. Many human rights staffers understood how we might be able to help in that space. When Rebecca Linder Blachly joined our staff, she took primary responsibility for our work here. When Matt Nosanchuk joined us from the White House, he, too, did some work in this space for the last six months or so of the Obama administration. In addition to being a part of the working group, our modest contribution to the administration's work here was to help stand up the Special Envoy for the Human Rights of LGBT Persons when the position was created and Randy Berry was the first person appointed to the post. I did meet with LGBT human rights activists in a small number of countries. All of these meetings took place in US embassies, and every conversation was centered on how US posts could help these communities and do no harm in the process. Without exception, the message we got from activists was for us not to talk about the promotion of gay marriage! Such an effort would have increased the targeting and violence against LGBT people in the countries where we had these conversations. There was no global gay marriage campaign, and we were not the leaders of any such nonexistent campaign. We did try to make sure our embassies found ways to support these leaders in ways that would be productive and not harmful. When religious leaders did query me about US government policies on LGBT rights, we were clear that the United States did not support criminalization of LGBT people and that religious groups should not foment abuse of LGBT people by any means. We argued for protecting life and limb of LGBT folk everywhere as part of US policy. We saw human rights as indivisible and rejected the notion that LBGT rights posed a threat to religious freedom rights, as I commonly heard from some religious freedom advocates.

The remaining critiques about not engaging the regional bureaus and domestic religious groups were easily countered with publicly available documents S/RGA had produced over the years. The malice behind all these charges was palpable. My interlocutor expressed surprise and shock at the evidence I gave. Our meeting ended with the staffer telling me Secretary Pompeo had not decided yet about the fate of S/RGA and that my evidence would be factored into their analysis. Alas, Pompeo authorized Tillerson's proposed changes, and S/RGA was killed. The power of the three slanders against us proved to be too much.

There are three questions left for me to answer. First, just who or what do I mean by the "devil" in the title of the book? Second, what are the current prospects for restarting S/RGA by the Biden administration? And finally, what should a renewed S/RGA look like, based on what I learned from its first incarnation?

What about the devil? When I mentioned my working title to a friend, he immediately asked me which undersecretary I was calling the devil. I demurred and did not take the bait. At the risk of disappointing many of my readers, let me clarify now, I am not referring to any particular person or persons as the devil. I am, however, pointing to a collection of malign global forces that were apparent during my time at the State Department and, in most cases, are still at work around the planet. Satan is the English transliteration of a term in the Hebrew Bible whose literal meaning is "adversary."[1] So I am taking the devil to be a symbol of those malign and oppositional forces I saw at work around the world. And their number was large, and not all of those forces were external to the United States. And to be clear, those malign forces posed a vast array of threats to our work, from the existential to the level of minor irritant and also to the work of others in the State Department. I am not equating, for instance, the evil wrought by ISIL with the minor headaches leaders of right-wing Christian religious freedom advocates caused for the work of the Office of Religion and Global Affairs. If the metaphor of "the devil" offends, I'm sorry. But as a symbol of the collective range and magnitude of malign forces we faced, I think it is apt. While we were occupied trying to make the world a better place, we were always aware of various adversaries working at cross purposes with ours. Nevertheless,

I would argue that we were never overwhelmed by those threats, and it would be hard to overstate the joy and camaraderie we felt in our work.

I think historians will look back on the Obama presidency as a time of real global peril. And I think it is fair to say I felt a good bit of daily pressure to make contributions to help address some of those issues, as I try to show in the previous chapters. Let's start with the truly evil. I was often asked if we saved any lives directly. That question always irritated me a little. I don't believe the major criterion for evaluating our work should be based on how many burning buildings we ran into. For the most part, that represents a gross misunderstanding of what diplomacy actually entails, especially for a Washington-based office. It is true that two of our staff members were deeply involved in rescuing a small set of families of a minority religion from a life-threatening situation and relocating them to a safer, more hospitable environment. Likewise, I was brought in to consult on a hostage case that ultimately failed, and I will carry the memory of that failure with me until I die. We made marginal contributions to the effort to relocate Guantanamo Bay detainees, one of the many moral stains left by the George W. Bush administration. And that pretty much exhausts any work we did that might have been close to headline status. There isn't a lot more to be said about that.

There were, however, many global hot spots where we made routine diplomatic contributions to government-wide efforts to push back on efforts that had significant negative moral implications, including some of the work I have already mentioned but have not described at any length. When I look back at these years, I see the expansion of autocratic nationalist leaders and their fruit. Putin, Xi Jinping, Modi, ISIL, even Aung San Suu Kyi will all be remembered for their atrocities. And in each case, religion was a significant vector, and we made contributions on the policy side resisting their evil. I was particularly proud of the work we did supporting Secretary Kerry in the policy process of declaring that ISIL was guilty of genocide against multiple religious communities in Iraq.

I have covered the domestic adversaries we encountered: the religious freedom folk who saw our work as threatening their exclusive hegemony in the religion and diplomacy space; some leaders in the countering violent extremism sector who tried to enlist us in their work to create "moderate" Muslims; Republican politicians who advanced bad-faith arguments about refugees, immigrants, and the administration's policy change in Cuba; and the occasional religious leader who put personal success over political success in some contexts. It is a chaotic world, and confronting adversaries, whether in the form of international bad actors, evil global movements that compound human suffering, or human-induced climate change, will always be a part of American diplomacy. Against this background, the work of persuading religious communities to work together on issues of mutual concern with US foreign policy goals was never boring, always challenging, and, for the most part, pathbreaking work.

Just what is the future of the analysis of religion for US diplomacy? The story might be over, or it might reappear to build on the sophistication we brought to the space. My conversations with members of the Biden administration to this point in time have been decidedly mixed. At the point of this writing in 2022, the answer for the moment is "not now." Given the radical staffing cuts of State Department staff by the Trump administration, and given the obstruction of confirming appointees by insurrection-supporting Senators Ted Cruz and Josh Hawley, and the diplomatic wildfires erupting around the planet, it is not surprising Secretary Blinken's senior staff have not had the bandwidth to assess the question. It is disappointing but understandable. My fear is that some of the historical reticence of liberal Democrats to sufficiently grasp my arguments on why this work is important may feed the bureaucratic inertia against embracing the value of the sort of work we did. I've learned never to underestimate the power of reticence combined with inertia, to say nothing of fear. But I remain hopeful that will change, and at some point the Office of Religion and Global Affairs will be restarted.

There are several senior leaders at State today who support the reopening of S/RGA. I think in time crises could easily erupt that demonstrate the need for that skill set, and its absence will be noted. But I hope it does not take a crisis to make this clear. The truth is, as several of my colleagues there have told me, the State Department is broken after the Trump years, and it is going to take years to repair it. But there are many fronts at State where similar stories to mine can be told. The rebuilding of the department is off to a slow start. The recovery of US diplomacy may require a generation.

This is a natural time to pivot to the final question about what a refashioned S/RGA might ideally look like. In terms of structure, I think there are three lessons to be learned here. First, I would jettison the so-called Specials.

The Trump era killed the Special Representative for Muslim Communities position, and I don't believe the Biden administration will restart it. If there is a need for a diplomatic initiative here, it is probably more akin to the current proposal from Representative Ilhan Omar to establish a Special Envoy to Combat Islamophobia and would be analogous to the current Special Envoy to Monitor and Combat Anti-Semitism. But it should be located in the Bureau of Democracy, Human Rights, and Labor. Similarly, President Biden had upgraded the Special Envoy to Monitor and Combat Anti-Semitism to an ambassadorial position and spun it off as an independent office. And the Special Envoy to the Organization of Islamic Cooperation should be folded back into the Bureau of International Organizations, where it was before S/RGA. It looks like the Biden team is going to make that move.

These three offices were tiny—two or three staff members at best—with very limited budgets, and were scattered all across the sprawling State Department bureaucracy with limited impact before the Kerry era. They were merged into S/RGA before my arrival on the advice of a consultant. I was charged with making them successful, and I did that by giving them more staff and budget resources than they ever had. But now I think it is clear they need to be housed in more appropriate locations for their respective missions. They will lose some of their access to the secretary as a result, but they will be closer to relevant mission-oriented senior leadership. I did not tell their stories in this book because the special envoys or representatives, Shaarik Zafar, Ira Forman, and Arsalan Suleman, may want to tell their own stories of their work in S/RGA instead of hearing my version of what they did. To a person they performed admirably, and I could not have asked for better partners.

I believe our original threefold mission of advising the secretary, equipping posts to assess religious dynamics and engage religious actors, and being the public connection point for external partners still holds up. If a new office reappears, it will be the second mission, equipping more posts to do this important work, that will need the most additional attention. America's diplomatic footprint has never been fainter in my lifetime as a result of the great Pompeo purge. Personnel at all levels is depleted. Expertise in religion is virtually nonexistent, and senior leaders are confronting a global to-do list that would be intimidating in any time period and even with a fully staffed department. Without an analogue office to S/RGA, opportunities will be missed, bad policies are more likely, and a generation of willing partners to help advance US interests will be turned away. None of these outcomes are foreordained, and all of them can be avoided.

One of the dynamics we began to see in the Obama era, the rise of global right-wing populism and nationalism, is only spreading and becoming more intense, in the United States and around the planet. The impact of religious dynamics plays out differently in almost every national context. But religion is a constant vector. At a minimum, there always seems to be targeted religious minorities, as well as majority religions that are co-opted by the authoritarian governments to the benefit of the authoritarian leaders. My suspicion is that US efforts to push back against these forces will mirror its earlier work on countering violent extremism in that it will approach the religious dynamics of these various movements primarily from a security perspective and not one of direct diplomatic engagement based on contextual historical understanding. The FBI, the Department of Homeland Security, the NSA, and the Pentagon do not have a capacity to analyze the religious dynamics of these movements, and they probably never will. At the moment, the State Department doesn't have such a capacity either. If there is a new advisory office on global religion, it will have to have a greater analytical capacity than we had in my day on how to counter the flood of right-wing religion-fueled populism.

There is language coming out of the State Department to the effect of renewing a commitment to expand engagement with civil society organizations and universities. I believe our work to expand and strengthen public engagement made a huge contribution to the overall public diplomacy of the department in the Kerry era. What we did with very limited resources in the Kerry era would be a good place to look for great ideas in how to do this work. I believe there is even greater demand today across the globe from religious communities, religion scholars, media, and religiously affiliated NGOs to engage US diplomacy than there was during the Kerry years. Expanding relationships with those networks will increase the influence and effectiveness of US diplomacy.

And the one area I have mentioned briefly that needs a complete overhaul would be the integration of knowledge and expertise on religion throughout the executive branch. A strong research capacity on religion, once housed in the intelligence community, was shuttered by the Trump administration.

While the National Security Council under Biden has restarted the Global Engagement Directorate, there is no longer an Interagency Policy Council on religion, which in the Obama era included S/RGA, the intelligence community, the Pentagon, and USAID. As a consequence, any relevant work within the wider executive branch, shrunken though it may be, no longer has an information pipeline through which to communicate routinely to the White House. Right now, the Biden administration has a degraded capacity to understand religion and is without a mechanism to share the benefits if the old capacity is restored.

I am by nature both hopeful and realistic. The realistic side of me fears the State Department will go back to its ill-educated reticence with respect to religion. The hopeful side of me believes we made a compelling case in our short tenure and that our narrative will eventually be recovered. Only time will tell what the future of a better understanding of religion in US diplomacy will be. But at this moment, the capacity of our diplomacy to understand religious dynamics is near to that which prevailed at the beginning of our forever wars at the beginning of the millennium. To be sure, the foreign policy leaders of the current administration do not harbor the grandiose illusions the Bush administration did and their thirst for war. But the ability to understand the complex dynamics of religion now is virtually nonexistent in the current administration, and that is a troubling prospect against the background of our increasingly unruly world.

NOTES

Acknowledgments

1. Augustine, *City of God*, trans, Henry Bettenson, ed. David Knowles (Harmondsworth: Penguin, 1972), book 22, chapter 30.

Chapter One

1. For Kerry's account of learning about Pershing's death, see John Kerry, *Every Day Is Extra* (New York: Simon & Schuster, 2018), 54–55.

2. See Michael Oren's account of the religious aspects of the tense negotiations between the United States and the Barbary Pirates even before the passing of the Constitution. Michael Oren, *Power, Faith, and Fantasy: America in the Middle East; 1776 to the Present* (New York: Norton, 2007), 23–32.

3. William Burns reinforces the point in the conclusion of his magnificent book *The Back Channel: A Memoir of American Diplomacy and the Case for Its Renewal* (New York: Random House, 2019), 408. He argues for a trinity of qualities every diplomat should have: judgment, balance, and discipline. All three require a nuanced grasp of history and culture, mastery of foreign languages, hard-nosed facility in negotiations, and the capacity to translate American interests in ways that other governments can see as consistent with their own interests. See also John Campbell, *Nigeria and the Nation-State: Rethinking Diplomacy with the Postcolonial World* (Lanham, MD: Rowman & Littlefield, 2020), ix, where he cites the need for diplomats to understand the dynamics of how countries work in order to be able to communicate effectively back to Washington. He specifically cites the need to better understand the complex religious landscape of Nigeria.

4. For a detailed explanation of the paradox of the failure of analysts to grapple with religion in international affairs despite the long-standing influence of religion in global politics, see J. Bryan Hehir, "Why Religion? Why Now?," in *Rethinking Religion and World Affairs*, ed. Timothy Samuel Shah, Alfred Stepan, and Monica Duffy Toft (New York: Oxford University Press, 2012), 15–35.

5. I do not know why Secretary Clinton never launched a version of the office. Once inside, I heard three different reasons for why she never pulled the trigger. The first reason was that someone on her legal affairs team thought it was unconstitutional. Since several members of the White House Counsel's Office seemed to believe it was constitutional, this doesn't sound right to me. The second reason I heard was that the proposal sat on Clinton's chief of staff's desk and just disappeared. This strikes me as a very possible explanation, as gatekeepers have tremendous power in making things disappear by just sitting on them. And finally, I learned that a version of the office was in the works but fell victim to the chaos surrounding Benghazi at the end of her term as secretary. The office was to be called the Office of Religious Engagement, and a director had been tapped to lead it.

6. See John Lewis Gaddis, *On Grand Strategy* (New York: Random House, 2018). I see Gaddis and my own professor, Richard Neustadt at Harvard, attempting to do similar things in their respective works. Neustadt attempted to theorize how to make government institutions think smarter, to organize decision making, and to strengthen and preserve the institution of the presidency. Gaddis, ever the historian, also tries to teach the would-be grand strategists on what qualities to learn and master in order to develop better diplomatic strategies.

7. See Gaddis, *On Grand Strategy*. I am not claiming that Gaddis would endorse my application of his theses, nor do I want to imply that I agree with all Gaddis argues. However, his provocative work strikes me as incredibly rich and nuanced, and for my immediate purposes highly instructive.

8. Gaddis, *On Grand Strategy*, 4–5. I am by training and experience very uneasy about universalizing such things as being general to all human beings. Yet it is still possible to identify common traits and tendencies in historical characters.

9. Gaddis, *On Grand Strategy*, 8.

10. Gaddis, *On Grand Strategy*, 66–67. Gaddis points to Abraham Lincoln's strategic prowess in fighting the Civil War as an exemplar of the sort of strategic thinking he is commending. The best case I have seen for Lincoln along these lines is Richard Carwadine, *Lincoln: A Life of Purpose and Power* (New York: Vintage Books, 2006).

11. Gaddis, *On Grand Strategy*, 250–51.

12. One telling episode is illustrative of the fox-like nature of some of our religion experts. A staffer in our office once proposed a series of over a dozen international trips over the course of a summer to me. It looked more like a research trip for a new book than it did a rational plan for shaping our policy recommendations to the secretary. I demurred and did not approve the trip. I'm sure the staffer would have learned many interesting and possibly valuable things. But the relevance to particular policy initiatives was just not there. We were constantly seeking to anchor our work and research to concrete policy priorities of the secretary. And sometimes I had to be the bad guy in our shop.

Chapter Two

1. José Casanova, *Public Religions in the Modern World* (Chicago: University of Chicago Press, 1994), 3.

2. Casanova, *Public Religions*, 3.

3. Douglas Johnston and Cynthia Sampson, eds., *Religion, the Missing Dimension of Statecraft* (New York: Oxford University Press, 1994).

4. See Samuel P. Huntington, "The Clash of Civilizations?" *Foreign Affairs* 72, no. 2 (Summer 1993): 22–49; Samuel P. Huntington, *The Clash of Civilizations and the Remaking of World Order* (New York: Simon & Schuster, 1996).

5. Huntington, *The Clash of Civilizations*, 13.

6. Huntington, *The Clash of Civilizations*, 13.

7. Huntington does not actually claim universal validity for Western democracy and values, which separates him from many of his epigones who did in fact invoke his name as a source of warrants around the American invasion of Iraq, as an extension of American exceptionalism.

8. Huntington, *The Clash of Civilizations*, 43.

9. See "Christopher Dawson 12 October 1889–25 May 1970 First Incumbent of the Charles Chauncey Stillman Chair at Harvard," *Harvard Theological Review* 66, no. 2 (April 1973). Did Dawson and Huntington overlap at Harvard? Did they share a Eurocentric view that knowingly or perhaps unwittingly posits the moral and religious superiority of the Christian West? One senses that Huntington may be allied with a normative view that Europe was rescued from decline by the healing work of Christian royals.

10. Huntington, *The Clash of Civilizations*, 45.

11. Huntington, *The Clash of Civilizations*, 29.

12. Huntington, *The Clash of Civilizations*, 101.

13. See Madeline Albright, *The Mighty and the Almighty: Reflections on America, God, and World Affairs* (New York: HarperCollins, 2006).

14. See Ronald Thiemann, *Constructing a Public Theology: The Church in a Pluralistic Age* (Louisville: Westminster John Knox, 1991).

15. Thiemann also wrote a hauntingly accurate critique of theologians such as Stanley Hauerwas some thirty years ago who embraced antiliberal theology at a time when liberal democracy was under attack from both ends of the political spectrum. Thiemann's worry then was that such attacks on liberal democracy could undermine democracy over the long haul. In a time when American democracy is under literal attack today, it is worth pondering how antiliberal theologians such as Hauerwas have paved the way for the embrace of Donald Trump and the attendant rise of violence attached to certain quarters of evangelical and other American Christian communities. See Thiemann, *Constructing a Public Theology*, 23–24.

16. See Shahab Ahmed, *What Is Islam? The Importance of Being Islamic* (Princeton: Princeton University Press, 2016).

17. Ahmed, *What Is Islam?*, 245.

18. Neta Crawford, "US Budgetary Cost of Wars through 2016: $4.79 Trillion and Counting; Summary of Costs of the US Wars in Iraq, Syria, Afghanistan and Pakistan and Homeland Security," Watson Institute Brown University, November 2017.

19. See Lindsey Hines et al., "Posttraumatic Stress Disorder Post Iraq and Afghanistan: Prevalence among Military Subgroups," *Canadian Journal of Psychiatry* 59, no. 9 (September 2014): 468–79.

20. See the latest costs of the post-9/11 wars compiled by the Watson Institute for International and Public Affairs at https://watson.brown.edu/costsofwar/figures. Their accounting includes the budgetary costs to the United States ($8 trillion), the human cost (over 929,000 people), the geographic reach (over eighty-five countries), and the number of displaced persons (38 million).

21. See https://www.oprm.va.gov/docs/foia/GWOT_Rpt-Jun_2014_Final_Rerun_NoEDU.doc.

22. UNHCR: The UN Refugee Agency, "Global Trends: Forced Displacement in 2016," 67, https://www.unhcr.org/5943e8a34.pdf.

23. See "Iraq 2012 International Religious Freedom Report," in *International Religious Freedom Report for 2012*, US Department of State.

24. For the first comprehensive attempt to put a price tag on Iraq, see Jo-

seph E. Stiglitz and Linda Bilmes, *The Three Billion Dollar War: The True Costs of the Iraq Conflict* (New York: Norton, 2008). This is the most comprehensive analysis of the cost of the invasion. This book was written over a decade ago, and the cost has gone up according to the latest figures from the Watson Institute.

25. See https://watson.brown.edu/costsofwar/figures.

26. See C. J. Chivers, *The Fighters: Americans in Combat in Afghanistan and Iraq* (New York: Simon & Schuster, 2018), xxi. In the voluminous accounting of the wars, this book is the best single account I know in telling the story clearly that US strategy was not waged in a well-informed manner about the implications of religious belief and practice of Afghan and Iraqi civilians.

27. The best single account of the failures of the president to authorize and conduct a thorough policy assessment of the invasion is found in Richard Haass, *War of Necessity, War of Choice: A Memoir of Two Iraq Wars* (New York: Simon & Shuster, 2009).

28. Haass, *War of Necessity*, 279. Haass includes his fifteen-page memo from the Office of Policy and Planning in the State Department to Secretary Colin Powell titled "Reconstruction in Iraq—Lessons of the Past." This otherwise deep and helpful memo only refers to religion once, and that by noting that Iran might meddle in postconflict reconstruction efforts by exploiting historic relations with Iraqi Shiite leaders. There is no suggestion on how to engage such Shiite leaders. Haass requested two intelligence community products, "Regional Consequences of Regime Change in Iraq" and "Principal Challenges in Post-Saddam Iraq," that were done in January 2003. While both made perfunctory acknowledgments of Sunni-Shia dynamics in Iraq, neither signaled the disruptive forces that religious dynamics ended up posing for the invasion and its aftermath. Economic recovery and democracy building were seen as tools to mitigate any religious problems.

29. See David Kilcullen, *Counterinsurgency* (New York: Oxford University Press, 2010).

30. See *The U.S. Army/Marine Corps Counterinsurgency Field Manual* (Chicago: University of Chicago Press, 2007).

31. I attended a war game in 2007, and during a break I asked a marine who trained soldiers for deployment in Iraq if it was feasible to add instruction on how to interpret religious dynamics on the ground. He scoffed at the premise. He told me he did not have enough time to do much other than marginally increase the odds his pupils would not be killed, much less turn them into expert interpreters of local Muslim communities.

32. See *Religious Affairs in Joint Operations*, Joint Publication I-05, November 20, 2013; Chaplain William Sean Lee, Lt. Col. Christopher Burke, Lt. Col. Zonna M. Crayne, *Military Chaplains as Peace Builders Embracing Indigenous Religions in Stability Operations* (Maxwell Air Force Base, AL: Air University Press, 2005); Douglas Johnston, *Religion, Terror, and Error: U.S. Foreign Policy and the Challenge of Spiritual Engagement* (Santa Barbara, CA: Praeger, 2011); S. K. Moore, *Military Chaplains as Agents of Peace: Religious Leader Engagement in Conflict and Post-Conflict Environments* (Lanham, MD: Lexington Books, 2013); Eric Patterson, ed., *Military Chaplains in Afghanistan, Iraq, and Beyond: Advisement and Leader Engagement in Highly Religious Environments* (Lanham, MD: Rowman & Littlefield, 2014).

33. See https://www.pbs.org/wgbh/pages/frontline/yeariniraq/interviews /rajiv.html. See also Rajiv Chandrasekaran, *Imperial Life in the Emerald City: Inside Iraq's Green Zone* (New York: Vintage Books, 2007), 184–87.

34. In his defense, Bremer spins his relationship with Sistani in a different direction in his own telling of his time in Iraq. While acknowledging that Sistani never met directly with any American officials, Bremer suggests they had a warm relationship in a correspondence comprised of a dozen letters. A hermeneutic of suspicion leads one to see in this odd passage an attempt to address the widespread perception that he mismanaged the relationship early on and never recovered. See Paul Bremer, *My Year in Iraq: The Struggle to Build a Future of Hope* (New York: Threshold Editions, 2006), 164–67.

35. In this section I am relying on the account given by Anna Su in her masterful critical historical account of US religious-freedom policy. See Anna Su, *Exporting Freedom: Religious Liberty and American Power* (New York: Oxford University Press, 2016).

36. See especially Su, *Exporting Freedom*, chap. 6, "Age of Exceptionalism." I am in deep sympathy with her view that human rights are socially constructed over time and that religious freedom is not somehow the most valuable human right in a long hierarchy of other rights. In addition, see the work of Noah Feldman, *After Jihad: America and the Struggle for Islamic Democracy* (New York: Farrar, Straus & Giroux, 2003); Noah Feldman, *What Do We Owe Iraq: War and the Ethics of Nation Building* (Princeton: Princeton University Press, 2004); Noah Feldman, "The Democratic Fatwa: Islam and Democracy in the Realm of Constitutional Politics," *Oklahoma Law Review* 58, no. 1 (Spring 2005); Noah Feldman, "Imposed Constitutionalism," *Connecticut Law Review* 37, no. 4 (Sum-

mer 2005); Noah Feldman and Roman Martinez, "Constitutional Politics and Text in the New Iraq: An Experiment in Islamic Democracy," *Fordham Law Review* 75, no. 2 (2006): article 20. See also Peter Danchin, "U.S. Unilateralism and the Protection of Religious Freedom: The Multilateral Alternative," *Columbia Journal of Transnational Law*, 2002, and Elizabeth Castelli, "Praying for the Persecuted Church: US Christian Activism in the Global Arena," *Journal of Human Rights* 4, no. 3 (2005).

37. See Eric Schmidt, "Threats and Responses: Military Spending; Pentagon Contradicts General on Iraq Occupation Force's Size," *New York Times*, February 28, 2003.

38. The Center for Strategic and International Studies published two landmark evaluations of the reconstruction efforts, both of which were grim in their analysis. See "Iraq's Post-Conflict Reconstruction: A Field Review and Recommendations July 17, 2003" and "Progress or Peril: Measuring Iraq's Reconstruction," September 2004. See also the scathing analysis of an insider, Larry Diamond, *Squandered Victory: The American Occupation and the Bungled Effort to Bring Democracy to Iraq* (New York: Holt, 2005). For a historical chronicle of the reconstruction effort, see James Dobbins et al., *Occupying Iraq: A History of the Coalition Provisional Authority* (Santa Monica, CA: Rand Corporation, 2009).

39. See John Lewis Gaddis, *On Grand Strategy* (New York: Random House, 2018). I am not claiming that Gaddis would endorse my application of his theses, nor do I want to imply that I agree with all Gaddis argues. However, his provocative work strikes me as incredibly rich and nuanced, and for my immediate purposes highly instructive.

40. Gaddis, *On Grand Strategy*, 8.

41. Gaddis, *On Grand Strategy*, 66–67.

42. The literature on the invasion of Iraq is immense and complex. I have relied particularly on Haass, *War of Necessity, War of Choice*; George Packer, *The Assassin's Gate* (New York: Farrar, Straus & Giroux, 2005); Thomas Ricks, *Fiasco* (New York: Penguin Press, 2006); and Ron Suskind, *The One Percent Doctrine* (New York: Simon & Shuster, 2006). See also Rajiv Chandrasekaran, *Imperial Life in the Emerald City: Inside Iraq's Green Zone* (New York: Vintage Books, 2006); Derek Chollet, *The Long Game: How Obama Defied Washington and Redefined America's Role in the World* (New York: Public Affairs, 2016); Chivers, *The Fighters*; Diamond, *Squandered Victory*; Dobbins et al., *Occupying Iraq*; John Kerry, *Every Day Is Extra* (New York: Simon & Schuster, 2018);

Phoebe Marr, *The Modern History of Iraq* (Boulder, CO: Westview, 2012); Barack Obama, *A Promised Land* (New York: Crown Books, 2020); George Packer, *Our Man: Richard Holbrooke and the End of the American Century* (New York: Knopf, 2019); and Ben Rhodes, *The World as It Is: A Memoir of the Obama White House* (New York: Random House, 2018).

43. Suskind, *The One Percent Doctrine*, 123.

44. Gaddis, *On Grand Strategy*, 66–67. Gaddis points to Abraham Lincoln's strategic prowess in fighting the Civil War as an exemplar of the sort of strategic thinking he is commending. The best case I have seen for Lincoln along these lines is Richard Carwadine, *Lincoln: A Life of Purpose and Power* (New York: Vintage Books, 2006).

45. Gaddis, *On Grand Strategy*, 250–51.

46. Albright, *Mighty and the Almighty*, 8.

Chapter Three

1. You know you are getting old when the hospital you were born in has been closed. This region continues to suffer from a variety of poverty-related ills. From the shrinking of adequate rural health care to the opioid crisis, the Bootheel is ground zero for rural poverty in America. See Jack Healy, "It's 4 A.M. The Baby's Coming. But the Hospital Is 100 Miles Away," *New York Times*, July 17, 2018, section F, p. 15; Sarah Brown and Karin Fischer, "Dying Town: Here in a Corner of Missouri and across America, the Lack of a College Education Has Become a Public-Health Crisis," *Chronicle of Higher Education*, January 5, 2018.

2. See Richard Neustadt and Ernest May, *Thinking in Time: The Uses of History for Decision-Makers* (New York, Free Press, 1986), 157. I do this exercise for two reasons. First, I want to clarify some early misperceptions of who I was when I was appointed. And second, I think this exercise can help people understand why we organized the mission of the work the way we did, in contrast to a multitude of other paths we might have taken.

3. Another version of the joke about three sacraments goes baptism, communion, and attendance.

4. See David Edwin Harrell, "The Sectional Origins of the Churches of Christ," *Journal of Southern History* 30, no. 3 (August 1964): 277. See also Richard T. Hughes, *Reviving the Ancient Faith: The Story of Churches of Christ in America* (Grand Rapids: Eerdmans, 1996).

5. The term "Campbellite" is a reference to one of the founders of the movement, Alexander Campbell. From what I can gather, this epithet gained currency in the nineteenth century and was a commonly heard term of derision in my childhood. Most of my contemporaries in the Churches of Christ were familiar with the term, but we did not possess any real grasp of where it came from.

6. See *Official Manual of the State of Missouri for the Years 1913–1914*, compiled and published by Cornelius Roach, Secretary of State (Jefferson City: Stephens Printing Company, n.d.). See also Leon Parker Ogilvie, "Populism and Socialism in the Southeast Missouri Lowlands," *Missouri Historical Review* 65, no. 2 (January 1971); David R. Thelen, *Paths of Resistance: Tradition and Dignity in Industrializing Missouri* (New York: Oxford University Press, 1986), especially chap. 5, "Communities, Economic Development and Vigilantes: On the Mixture of Racial and Religious Dynamics"; Jarod Roll, *Spirit of Rebellion: Labor and Religion and the New Cotton South* (Urbana: University of Illinois Press, 2010); Erik Gellman and Jarod Roll, *The Gospel of the Working Class: Labor's Southern Prophets in New Deal America* (Urbana: University of Illinois Press, 2011); Thad Snow, *From Missouri: An American Farmer Looks Back*, ed. Bonnie Stepenwolf (Columbia: University of Missouri Press, 2012); Bonnie Stepenwolf, *Thad Snow: A Life of Social Reform* (Columbia: University of Missouri Press, 2003); and Kerry Pimblot, *Faith in Black Power: Religion, Race, and Resistance in Cairo, Illinois* (Lexington: University Press of Kentucky, 2017). Pimblot's account of national African American religious leaders and their influence on the civil rights movement in the border region along the Ohio River is astonishing.

7. After the 2008 presidential election, I had a lovely conversation with Sen. John Danforth at an event in St. Louis where we discussed our common roots in the Bootheel region. When I told him my parents styled themselves as this type of Republican, Sen. Danforth threw his head back and roared. He said he hadn't heard that term used in years, and certainly not in Washington, DC. At that point he was frequently picketed in Missouri when he supported GOP candidates on the hustings as a RINO—Republican in name only!

8. For a compelling theological critique of this use of "natural," see Kathryn Tanner, *God and Creation in Christian Theology* (Minneapolis: Augsburg Fortress, 2004).

9. I cannot find much scholarly reflection on the history of Paducah. Exceptions are John E. L. Robertson, *Paducah, 1830–1980* (self-published, n.d.), and Glen Murrell, "The Desegregation of Paducah Junior College," *Register of the*

Kentucky Historical Society 67, no. 1 (January 1969): 63–79. Murrell provides a very interesting history of the attempts to desegregate higher education state-wide in Kentucky. He also notes the involvement of Thurgood Marshall as part of the support provided to the local plaintiffs as part of the work of the NAACP Legal Defense and Education Fund. Because of this work in the early 1950s, the local junior college was desegregated before *Brown v. Board of Education* was decided in 1954.

10. For an attempt to compile a comprehensive list of theological doctoral degrees earned by members of the Churches of Christ through 2004, see Don L. Meredith, "Educational Studies: Theological Doctoral Studies by Members of the Churches of Christ, 1904–2004," in *Restoring the First Century Church in the Twenty-First Century: Essays on the Stone-Campbell Restoration Movement in Honor of Don Haymes*, ed. Warren Lewis and Hans Rollman (Eugene, OR: Wipf & Stock, 2005). My work at Harvard Divinity School is one oversight in this list!

11. See Martin Indyk, *Innocent Abroad: An Intimate Account of American Peace Diplomacy* (New York: Simon & Schuster, 2009).

12. See Richard Neustadt, *Presidential Power and the Modern Presidents: The Politics of Leadership*, rev. ed. (New York: Free Press, 1990; originally published 1960). Readers should also consult Matthew J. Dickinson and Elizabeth A. Neustadt, eds., *Guardian of the Presidency: The Legacy of Richard E. Neustadt* (Washington, DC: Brookings Institution Press, 2007).

13. See a similar story in Willie Morris, *North toward Home* (New York: Vintage Books, 2000).

14. For those who are hoping that I lay out a systematic theological case for why I am drawn to the work of diplomacy, I do not have the space to do that here. As I hint here, I have been influenced by an eclectic cohort of theologians such as Karl Barth, Helmut Gollwitzer, Harvey Cox, Reinhold and H. Richard Niebuhr, Francis Fiorenza, Bryan Hehir, Margaret Miles, Emilie Townes, and Robin Lovin, to name a few.

Chapter Four

1. The best single source for understanding this bizarre, influential, and dangerous conservative Christian group in Washington is Jeff Sharlet's *The Family: The Secret Fundamentalism at the Heart of American Power* (New York: Harper, 2008). The Family, or the Fellowship as it is sometimes called, seems to have a

lot of members in prominent positions in the Trump foreign-policy team and not a few Obama staffers. As the sponsor for the National Prayer Breakfast, they conduct a shadowy set of meetings after the formal prayer breakfast event, where a toxic brew of foreign leaders, international mafia, conservative American Christians, and US political leaders all discuss the "teachings of Jesus" while simultaneously advancing all manner of global mischief under a cloak of secrecy. No American president should ever address this cabal.

2. Unfortunately, some of the papers generated under Clinton's watch made it into the public record before I started, and a handful of academics had a field day criticizing the framing of the work by the civil society working group. These critics assumed incorrectly that Kerry had hired me and commissioned me to follow the conception of the office he inherited. Several of these scholars believe to this day the documents they saw contained my marching orders. Neither Kerry nor I ever saw these documents in their entirety, and I only saw a fraction of them long after we launched. It did, however, give me some pretty powerful ammunition against them when their critiques continued to surface over the first two years of our work. For the collective criticism, see https://tif.ssrc.org/2013/07/30/engaging-religion-at-the-department-of-state/. I will note that there was significant support among members of the American Academy of Religion (AAR) for our work. The AAR teamed with the Henry R. Luce Foundation to fund fellowships for religion scholars Evan Berry and Jerome Copulsky to work in S/RGA. David Buckley received a Council on Foreign Relations fellowship to join us for a year.

3. Among the cohort Robin Lovin and Will Storrar brought together were Vera Shevzov from Smith College, John Burgess from Pittsburgh Theological Seminary, Aristotle Papanikolaou from Fordham University, and Nadieszda Kizenko from Syracuse University.

4. See Reinhold Niebuhr, *The Irony of American History* (New York: Scribner's, 1952).

5. For our remarks, see https://2009-2017.state.gov/secretary/remarks/2013/08/212781.htm.

6. See the White House, "Empowering Local Partners to Prevent Violent Extremism in the United States," August 2011. See also the White House, "FACT SHEET: The White House Summit on Countering Violent Extremism," February 18, 2015, and "FACT SHEET: Leaders' Summit to Counter ISIL and Violent Extremism," September 29, 2015.

7. Will McCants and Clinton Watts, "U.S. Strategy for Countering Violent Extremism: An Assessment," Foreign Policy Research Institute, December 2012.

8. See these seven speeches by Sewall: "Combatting Terrorism: Looking over the Horizon," Geneva, Switzerland, June 15, 2015; "Why Counterterrorism Needs Countering Violent Extremism (CVE): How Human Rights and Good Governance Help Prevent Terrorism," Columbia Law School, New York City, September 22, 2015; "Preventing the Next ISIL: An Evolving Global Approach to Terrorism," Boston University, Boston, October 9, 2015; "Mobilizing against a Preeminent Challenge of the 21st Century: Countering Violent Extremism," Washington Institute for Near East Policy, November 20, 2015; "Countering Violent Extremism: How Human Rights and Good Governance Help Prevent Terrorism," Josef Korbel School of International Studies, Denver, February 29, 2016; "Our Common Struggle against Violent Extremism," Dhaka University, Dhaka, Bangladesh, March 30, 2016; "Religious Extremism in Africa," Center for Strategic and International Studies, Washington, DC, August 1, 2016.

9. For the text of the letter, see https://www.mercycorps.org/sites/default /files/20July2015_Statement_U.S.GlobalCounteringViolentExtremismAgenda .pdf.

10. See Peter Mandaville and Melissa Nozell, "Engaging Religion and Religious Actors in Countering Violent Extremism," United States Institute of Peace Special Report 413, August 2017.

11. For an in-depth view of Barton's work, see Rick Barton, *Peace Works: America's Unifying Role in a Turbulent World* (Lanham, MD: Rowman & Littlefield, 2018).

Chapter Five

1. See Will Steffen, "A Truly Diabolical Policy Problem," in *The Oxford Handbook of Climate Change and Society*, ed. John S. Dryzek, Richard B. Norgaard, and David Schlosberg (New York: Oxford University Press, 2014), 21–37.

2. See the following Yellowstone conference and National Park education staff efforts: https://medium.com/@HNRDems/how-climate-change-is-hurt ing-yellowstone-national-park-c128c27d580f; https://www.montana.edu /hansenlab/documents/downloadables/YS_18_2_Olliff_et_al_sm.pdf; https:// www.nps.gov/yell/learn/upload/Accessible-PDF-prepared-for-WEB-of -Yellowstone-Science-23-1.pdf; https://www.nps.gov/yell/learn/nature/cli mate-change.htm; https://greatnorthernlcc.org/sites/default/files/documents

/nps_ccar_2013_9.pdf; and https://esajournals.onlinelibrary.wiley.com/doi/full
/10.1002/ecs2.2380.

3. See the early study by CNA, "National Security and the Threat of Climate
Change," at https://www.cna.org/cna_files/pdf/national%20security%20and
%20the%20threat%20of%20climate%20change.pdf.

4. See https://cms.cern/collaboration.

5. To see the program at the Berkley Center visit https://berkleycenter
.georgetown.edu/events/symposium-on-religion-and-climate-change.

6. *Laudato Si*, par. 3. The full text of the encyclical can be found at https://
www.vatican.va/content/francesco/en/encyclicals/documents/papa-francesco
_20150524_enciclica-laudato-si.html.

7. *Gaudium et Spes*, par. 1.

8. *Gaudium et Spes*, par. 13.

9. *Gaudium et Spes*, par. 16.

10. For this text as well as the text for all his remarks, see https://aleteia
.org/2015/09/28/read-the-full-texts-of-all-of-pope-francis-addresses-during-his
-visit-to-the-u-s/.

11. Paris Agreement, 1. For the full text of the agreement see https://unfccc
.int/sites/default/files/english_paris_agreement.pdf.

12. Paris Agreement, 1.

13. Paris Agreement, 2.

14. Karl Barth once remarked, during his visit to the United States, on the
political activity of American churches, that this influence "may sometimes be
problematic and may promote a certain tendency toward self-righteousness."
See "1. Interview with Alexander J. Seiler November 28, 1962/January 23, 1963,"
in *Barth in Conversation*, vol. 2, *1963*, ed. Eberhard Busch (Louisville: Westminster John Knox, 2018), 2.

15. See Alice Hill and Madeline Babin, "Why Climate Finance Is Critical for
Accelerating Global Action," Council on Foreign Relations, May 18, 2021, http://
cfr.org.

16. Hill and Babin, "Why Climate Finance Is Critical for Accelerating Global
Action."

17. Hill and Babin, "Why Climate Finance Is Critical for Accelerating Global
Action."

18. Here I am following the analysis of Johannes F. Linn, "Mobilizing Funds
to Combat Climate Change: Lessons from the First Replenishment of the Green
Climate Fund," Brookings Institution, February 18, 2020.

19. See IPCC, "Frequently Asked Questions," https://www.ipcc.ch/site/as sets/uploads/sites/2/2018/12/SR15_FAQ_Low_Res.pdf.

20. For the most recent report by the Intergovernmental Panel on Climate Change see https://www.ipcc.ch/report/ar6/wg2/resources/spm-headline -statements.

21. See their first remarks at the White House regarding their respective jobs, https://www.whitehouse.gov/briefing-room/press-briefings/2021/01/27/press -briefing-by-press-secretary-jen-psaki-special-presidential-envoy-for-climate -john-kerry-and-national-climate-advisor-gina-mccarthy-january-27-2021/.

22. See, for example, https://www.whitehouse.gov/?s=readout+of+the +third+national+climate+task+force+meeting. Here you will find the sort of nitty-gritty diverse policies being implemented to see how the government is increasing carbon capture and preserving migratory bird habitats, nature-based projects to restore and enhance natural features to protect coastal communities, and other policies.

23. See https://www.whitehouse.gov/?s=President+invites+40+world+lead ers+to+leaders+summit+on+climate; https://www.whitehouse.gov/?s= fact+sheet%3A+president+biden+sets+2030+greenhouse+gas+pollution+re duction +target+aimed+at+creating+good-paying+union+jobs+and+securing +U.S.+leadership+on+clean+energy+technologies; and https://www.white house.gov/?s=leaders+summit+on+climate+summary+of+proceedings.

24. See https://www.whitehouse.gov/?s=Executive+Summary%3A+U.S .+international+climate+finance+plan.

25. See Riley E. Dunlap and Aaron M. McCright, "Organized Climate De- nial," in *The Oxford Handbook of Climate Change and Society*, ed. John S. Drydek, Richard Norgaard, and David Schlosberg (New York: Oxford University Press, 2014), 144–73.

Chapter Six

1. The title of this chapter comes from a poem by Emma Lazarus, "The New Colossus"; see https://poets.org/poem/new-colossus?gclid=CjwKCAjw8Km LBhB8EiwAQbqNoEReHkw_PwVUQkzEbhFvnlWsomV6sJlA46K8GyACSvN HYZ3Q58ZCUhoCIroQAvD_BwE.

2. These figures are as of June 2021. See https://www.unhcr.org/refugee -statistics/.

3. The best single-volume collection of essays on the history and background of the convention is Andreas Zimmermann, ed., *The 1951 Convention relating to the Status of Refugees and Its 1967 Protocol: A Commentary* (Oxford: Oxford University Press, 2011).

4. See the resulting document, *Guidelines on International Protection: Religion Based Refugee Claims under Article 1A (2) of the 1951 Convention and/or the 1967 Protocol relating to the Status of Refugees.* In particular, see paragraph 27, where I can see traces of my suggestions and those of other religion scholars in attendance on how to handle religiously based claims with more sophistication and reject the use of analogies to the personal experience of the judges and administrators. This document can be found at https://www.unhcr.org/en-us/publications/legal/40d8427a4/guidelines-international-protection-6-religion-based-refugee-claims-under.html.

5. This distinction between interreligious work as praxis and interreligious work as theater came from a professor of sociology at Bethlehem University who greeted me skeptically at a small gathering of faculty in Bethlehem. With folded arms, he viewed my arrival with the weary air of one who had seen a long trail of Americans coming to the region as do-gooder promoters of feel-good interreligious dialogue who should have probably never come to the region. When he asked me which mode of interreligious engagement I supported, I burst out laughing and told him that was the greatest single framing phrase I had heard. I had no interest in theater.

6. See https://www.pewforum.org/2019/07/23/feelings-toward-religious-groups/#familiarity-with-a-religion-leads-to-morefavorable-views. The vast data Pew has generated since 9/11 remain a treasure trove of useful information for anyone wanting to learn more about Islam either in the United States or globally.

7. Goudeau's brilliantly written book, *After the Last Border: Two Families and the Story of Refuge in America* (New York: Viking, 2020), is a powerful primer on refugee resettlement in the United States. And her attention to the complexities of refugees and agency as well as representation is exemplary. See especially her afterword, 303–8.

8. See, for instance, Mark Hamilton, *Jesus King of Strangers: What the Bible Really Says about Immigration* (Grand Rapids: Eerdmans, 2019); David Hollenbach, *Humanity in Crisis: Ethical and Religious Responses to Refugees* (Washing-

ton, DC: Georgetown University Press, 2019); and Rabbi Jonathan Sachs, *The Home We Build Together: Recreating Society* (London: Bloomsbury, 2007).

9. See Alexander Betts and Paul Collier, *Refuge: Rethinking Refugee Policy in a Changing World* (New York: Oxford University Press, 2017).

10. You can find the text at https://www.un.org/en/about-us/universal -declaration-of-human-rights.

11. This text can be found at https://www.unhcr.org/en-us/1951-refugee -convention.html.

12. Report of the United Nations High Commissioner for Refugees Part II Global Compact on Refugees, September 13, 2018, p. 1.

13. See https://www.raptim.org/largest-refugee-camps-in-2018/.

Chapter Seven

1. I've probably offended every religion scholar reading this book while boring the readers who don't know and don't care about current fights in the guild of religion scholars. I beg everyone's forgiveness. But I mention this because the work we did in S/RGA provoked a wide range of reactions among scholars of religion, some of which I detail in this book. I have chosen not to kill more trees by attempting to map systematically the current territory of the study of religion and the different responses to our work. In the final chapter I will mention some of those reactions only in passing, to correct some of the more egregious attempts to analyze our work. But on the whole, we got a positive reaction among religion scholars of various theoretical orientations.

2. A good place to get an orientation to the current state of scholarly discussions on religion and conflict is Atalia Omer, R. Scott Appleby, and David Little, eds., *The Oxford Handbook of Religion, Conflict, and Peacebuilding* (New York: Oxford University Press, 2015).

3. I should note that I benefited from the professional advice of several of my professors at Harvard Divinity School who were pretty consistent in not trying to make clones of themselves out of the doctoral students they taught. My immediate doctoral committee of Bryan Hehir, Ron Thiemann, Harvey Cox, and Francis Fiorenza never insisted on any "party" affiliation regarding theory, and in their own work they were all quite eclectic and interdisciplinary.

4. I cannot provide a comprehensive and deep assessment of the complex issues and history surrounding Middle East peace. I will point out a few helpful

sources for those who want to learn more. A good start for getting a grasp of the major issues and the Israeli and Palestinian views is a primer produced by the S. Daniel Abraham Center for Middle East Peace (http://centerpeace.org), which can be found at https://www.ispeacestillpossible.com/.

5. See https://www.usip.org/programs/alexandria-declaration. See also Yvonne Margaretha Wang, "How Can Religion Contribute to Peace in the Holy Land? A Study of Religious Peacework in Jerusalem" (PhD diss., University of Oslo, 2011), 197.

6. They would get their photo op later with Trump's envoy Jason Greenblatt, but the incoherence of the Trump Middle East "plan" and the internal bickering of the CRIHL led to its demise. The CRIHL did not survive the Trump peace effort and had disbanded, according to Trond Bakkevig. See Raphael Ahren, "In 'Historic Move,' Trump Envoy Hosts Interfaith Meeting," *Times of Israel*, March 16, 2017.

7. Naim Ateek's writings include *Justice and Only Justice: A Palestinian Theology of Liberation* (Maryknoll, NY: Orbis, 1989) and *A Palestinian Christian Cry for Reconciliation* (Maryknoll, NY: Orbis, 2013).

8. I call this technique of searching for an overlap in two people's family background or experience "Who's your Daddy?" For Southern men from a certain age, that is, old guys, this means trying to establish some mutual connection between families—not just individual men but entire lines of families. In Mississippi in the 1980s, the deepest metaphysical bond two white males could discover was if they had attended Ole Miss and were members of the same fraternity. If such a tie could also be discovered among their fathers, it would take an act of God to break the friendship. I didn't have much social capital to invest in the Mississippi version of this game. Obviously, the historic problems attached to this type of male bonding are beyond redemption today. But my point is that attempting to find some overlapping vectors of connection is an important part of formal and informal diplomacy. I could also relate a story where I attempted to do this with a senior US diplomat, and it ended in disaster, so one has to be prudential about this technique. I must refrain to protect the guilty.

9. For more on Rabbi Melchior, see https://www.rabbimichaelmelchior.org /welcome.

10. An exhaustive list of all our engagements during our visits there as well as our domestic engagements would be too long to recite. We did have multiple visits with the Waqf, with Sharia courts, with Danny Seideman, with World Vision

staff both there and in the United States. I had several interactions with Bishop Munib Younan, several Lutheran groups, the Tent of Nations, and Bethlehem University and Bethlehem Bible College.

11. For a transcript of the speech, see https://www.thejewishstar.com/stories /transcript-of-secretary-john-kerrys-speech-attacking-israeli-policies,11813?.

12. See https://www.deseret.com/2016/11/20/20600825/q-a-religious-free dom-ambassador-reflects-on-work-looks-toward-future.

13. It is important to see his elaboration on all six of these principles.

14. See the 2009 proposal by Michael Bell and Daniel Drezner at https:// www.foreignaffairs.com/articles/middle-east/2009-03-01/missing-peaces, as well as the more recent analysis by the International Conflict Group example at https://d2071andvipowj.cloudfront.net/b48-how-to-preserve-the-fragile-calm -at-jerusalem-s-holy-esplanade.pdf.

15. It was an unfortunate unforced error on the part of Trump's foreign policy when Secretary Pompeo tweeted out his support for Bartholomew's issue of the Tomas granting autocephaly because it reeked of precisely the sort of ecclesias-tical interference Russian had been alleging for years.

16. It would be impossible to list a full bibliography here of Orthodox history even on political theology, much less Orthodox theology. Here a few useful sug-gestions: Kristina Stoeckl, Ingeborg Gabriel, and Aristotle Papanikolaou, eds., *Political Theologies in Orthodox Christianity: Common Challenges—Divergent Po-sitions* (London: T&T Clark, 2018), and John P. Burgess, *Holy Rus': The Rebirth of Orthodoxy in the New Russia* (New Haven: Yale University Press, 2017).

17. See Vladimir Putin, "On the Historical Unity of Russians and Ukrainians," July 12, 2021, https://www.newagebd.net/article/164936/on-historical-unity-of -russians-and-ukrainians-i.

18. I am going to resist the temptation to say more about the tragic unfold-ing events at the moment of this writing in the Tigray region of Ethiopia under Abiy's direction. All I will say is that the evolving conflict there has a religious dimension woven throughout it, and that is not to say that somehow religion explains everything.

Chapter Eight

1. For the work and history of the dicastery, see https://www.humandevelop ment.va/en.html. For Tomasi's work at the UN, see H. E. Archbishop Silvano M.

Tomasi, *The Vatican in the Family of Nations: Diplomatic Actions of the Holy See at the UN and Other International Organizations in Geneva* (Cambridge: Cambridge University Press, 2017).

2. September 18, 2020.

3. John L. Allen Jr., "As Pompeo Arrives in Rome, We're through the Looking Glass," *Crux*, September 30, 2020.

4. Nicole Winfield, "Pompeo, Vatican Clash over China after Tensions Spill Out," Associated Press, October 1, 2020.

5. See Aaron Blake, "Bolton Says Trump Didn't Just Ignore Human Rights but Encouraged China's Concentration Camps," *Washington Post*, June 17, 2020, https://www.washingtonpost.com/politics/2020/06/17/bolton-says-trump -didnt-just-ignore-human-rights-encouraged-chinas-concentration-camps/.

6. The best account of the Vatican's role in the Cuba diplomatic normalization is Ben Rhodes, *The World as It Is: A Memoir of the Obama White House* (New York: Random House, 2018), see especially chap. 28, "Havana."

7. See statement by the president on Cuba policy changes at https:// obamawhitehouse.archives.gov/the-press-office/2014/12/17statement-pres ident-cuba-policy-changes. See also Peter Baker, "U.S. to Restore Full Relations with Cuba, Erasing a Last Trace of Cold War Hostility," *New York Times*, December 17, 2014.

8. A detailed account of the performance of the Cuban government on religious freedom can be found at https://www.state.gov/wp-content/uploads /2019/01/Cuba-3.pdf. It is clear that, even in 2016, when I found an overall better environment for religious communities in Cuba, the government was deeply involved in malign activity.

9. See the 2015 Benin section of the *International Religious Freedom Report for 2015*, United States Department of State, Bureau of Democracy, Human Rights, and Labor.

10. This collection of data I am relying on here in this section was led by Rebecca in both sessions at the end of each workshop. A cable was drafted by consulate staff in consultation with Rebecca's concurrent note taking during the sessions and distributed to a wide list back in Washington across several US government agencies summarizing the event and its outcomes.

11. See John Campbell, *Nigeria and the Nation-State: Rethinking Diplomacy with the Postcolonial World* (Lanham, MD: Rowman & Littlefield, 2020), especially chap. 4, "Sharing the Cake."

Chapter Nine

1. See James M. Efird, "Satan," in *The Harper-Collins Bible Dictionary*, ed. Paul
Achtemeier, rev. ed. (San Francisco: HarperCollins, 1996), 974–75.

INDEX

ABC News, 61–63
Abilene Christian University (ACU),
    47–48, 50, 163–64
actors, 31–32
Afghanistan, 4, 17, 18, 20, 28
African Council for Accreditation and
    Accountability, 216
"African Initiative on Education for Peace
    and Development through Inter-
    religious and Intercultural Dialogue,"
    210–11
Ahart, Thomas, 136–37
Ahmed, Abiy, 182
Ahmed, Shahab, 16
Al-Azar University, 86
Albright, Madeline, 14–15, 29
Al-Khatib, Azzam, 166
Allen, John, 157, 172, 195
antiliberalism, 232n15
Arab Spring, 182
Ateek, Naim, 163–64
Axelrod, David, 62

Babin, Madeline, 118
Baer, Lauren, 71, 77
Bakkevig, Trond, 161
Barkley Lake, 44
Bartholomew, Ecumenical Patriarch, 98,
    110, 174–75, 178–80
Barton, Rick, 92
Bean, Alice, 108
Benedict XVI, Pope, 189, 190

Benin, 210–11
Berkley Center for Religion, Peace, and
    World Affairs, 108
Berlin, Isaiah, 7, 25
Berry, Randy, 222
Berry, Wendell, 49
Betts, Alexander, 144, 145
Biden administration, 120–21, 142, 151,
    152, 167–68, 225–26, 228
Birch, Bruce, 57
Blachly, Rebecca Linder, 210–12, 213–14,
    222
Blinken, Antony, 146, 225
Blumenfeld, Laura, 155
Boehner, John, 111
Boston, 52, 54
Boycott, Divest, and Sanctions (BDS),
    160
Bremer, Paul, 22–23, 234n34
BudgIT, 215
Buhari, Muhammadu, 211–12
bullying, 49
bureaucracy, 3, 54–55, 79
Bureau of Conflict Stabilization Opera-
    tions (CSO), 78, 91, 92, 153
Bureau of Democracy, Human Rights,
    and Labor, 203, 226
Bureau of International Organizations,
    226
Bureau of Population, Refugees, and
    Migration (PRM), 132

Bureau of Western Hemisphere Affairs (WHA), 198
Burke, Raymond, Cardinal, 2
Burton, Bill, 62
Bush administration, 18, 19, 25–28, 57, 58, 70, 83–84, 103

Cambridge (MA), 48, 49–50
Campbell, Alexander, 35
Campbell, John, 218
Campbellites, 34, 237n5
Carter, Pat, 199
Casanova, José, 9, 10
Casey, George Washington, 37
Casey, Karen, 49
Catholic Relief Services (CRS), 190–91
Cats, 53
Center for Strategic and International Studies (CSIS), 60, 92, 210
Challenge of Peace (USCCB), 53–54, 56
Chandrakekaran, Ravi, 22–23
chaplains, 21, 87
Cheney, Dick, 27
Chicago, 139–41
Chicago Council on World Affairs, 141
China, 195–96
Christianity: Churches of Christ, 35; corruption, Nigeria, 212, 214–17; CVE, 87; fundamentalist, 61, 93, 166, 194–95; history, 175–76; Huntington, 13; and Iraq, 18, 23–24; and Islam, 87; nationalism, 116, 142, 221; and Obama, 64–65; public policy, 56; public theology, 15–16; and UN, 116. See also evangelicalism
Chomsky, Noam, 12
Christie, Chris, 130
Churches of Christ, 32–36, 52–53, 56–57
Church World Service (CWS), 126, 129, 130
civilization, 12–13
Civil War, 37
Clash of Civilizations (Huntington), 11–13
class, 44–45, 47
climate change: Biden, 120–22; Catholics, 106; disinformation, 123–24; finance, 117–18, 121–22, 123; Francis, 108–15;
Kerry, 44, 103, 104; moral principles, 116; Obama administration, 101; planetary warming, limiting, 119–20; policy, 105, 117; policy shops, 105, 106–7; problem of, 102–3; and religion, 101, 104–6, 115, 119, 122–23; secular environmental groups, 104, 107; and S/RGA, 104, 105–6, 119, 122–24; Trump, 120, 121; United Nations, 115–18; US, 121–22. See also Paris Accord on Climate Change
Clinton, Hillary, 75–77, 153, 220
Clinton, Bill, 57, 230n5
Coe, Doug, 73
Colecchi, Steve, 106, 190
Collier, Paul, 144, 145
Conference of Cuban Catholic Bishops, 204
conflict, 10–11, 153–54, 187. See also Israel-Palestine peace negotiations; Russia; violence
Congress, US, 74–75, 109, 111, 112, 114, 115, 201
Cook, Susan Johnson, 75
Copulsky, Jerome, 82
corruption, Nigerian, 212–18
costs of 9/11 wars, 17–18, 232n20
Council of the Religious Institutions of the Holy Land (CRIHL), 161–62
countering violent extremism (CVE), 83–92
counterinsurgency, 20–21
Cownie, Frank, 138
Cremisan Monastery, 160
Cronkite, Walter, 41
Cuba: Castros, 198, 201, 205–6, 208; Catholic Church, 204, 210; Diego, 207–9; diplomatic relations, 197–98; evangelicals, 206–7; Islam, 204; Judaism, 205–6; Kerry, 201; Obama, 197–98, 200, 206, 208, 209–10; Office of Religious Affairs (ORA), 207–8; religious communities, 204–6; religious freedom, 203, 209; Rubio, 202–3; S/RGA, 201–2, 210; State Department, 198–200, 202; status, agents, 201; ter-

rorism, 201; travel and commerce, 201;
Vatican, 201; visit, 202–5; White House,
secret meeting, 196–97
Cuban Council of Churches, 198, 203
culture, 13, 79–80
Cuomo, Chris, 61, 62–63
Cuomo, Mario, 63
Curtis, Laterica, 199–200, 202

Daalder, Ivo, 141–42
Dallas, 132–33
Danan, Liora, 60, 68, 70, 77, 79–80, 99,
107, 131, 155, 160, 199–200, 210
Danforth, John, 237n7
Dawson, Christopher, 13, 231n9
Day, Barbara, 72
Day, Dorothy, 112–13
Dean Acheson Auditorium, 168–69
Debs, Eugene, 37
DeLaurentis, Jeffrey, 203–4
Democratic Party, 42, 61, 74, 112
Department of State. *See* State
Department
Des Moines, 136–39
Des Moines Area Religious Council, 138
Des Moines Public Schools (DMPS),
136–37
devil, the, 223–24
Dicastery for Promoting Integral Human
Development, 192
Diego, Caridad, 202, 207–9
dignity, 80–81
diplomacy: Albright, 14–15, 29; Biden,
225; Burns, 229n3; conversations,
163; Cuba, 197–98; and CVE, 91–92;
expertise, 29; Israel-Palestine peace
negotiations, 154, 163, 165; Kerry, 2–3;
points of contact, 183–84; Pompeo,
195; questions, 3, 140; and religion, 3–5,
14–15, 28, 29–30, 82–83, 89–90, 92,
101, 124–25, 159, 181–82, 184–85, 225;
respect, 80; S/RGA, 28, 71, 77, 160–61,
181–82, 224; Trump, 194; and Vatican,
191, 194
Disabilities Treaty. *See* United Nations

Convention on the Rights of Persons
with Disabilities
disinformation, 123–24
Dole, Robert, 93
Dome of the Rock, 165–66
Dubois, Joshua, 61–62, 64, 75
Dworin, Adela, 205

Ecumenical Advocacy Days, 158
education, 36, 38–39, 45–46, 47–52, 81,
134, 136–37
embassies, 29, 30, 78, 89, 181, 183, 185, 186
ends and means, 7, 26–27
"Engaging Religious Communities
Abroad: A New Imperative for US
Foreign Policy," 141
environmentalism, 43–44, 93, 94. *See also*
climate change
Erdogan, Recep Tayyip, 179
Ethiopia, 181–87
evangelicalism, 30, 35, 64, 93–94, 123,
194, 206–7
Executive Order on Tackling the Climate
Crisis at Home and Abroad (EO
14008), 121

Farris, Mike, 93
Fellowship (the Family), 73, 238n1
Filaret, Metropolitan, 177
First Things, 195
Florini, Karen, 105
foreign policy, US: and Islam, 87–88;
Obama administration, 5–6; and
religion, 5–6, 8, 54, 75–76; S/RGA,
189; surprises, 189. *See also* diplomacy;
policy
Ford, Gerald, 41
Ford, John, 97
Foreign Service, 11, 29, 78, 186, 199–200
Forman, Ira, 226
foxes and hedgehogs, 7–8, 25–26, 153
Francis, Pope, 97–99, 106, 108–15,
146–48, 189–90, 191, 192–93, 195, 201
Francis of Assisi, 110
Franken, Al, 112

Gaddis, John Lewis, 6–8, 25–26, 27–28, 230nn6–7
Gaudium et Spes, 110
gay marriage, 222–23
Gingrich, Callista, 194
Global Compact on Refugees, 148–49, 151
Global War on Terror, 83
Gonzales, Aldo, 202, 209
Good Morning America, 61–62
Goudeau, Jessica, 143
Greater Yellowstone Ecosystem, 102
Green Climate Fund, UN, 101, 118–19
Gross, Alan, 200–201

Hackett, Ken, 98, 190–91, 193
Hamre, John, 60
Hardin-Simmons University, 163–64
Harrell, David Edwin, 33
Harvard Divinity School (HDS), 48–49, 50–51, 52, 55–56
Harvard University, 54–55
Haslach, Patricia, 182, 185, 186
Hauerwas, Stanley, 232n15
Hehir, Bryan, 4, 54, 56, 57, 193, 196–97
Hernandez, Juan de Dios, 204
Heumann, Judy, 93–94
hierarchy of needs, 84–85
Higginbottom, Heather, 6
Hill, Alice, 118
Holy and Great Council of the Orthodox Church, 178
Home School Legal Defense Association, 93
Huda, Qamar-Ul, 154
Huntington, Samuel, 11–14, 231n9
Hussein, Saddam, 19, 26

imam-training curriculum, 85–87
Indyk, Martin, 52, 99, 155, 156
Innocent Abroad (Indyk), 52
Interagency Policy Council (IPC), 180
interfaith dialogue, 95–96, 138–39, 243n5
Intergovernmental Panel on Climate Change (IPPC), 120
International Religious Freedom Act, 24, 83

International Religious Freedom Office/Report, 74–75, 83, 203, 208–9. *See also* religion: freedom of
Iraq: Bremer, 22–23; Bush/Bush administration, 19–20, 25–28; constitution, 22–24; and CVE, 87–88; ends and means, 26–27; foxes and hedgehogs, 26–27; government, rebuilding, 22; Haass, 233n28; insurgency, 20; intelligence, 19, 26; and Israel/Palestine, 158–59; and Islam, 22–24, 25, 158–59; Kilcullen, 20–21; Provisional Governing Authority, 22–23; reconstruction, 24–25; refugees, 127, 135; religion, 17, 18–21, 23, 25, 233n28, 233n31; religious freedom, 23–24; and S/RGA, 17; strategy, 25, 28; War, 4, 15, 17–22, 25–26, 28, 57–58
ISIS/ISIL, 84, 85, 89, 224
Islam: Ahmed, 16; analysis, 154–55; and Christianity, 87; Cuba, 204; and CVE, 83–87, 89; Ethiopia, 182–83, 185; and foreign policy, US, 87–88; Huntington, 11–13; Iraq, 22–24, 25, 158–59; Kilcullen, 20–21; Nigeria, 212, 213, 217; refugees, 139; stereotypes, 155
Israel, 87–88, 98–99, 157–60, 166–67
Israel-Palestine peace negotiations: Abraham Accords, 167, 172; Ateek, 163–64; Biden administration, 167–68; Cremisan Monastery, 159–60; CRIHL, 161–62; diplomacy, 154, 163, 165; embassy, US, 160; future, 169–70; Gaza, 167–68; holy sites, 171–73; and Iraq, 158–59; Kerry, 156–58, 164, 168–71; Melchior, 164–65; Noah's ark problem, 157; principles, 170–71; religions, three, 165, 166, 171; skepticism, public, 170; S/RGA, 154–55, 160–61; support, public, 156; Trump, 162, 167–69, 172; two-state solution, 168, 169; US embassy, 167; Waqf, 165–66

Jackson (MS), 52–53
Jefferson Science Fellowship (JSF), 107
Jerusalem, 156
Johnson, Lyndon B., 46

Johnson, Toiyriah, 73
Johnston, Douglas, 10
John XXIII, Pope, 109
Joint Chiefs of Staff, 21
joy, 80

Kano, Malineh, 140–41
Kansara, Jay, 72–73
Kennan, George, 70
Kennedy, John F., 38, 61, 109
Kennedy School, 54, 55, 56
Kennet (MO), 31, 33
Kerry, John, 1–3, 6, 7, 8, 15, 30, 44, 67–68, 70–71, 73–75, 76, 82, 92, 97–99, 101, 103–4, 109, 121, 156–58, 159, 160, 164, 168–71, 190, 193, 201, 217, 224
Kessler, Michael, 82
Kilcullen, David, 20–21
King, Martin Luther, Jr., 39, 112–14, 213–14
King Abdullah International Center for Interreligious and Intercultural Dialogue (KAICIID), 95–97
Kirill, Patriarch, 174–75
Kissinger, Henry, 41

Latter-day Saints, 95
Laudato Si (Francis), 106, 108–11
leadership, 65
lead levels, water, 44
Lempert, Yael, 166
Leslie, Rachel, 78–79, 131–32, 135, 160, 202
Lewis, LeMoine, 47–48, 50
Lillis, Amy, 77–78, 79, 191, 212
Lincoln, Abraham, 7–8, 27–28, 112–13, 230n10
Lincoln Memorial, 39
Louisville Courier Journal, 40

Madani, Iyad bin Amin, 97
Mahmoud, Mahmoud, 131
Mandaville, Peter, 86, 90–91, 154
Markey, Ed, 111–12
Marshall, Katherine, 213, 214
Maslow, Abraham, 84–85
May, Ernest, 31, 54

McCants, Will, 84
McCarthy, Gina, 121
McCurry, Mike, 59–60, 103–4
McDonough, Denis, 220
McGovern, Jim, 192
McKean, David, 70
megachurches, US, 207
Melchior, Michael, 164
Merton, Thomas, 112–13
Middle East peace process. *See* Israel-Palestine peace negotiations
Missouri, 31, 37
Mixed Blessings: U.S. Government Engagement with Religion in Conflict-Prone Settings (CSIS), 60
Moore, Russell, 94
Mount Zion Cemetery, 41
Murphy, Chris, 112

National Association of Evangelicals, 94
National Capital Semester for Seminarians, 57, 58–59
National Climate Task Force, 121
National Intelligence Council, 19
National Prayer Breakfast, 73–74
"National Strategy for Integrating Religious Leader and Religious Community Engagement into U.S. Foreign Policy," 180
Netanyahu, Benjamin, 157
networking, 59–60, 69
Neustadt, Richard, 31, 54, 55, 230n6
newspapers, 39–40
Nguyen, Viet Than, 143
Nguyen, Vinh, 137
Niebuhr, Reinhold, 70, 82
Nigeria, 211–18
Nixon, Richard, 61
nongovernmental organizations (NGOs), 184
Nosanchuk, Matt, 222
Nozell, Melissa, 90–91
nuclear weapons, 53–54, 56
Nuland, Victoria, 174, 175, 191

Obama, Barack, 6, 8, 114, 118, 130

Obama administration: and Christianity, 64–65; climate change, 101; Cuba, 197–98, 200, 206, 209–10; CVE, 83–84, 85–87, 90; foreign policy, 5–6; Iraq, 18; peril, 224; and refugees, 130, 132, 148; and religion, 5–6, 61, 64; S/RGA, 124, 222; Wright, 61–62, 63–64
Office of Conflict Stabilization Operations. *See* Bureau of Conflict Stabilization Operations
Office of Evangelization, Natchez-Jackson Diocese, 53–54
Office of International Religious Freedom. *See* International Religious Freedom Office/Report
Office of Policy Planning, 19, 70–71, 221
Office of Religion and Global Affairs (S/RGA): accomplishments, 220; adversaries, 223–25; Albright, 15; ALDAC, 181; and Biden, 224–25; chief of staff, 68–69; and climate change, 104, 105–6, 119, 122–24; and conflict, 154, 187; criticisms, 221–23; Cuba, 201–2, 210; and CVE, 83, 85–89; Danan, 68–69; diplomacy, 28, 71, 77, 160–61, 181–82, 224; equipping posts, 226–27; establishment, 3; Ethiopia, 181–82, 185–87; foreign policy, 189; foxes, 28; future of, 225–26; instrumentalization, 124; and Iraq, 17; Israel-Palestine peace process, 154–55, 160–61; Jefferson Science Fellows, 107–8, 124; and LGBT rights, 222–23; lives saved, 224; map-making, 181; and Obama, 124, 222; Policy Planning, 71; and Pompeo, 221, 223; and Russian Orthodox Church, 173; scholars, 244n1; and Specials, 79, 225–26; staff, 77–78, 147–48; and State Department, 3, 69–70; and Trump, 221; and Vatican, 210
Office of the Special Envoy for Israeli Palestinian Negotiations, 99, 155
Olbricht, Thomas, 48
Olupona, Jacob, 215
O'Malley, Seán Patrick, Cardinal, 197
Onuphrius, Metropolitan, 177–78

Organization of Economic Cooperation and Development, 118
Organization of Islamic Cooperation (OIC), 146–47
Ortega, Cardinal, 197
Orthodox Church, 81, 98, 173–80
Otero, Maria, 75

Pacem in Terris (John XXIII), 109
Paducah (KY), 35–36, 38, 41, 43, 45, 46, 237n9
Palestine, 79, 87–88, 99, 167. *See also* Israel-Palestine peace negotiations
Paris Accord on Climate Change, 44, 101, 105, 108–10, 115–18, 119–21
Parolin, Pietro, 98, 99, 191
Pershin, Richard, 1, 2
Phoenix, 134–36
placement, 31–32
policy: Albright, 15; Christianity, 56; climate change, 105, 117; CVE, 90–91; foreign, 54, 75; moral questions, 146; Neustadt, 54; refugee, 144, 146; and religion, 15, 75–76. *See also* foreign policy, US
Pompeo, Mike, 195–96, 221, 223
preaching, 35
prosperity gospel, 182, 212
Protocol relating to the Status of Refugees, 129
public sphere, 10, 15–16
Putin, Vladimir, 173–74, 180
Pyatt, Gregory, 173–74, 175

race, 36–38, 44–46, 63
RadCon, 220
radio stations, 211
Reagan, Ronald, 52, 53–54
Refugee Convention relating to the Status of Refugees, 144–45
Refugee One, 140–41
refugees: agency, 142, 143; asylum, 145; camps, 150; Biden, 151, 152; Bhutanese, 72–73; Chicago, 139–41; cities, 142; community liaisons, 138; Dallas, 132–34; definition, 145; Des Moines, 136–39; diaspora, 136; education, 134, 136–37;

European Union, 145–47, 148; funding, 145; global population, 128–29; global system, 140–41, 149; hate rhetoric, 132, 133, 135, 142–43; Iraqi, 127, 135; Jersey City, 126–28, 130–31; languages, 136–37; moral fatigue, 145–46; moral questions, 143–44, 146; Muslim, 139; non-refoulement, 145, 150–51; and Obama administration, 130, 132, 148; Phoenix, 134–36; policy, 144, 146; political hurdles, 150; and populism, 142–43; proximity, 142–43; and religion, 100, 129–30, 131, 135–36, 138–39, 144, 151–52; Republicans, 141; resettlement, 72; and State Department, 130, 132, 136, 142, 151–52; Syrian, 127, 130; Trump, 131, 141, 149, 150; and UN, 129, 144–45, 148–49, 150, 151; US, difficulty in, 126–28; Vatican, 146–48

Refuge: Rethinking Refugee Policy in a Changing World (Betts and Collier), 144
Reid, Harry, 92
religion: Albright, 14–15, 29; author's, 32–34, 159; Biden, 225, 228; Bremer, 22; and climate change, 101, 104–6, 115, 119, 122–23; and conflict, 10–11, 153–54; and CVE, 84, 90–91; Democrats, 61; and diplomacy, 3–5, 14–15, 28, 29–30, 71, 82–83, 89–90, 92, 101, 124–25, 159, 181–82, 184–85, 225; and executive branch, 227–28; extremism, 227; finances, climate change and, 123; foreign policy, 15, 75–76; Foreign Service, 29; foxes, 230n12; freedom of, 23–24, 194–96, 203, 209; and GOP, 65, 74; HDS, 55–56; and Huntington, 11–14; ignorance of, 4, 17, 18–19, 25; international relations, 10–11; and Iraq War, 15, 17–22, 23, 25, 233n28, 233n31; Israel-Palestine peace negotiations, 165, 166, 171; Kennedy vs. Nixon, 60–61; Kilcullen, 20–21; and military, 20–21; and money, 95–96; Noah's ark problem, 157, 212; Obama administration, 5–6, 61, 64; and peace, 153; powerful, 4, 9; and the press, 65; public, 10, 55–56; and refugees, 100, 129–30, 131, 135–36, 138–39, 144, 151–52;

registration laws, 206–7; and statecraft, 10–11; and State Department, 3–5, 9–10, 11, 15, 28, 156–57; stereotypes, 153; Trump, 194–96, 227; Ukraine, 176; and violence, 153
Religious Affairs in Joint Operations, 21
Religious Right, 53
Republican Party, 37, 39, 42, 52, 53–54, 58, 65, 74–75, 92–93, 112, 115, 141
Richards, Ann, 70, 72, 132
Rodrigues, Cardinal, 191
Rogers, Melissa, 82
Roman Catholicism: climate change, 106, 114; Cuba, 204, 210; Cuomo, 63; Kerry, 2, 103–4, 190; and Reagan administration, 53–54; refugees, 146–47. *See also* Vatican
Romero, Oscar, 192
Ross, Brian, 62
Ross, Carly, 137–38
Ross Barnett Reservoir, 53
Rubio, Marco, 74–75, 202–3
Russia: Crimean invasion, 173; Orthodox Church, 173–80; patriarchate, 174–75, 177, 178–79; propaganda, 174, 175; Putin, 173–74, 180; and S/RGA, 173; and Ukraine, 173–74, 175; and US, 175

Sabeel, 163
Sampson, Cynthia, 10
Saperstein, David, 168
scale, 27–28
Scottish commonsense realism, 35
secularization theory, 10
segregation, 36–37, 38, 45–46
Seiple, Chris, 75
Seiple, Robert, 75
Selective Service, 41
self-actualization, 84–85
Senate Climate Caucus, 111–12
senior leadership meeting, 67
Sewall, Sarah, 84–86, 90, 92
Shannon, Thomas, 194
Sherman, Wendy, 146, 147
Shinseki, Eric, 24–25
Sistani, Ayatollah Ali, 22–23, 24, 234n34
situational awareness, 42

Sneed, Claire, 78
soil erosion, 43–44
Souraphiel, Cardinal, 191
sources, historical, 51
Southern Baptists, 94
southern strategy, 52
space, 27–28
speaking up, 65
Special Envoy to Monitor and Combat
  Anti-Semitism, 79, 226
Special Envoy to the Organization of
  Islamic Cooperation, 79, 226
Special Representative to Muslim Communities, 79, 226
Sperry, Willard, 48
S/RGA. See Office of Religion and Global
  Affairs (S/RGA)
State Department: Albright, 15; Casey,
  8; and conflict, 153; and Congress, 75;
  Cuba, 198–99, 202; culture, 80; and
  CVE, 91; and Disabilities Treaty, 93–94;
  engagement, public, 227; and GOP, 75;
  information, 183; and Israel-Palestine,
  158; Main State, 6; real estate, 67–70;
  and refugees, 130, 132, 136, 142, 151–52;
  and religion, 3–5, 9–10, 11, 15, 28, 76,
  78–79, 156–57; science, 123–24; S/RGA,
  3, 69–70; tour, US, 185–86
Stern, Todd, 105, 108
Stivers, C. J., 18
stock market, 46–47
Storrar, Will, 176
Strategic Dialogue with Civil Society, 75
Strategy for Integrating Religious Leader
  and Religious Community Engagement, 5–6
Strider, Burns, 61
Su, Anna, 23
suffering, 49
Suleman, Arsalan, 155, 226

Tefft, John, 175
Teklemariam, Shiferaw, 182, 183, 186–87
Temple Mount, 166, 172
Thames, Knox, 168
theology, 15–16, 32, 35, 154

Thiemann, Ronald, 15–16, 55, 232n15
Thomas-Greenfield, Linda, 212, 217–18
Tillemann, Tomicah, 75
Tillerson, Rex, 221
Tomasi, Silvano, 192–93
Trump, Donald, 52, 58, 101, 118, 120, 121,
  131, 141, 150, 220
Trump administration, 5, 30, 149, 162,
  167–69, 172, 193–96, 221, 227
Turkey, 179
Turkson, Peter, Cardinal, 192
Twal, Fouad, 159

Ukraine, 173–75, 178, 180
Ukrainian Orthodox Church, 180
Union of Orthodox Rabbis, 158
United Nations, 93, 115–16, 129, 148–49
United Nations Convention on Refugees,
  126, 150, 151
United Nations Convention on the Rights
  of Persons with Disabilities (Disabilities
  Treaty), 92–95
United Nations Framework Convention
  on Climate Change, 116, 121
United Nations High Commissioner for
  Refugees (UNHCR), 129–30
United Nations Universal Declaration of
  Human Rights, 144, 145
United States Commission of Interna-
  tional Religious Freedom, 23
United States Committee for Refugees
  and Immigrants, 137
United States Conference of Catholic
  Bishops, 53, 56, 190
University of Chicago Divinity School, 78
U.S. Army/Marine Corps Counterinsur-
  gency Field Manual, 20

Vanderslice, Mara, 75
Vatican, 94, 98, 146–48, 159–60, 190–91,
  192, 193–96, 210. See also Roman
  Catholicism
Vendley, William, 75
Vietnam War, 1, 2, 38, 40–43
violence, 43–44, 86–88, 153. See also
  conflict
Vote-a-Rama, 2

Wade, David, 6, 92, 93, 98, 99, 146, 197
Walker, Newman, 45
Wallace, Ann, 47–48, 52
Waqf, 165–66
Warren, Rick, 94–95
Washington, DC, 39, 57–60, 69, 102, 160
Watson Institute, 17, 18
Watts, Clinton, 84
Wesley Theological Seminary, 6, 57–58, 69, 102
White, Jerry, 182
White, Theodore, 50
White House Evangelical Advisory Board, 30

White House Office of Faith-Based and Neighborhood Partnerships, 72
Wilson, David McAllister, 57, 60
Wistrand, Jennifer, 176
Wolfowitz, Paul, 25
workplace, 81–82
Wright, Jeremiah, 61, 62–63
Wuerl, Donald, 190

Xi Jinping, 196

Yahya, Pedro, 204
Yellowstone National Park, 102, 103

Zakar, Shaarik, 154–55, 180, 226
Zogby, Eileen, 112
Zogby, James, 112